Football in the Ne

Football is rarely out of the headlines, with stories about star players mis-behaving, clubs facing financial meltdown, or TV companies battling over broadcast rights dominating much of the mainstream news and current affairs agenda. The impact of the vast amounts of money paid to elite footballers, and the inability of young men to cope with this when combined with their media-fuelled celebrity status, have frequently made headlines. However, at the core of this process is the battle to control a game that has exploited its position as a key 'content provider' for new media over the last decade.

Football in the New Media Age analyses the impact of media change on the football industry, drawing on extensive interviews with key people in the media and football industries. It examines the finances of the game; the rising import-ance of rights and rights management in the industry; and attempts by clubs to develop their own media capacity. At the core of the book is an examination of the battle for control of the game as media, business and fans all seek to redefine the sport in the twenty-first century.

Raymond Boyle and **Richard Haynes** both teach in the Department of Film and Media Studies at the University of Stirling and are members of the Stirling Media Research Institute. Raymond Boyle is co-author of *Sport and National Identity in the European Media* (1993) and, with Richard Haynes, of *Power Play: Sport, the Media and Popular Culture* (2000). Richard Haynes sits on the Editorial Board of *Media, Culture and Society* and is the author of *The Football Imagination: The Rise of Football Fanzine Culture* (1995).

Football in the New Media Age

Raymond Boyle and Richard Haynes

Routledge
Taylor & Francis Group

LONDON AND NEW YORK

First published 2004
by Routledge
11 New Fetter Lane, London EC4P 4EE

Simultaneously published in the USA and Canada
by Taylor & Francis Inc
29 West 35th Street, New York, NY 10001

Routledge is an imprint of the Taylor & Francis Group

© 2004 Raymond Boyle and Richard Haynes

Typeset in Galliard by Wearset Ltd, Boldon, Tyne and Wear
Printed and bound in Great Britain by Antony Rowe Ltd,
Chippenham, Wiltshire

British Library Cataloguing in Publication Data
A catalogue record for this book is available from the British
Library

Library of Congress Cataloging in Publication Data
Boyle, Raymond, 1966–
    Football in the new media age / Raymond Boyle and Richard Haynes.
        p. cm.
    1. Soccer—Social aspects—Great Britain. 2. Mass media and
sports—Great Britain. 3. Digital media—Social aspects. I. Haynes,
Richard. II. Title.
    GV943.9.S64B69 2004
    796.334'0941—dc22   2003026225

ISBN 0–415–31790–8 (hbk)
ISBN 0–415–31791–6 (pbk)

For Lauren – (RB)
For Susan, Alice and Adam – (RH)

Love it or hate it, there is no denying the sporting, cultural and even economic importance of football.

Will Hutton, 'Football pays the penalty';
the *Observer*, 16 March 2003

Contents

Acknowledgements   viii

Introduction: the game   1

1   Football and television: game on?   7

2   The digital revolution: a whole new ball game?   27

3   The European dimension: power and influence in new
    media football markets   51

4   Commercialising celebrity: player power and image rights   71

5   Battle for control: football clubs and new media strategy   95

6   A league of their own? The Old Firm and SPL TV   118

7   The new World Wide Web of football: interactivity and the
    fan   138

Conclusion: the only game? The media and the football
industry in the twenty-first century   159

Notes   168
Bibliography   169
Index   176

Acknowledgements

We would like to thank the people who agreed to speak with us during this project. They were drawn from across the media and football industries. Those who spoke on the record include: John Boyle, George Berry, Genevieve Berti, Denis Campbell, Nic Couchman, Stuart Cosgrove, David Elstein, Alex Fynn, Owen Gibson, Michael Grant, Patrick Harverson, Graham Lovelace, Gabriele Marcotti, Ashling O'Connor, John Nagle, Nialle Sloane, Peter Smith, Chris Tate, Gordon Taylor, Damian Willoughby and Will Muirhead.

Also thanks are due to colleagues with whom we have directly or indirectly discussed aspects of this work. In particular Will Dinan, Simon Frith, Matthew Hibberd and Stephen Morrow.

We gratefully acknowledge the assistance we received from the Carnegie Trust for the Universities of Scotland that helped facilitate the range of travel involved in this project.

Introduction

The game

> In an era of globalization, when people have more leisure time, football is the most global business of the lot. You tell me another product that is bought off the shelf by three billion consumers. Not even Coca-Cola comes close.
>
> Sergio Cragnotti, President of Lazio (Lovejoy, 2002: 188)

Football in the new media age can often appear ubiquitous. The month of October 2003 saw football related stories dominate much of the mainstream UK news and current affairs agenda. The stories of alleged sexual and criminal misdemeanours involving young, wealthy professional football stars merged with poor behaviour by players on the pitch. While the failure of the Manchester United and England player Rio Ferdinand to turn up for a drugs test resulted in his subsequent omission from the England national squad on the eve of a major international fixture. This 'crisis' was then escalated by the threat by the England national team to withdraw from the game and threatened to end in a major court battle between the biggest club in England and the governing body of the English national game.

These events served to illustrate some of the associated baggage that accompanies football in the digitised media age. The impact of vast amounts of money to elite footballers and the inability of young (predominately British) men often to cope with this when combined with their media-fuelled celebrity status has been clear to see. However at the core of this process is the battle to control a game which has exploited its position as the key 'content' of new media developments over the last decade or so. It is this process and the battle for control, between players, clubs, fans and media corporations that interests us in this project.

Blain and Bernstein (2002) have argued that the level of research that focuses on the relationship between the media and sport has now reached such a stage that it constitutes a significant field of research within academic activity. They argue that what characterises much of this research activity is an ability to both blur and push the boundaries between more traditional academic approaches, such as among others sociology, gender studies and leisure studies. They also suggest that much of this work is concerned with the struggle between the local and the global, with its attendant concerns of the impact of this process on issues of identity, media representation and political economy. It is within this broad frame of reference that this book is placed and we hope it makes some contribution to that ongoing debate and research trajectory.

While our previous book (Boyle and Haynes, 2000) has examined the broad sweep of the relationship between the media and sport, this book has a more specific area of enquiry. It turns our attention to the interplay between the football and the media industries and seeks to identify to what extent the evolution of this relationship helps to illuminate wider aspects of change within both the sporting and media environments. To this end we are interested in football *as a cultural form*; football *as an industry and business* and football *as a media product*. It seems to us, that at certain moments the game is clearly one of these, at others, it can appear to be all of them.

It's also important to say at this juncture what the book is not about, otherwise we leave ourselves open to the charge that we have set up false expectations for the reader. The book is primarily, but not exclusively focused on the relationship between the game and the broadcast and new media sectors of the cultural industries. At certain moments throughout this research we do engage with debates that encompass the print media. This is particularly the case when we discuss some of the wider issues related to journalistic access which the attempt by elite clubs to 'commercialise' all areas of their activity clearly raises (see Chapters 4 and 5). However the fascinating relationship between the game and the print media remains both beyond the scope of this book, and a project for another day.

Throughout the book there is a concern with tracking and making sense of the emerging political economy of the media–football relationship. This raises related concerns about issues of representation and the role of the audience and fans in this process. However given the constraints of time and space, we make no apology for the book's focus on the wider economic and regulatory framework within which football finds itself operating with regard to the media industries. In so doing, we do not underestimate the role that fans play in the structure of the sport, or their role in the increasingly mediated culture within which football is located.

Specifically this book attempts to examine the changing relationship between football and particular aspects of the media industries during a time of change in both sectors. This also raises the issue of what we mean by 'new media age'. The phrase itself suggests a particular moment in media development that marks both a new stage of evolution and some sort of break from the past. As Lievrouw and Livingstone (2002: 1) argue the term itself has had a long history within the field of social research since the 1960s. Often work in this area has been technology focused and centred on the developments of information and communication technologies (ICTs). From within a communication/media studies frame of reference, the work of Raymond Williams (1974) and his concern with the social, political and aesthetic impacts of new communicative forms in society is a good example of how debates about new media forms have long been circulating and informing research in this area.

Lievrouw and Livingstone (2002: 7) suggest that the parameters within which they place new media include:

> The artifacts or devices that enable and extend our ability to communicate; the communication activities or practices we engage in to develop and use these devices; and the social arrangements or organisations that form around the devices and practices.

In other words the concerns we are interested in with regard to new media are centred on issues of specific media (digital television, the Internet and mobile telephony) and their institutional context and social usage. In addition, we would argue that these technologies are themselves subject to wider shifts in the political, economic and social contours of society. For new media we might also refer to the digitised age, in which digital technology has enabled new forms and patterns of communication to emerge, while both shaping and being shaped by wider patterns of social usage or consumption.

Some other points are also worth noting at this stage. We would argue that while new media can be a helpful phrase in isolating some of the areas of interest we wish to look at, equally it can be misleading. When do new media become old media? In the 1980s for example, cable and satellite delivery systems were 'new media' and as we see in the first chapter they significantly helped shape the wider economic development of the game. In short, one might argue that there are no 'old' and 'new' media, rather simply media. Thus when we look at the key issue of the impact of digital television on the economics of the game through the selling of rights, we are in some cases discussing (new) digital television stations, in others we are focusing on existing (old) television companies who have either migrated to digital or set up digital arms of existing corporations.

It appears to us that some of the most fundamental issues within (old) media studies, a concern with; patterns of ownership, issues of control and access, representation and identity, and audiences and media consumption, remain equally valid in any new media studies project. What is required is a refinement of some of these issues to take account of a changing media and cultural land-scape. To that list we might add the broader regulatory social, economic and political framework, which attempts to police the boundaries of media develop-ment and by implication large aspects of popular culture.

However as we have argued elsewhere (Boyle and Haynes, 2002) there are also clearly areas that this current stage of media evolution has transformed. For example in the digital environment, the repackaging and re-formulating of images across a range of platforms clearly has implications for rights holders as well as raising issues of access across more traditional national boundaries/ markets. Centrally there have been attempts by a range of stakeholders in the game to exploit these new technological innovations to extract a commercial value from areas or activities previously not viewed as offering that potential.

One of the key issues which runs throughout the book is a concern with the interaction between differing models of media organisation. On the one hand we have broadcasting, which despite the rise of satellite and cable delivery systems throughout the 1980s is still primarily organised within national boundaries. So for example, the football rights deals done with broadcasters (for either domestic or international competitions such as the UEFA Champions League) remain wedded to the idea of national boundaries. By contrast, a platform such as the Internet, offers the possibility of a global, boundary-less audience for the sport and perhaps in time may come to challenge the primacy of the national broadcasting model. It is an interest in tracking and analysing these two related aspects of media development that runs throughout the following research and analysis.

Sport has been widely referred to as the 'battering ram' that has helped to open up the pay-TV market in the UK. In this country, football specifically has been viewed in the recent past as the 'cash cow' of the new media sport economy and has driven the rollout of cable, satellite and digital TV, albeit in an uneven process, including periods of retrenchment. It is the centrality of football as a form of 'content' for many of the digital platforms that make it such a compelling subject for an examination of the characteristics of the new media environment.

Another key theme that runs through the book then is that of control, and the shifting patterns of power that permeate the wider cultural industries. Too often sport is not included within these policy related discourses, yet we would argue that sport, and football in particular is more than worthy of the consideration given its impact on aspects of the cultural landscape.[1] Both culturally and economically football matters, whether policy makers and key publics like it or not.

The book

The opening chapter of the book presents an historical overview of the relationship between football and television in the UK, and sets out some of the previous writing that has engaged with the relationship between the sport and television in particular. While much of this material covers the relationship between the game and television in a pre-Internet and digital age, it remains important because the advent of technologies such as cable and satellite delivery systems (and the changing political climate which facilitated their entry into the media market) all helped to change the football industry and put in place a new template within which the game would forge its relationship with the broadcast media.

In this chapter we want to map out the various theoretical and analytical influences from which we draw upon for this book and place this work within a wider frame of reference which sees areas such as media studies turning its attention to key areas of the cultural economy, such as sport.

Chapter 2 focuses specifically on the impact that changes in the wider media environment have had on the game in the late 1990s and the early part of the new century. In particular we are interested in examining the way in which the launch of digital television in the UK marks a crucial moment in the relationship between the game and the main broadcasters in the UK. This analysis is extended in the following chapter to look at similar developments across various European markets and tracks how the arrival of digital technologies in the European broadcasting industry have helped to re-shape the football economy.

One of the key characteristics of the digital age has been the rise in the complexity in the value of a range of commercial rights as the ability to manipulate digital images across a range of platforms has taken shape. In the footballing context this has accelerated a process already underway, in which star players have enjoyed more power and influence than in previous decades. Chapter 4 examines the rise of the importance of players' image rights in the digital environment and how this is restructuring the relationship that elite performers have with the sport.

Chapter 5 then develops this theme by looking at the ways in which football clubs have attempted to exploit and develop business opportunities that new media platforms have offered (such as digital television, the Internet and mobile telephony) to extract additional value from club brands and rights. It highlights the tensions this process generates between traditional media and the clubs and also examines the various business models they are adopting in their new media strategies.

The next part of the book, Chapter 6, focuses on attempts by actual leagues to extend their control of the mediated game by setting up their own media companies to exploit the rights they hold. While this chapter acts as a case study looking at the SPL TV scenario in the Scottish Premier League, it serves to illustrate the fundamental structural tensions that now run through the game and which are being driven by wider shifts in the media environment. At the core of this process is the emerging relationship between traditional notions that have seen football mediated primarily within a national broadcasting culture, and the potentially global communicative system of the Internet as a means of creating a larger, more disparate footballing community and globalising the local appeal of particular football clubs.

Chapter 7 extends this concern with the global dimension of the game by looking at the role of the Internet in major world footballing events, such as the FIFA World Cup of 2002. In addition, this chapter examines the role and impact of interactivity – one of the distinctive features of digital technology – on football fans. We also ask to what extent the advent of the new media age will change the cultural contract supporters have with the game.

A couple of additional observations are also important at this stage.

The book is primarily about the elite of the game, in terms of clubs and leagues. Partly this is because it is in these areas that new media are impacting on most dramatically, but also because there is clearly a knock-on effect for the rest of the game of the changes at the top end of the sport. We focus mainly on the key new media platforms of digital television, the Internet and mobile telephony. A central aspect for some observers of these evolving technologies is the concept of convergence that theoretically the process of digitisation offers. We want to test this thesis in the book with regard to football and suggest that along with the patterns of change which emerge in the digital environment there are equally strong elements of continuity with longer more established forms of communicative practice and organisation.

Ultimately, it is hoped that by mapping out the new terrain that football as a sport and a cultural form now finds itself operating on, we can analyse the impact of this on the changing cultural contract the game has with the fans. We will argue that football in the new media age marks the latest stage of refinement in the sports ongoing commercialisation journey, a process whose roots stretch back into the nineteenth century. The book is about trying to understand the contemporary stage of this development and how both the sport and new media interact with, and are shaped by, a range of social, political, economic and cultural factors. As both football fans and media analysts we think it is a task worth undertaking.

Chapter 1

Football and television

Game on?

Anyone who still wondered whether football was a sport or a business should wonder no more. The vast majority of these men (and women) do their work, not in the crowded penalty-box, or the close quarters conflict of the midfield, but in boardrooms and corridors, on the mobile telephone or via the small screen. They are the administrators, lobbyists, club chairman and directors who run the game, the agents and broadcasters who live off it, and the politicians, policemen and bankers with the power to make telling interventions from outside. It is not a list to stir the soul.

Journalist Glenn Moore, introducing the 50 most influential people in
British football. The *Independent*, 13 January 2003

Here [Britain] it's football first, second and third.

David Hill, BSkyB's then Head of Sport, 1992

Introduction

Today it is difficult to imagine football without television or a television schedule bereft of football. As a result over the last decade or so academic writing about sport and football in particular has mushroomed. What we want to do in the first section of this chapter is outline some of the previous writing on the relationship between the football industry and the media. In particular we focus on that work which has traced the impact that television has had on the structure and financing of the sport in the UK. In the following section, we analyse the key milestones which characterise the relationship between television and football over the last few years. We argue that it is impossible to understand football in the new media age, without reference to the more general history of the sport in the television age. As we suggested in the Introduction, the new media environment is in many ways the latest staging post in a longer history of media evolution, which sees both continuity and change in its interaction with aspects of wider popular cultural activity. Thus in many ways this chapter sets the broader historical context within which the rest of the book is placed.

Approaches to the relationship between football and television

Television and football: economic issues and concerns

Concerns about the impact of the economic restructuring of the game and issues about its governance have become an area of growing concern during the last decade (Fynn and Guest, 1994, 1999; Conn, 1998; Conn *et al.*, 2003; Dempsey and Reilly, 1998; Morrow, 1999, 2003; Hamil *et al.*, 1999, 2000; Banks, 2002; Bower, 2003a). The increasing influence that television has exercised over the sport and the unhealthy degree to which clubs have become dependent on television income have meant that the economic aspects of the game have become of considerable interest to those coming from a more financial and or legal background (Morrow, 1999, 2003; Greenfield and Osborn, 2001).

An important aspect of this approach has been to focus in varying degrees on the relationship between football clubs and television in particular. Significantly many of these writers, while drawing on academic disciplines such as economics and law are often keen to highlight the unique cultural dimension that accompanies football, particularly, but not exclusively in the UK.

Stephen Morrow (1999: 13) notes how framing discussions between football and television in purely economic terms only offers a partial picture. He argues:

> In particular insufficient consideration is given to the peculiarities of the product [football] in economic terms. In these terms the customer concept is incomplete because it fails to consider the role played by supporters in creating the product they are asked to buy, i.e. the atmosphere. In other words football needs supporters not just as customers but because they form part of a unique joint product.

Thus while the economic aspects of the evolution of the football industry are important, so too is understanding that here is a business often heavily laden with cultural value, and political symbolism.

What many of these authors (Conn, 1998; Hamil *et al.*, 1999) demonstrate is the extent to which the language of the market and business has permeated football culture. This has happened in a relatively short period of time, and while vestiges of the football as business discourse can be traced back to the 1980s and clubs such as Tottenham Hotspur and their flotation on the stock market, by comparison with the 1990s, these were peripheral in the wider structure of the game. What could be argued is that football as an industry and business simply adopted many of the established commercial and market driven aspects of other areas of both public life and popular culture in Britain, a decade or so after most of these areas had been colonised by market forces. To put it simply, these commercial forces, with one or two exceptions, were simply not interested in football, which the *Sunday Times* (18 June 1985) in an infamous editorial in the 1980s could call 'a slum sport watched by slum people'.

However the powerful combination of forced governmental change, driven by the Taylor Report (1990), a cultural shift in the image of the national game in England facilitated by the relative success of that country at the Italia 90 World Cup, and the massive financial and marketing boost given to the game by money from BSkyB in 1992, all combined to open up the football industry to the commercial forces which had paid little attention to football in the previous decade. As David Conn has argued by the early 1990s:

> A new breed of financial adviser arrived – accountants, brokers, lawyers – schooled in the nihilism of market forces, looking at football in the most superficial ways. Football, according to the City, is an 'entertainment product', the clubs are 'brands'.
>
> Conn, 1998: 154

Economists such as Dobson and Goddard (2001: 423) argue that what they call 'the competitive imbalance' in the English game – and indeed the contemporary football industry more generally – is a result of the unleashing of market forces on the game, which in turn is closely allied with its changing relationship with television which we discuss later in the chapter.

Central to this area of research are the twin concerns about the distorting impact that the flow of television money is having on the game, specifically the more traditional aspects of the sport and the apparent lack of governance of a sport which increasingly appears to treat its supporters with disdain. Many of these writers (Hamil *et al.*, 1998, 2000; Bower, 2003a) highlight an inability for the structures of the sport to adequately deal with its new found wealth – centred on the elite end of the game – and balance this with the wider aspects of social responsibility that come from running a major cultural activity. One which forms part of a wider network of activities and constitutes an important component of various collective identity formation processes. As the economist and writer Will Hutton has argued:

> What football demonstrates more eloquently than any economic tract is how feeble are the self regulating tendencies of capitalist markets, of how easy it is for industries to succumb to perverse and self destructive incentives and of the necessity for external intervention by way of regulation and rules to make good those endemic shortcomings.
>
> The *Observer*, 16 March 2003

Thus concerns about the impact of massive television revenues on aspects of the footballing economy raise wider issues about control which go beyond the confines of this particular industry and find echoes across the wider economy.

It is not just in this area that economists and lawyers have raised concerns. One of the characteristics of the new media age has been a growing concern with the issue of intellectual property (IP) and image rights in general.

Media rights and competition law

The growth of media involvement in football has also spawned an increasing interest in the role that the law and wider regulatory frameworks play in the sport. Some of this has been clearly driven by the wider encroachment of issues of law and regulation within the field of the media industries themselves. We would argue that the relocating of elite football within the wider entertainment and cultural industries has also resulted in issues of rights and their regulation, often more closely associated with areas such as the music and the film industries, becoming increasingly part of the culture which surrounds elite football performers. We look at this in particular detail in Chapters 4 and 5.

More generally however, football as a business has found itself becoming immersed in the wider arena of law and regulation. For an industry which has spent most of its history apparently immune from such practices and has obstinately self-regulated its activity, this has been something of a culture shock (Morrow, 1999, 2003; Hamil *et al.*, 1999; Bower, 2003a). The structural shift in club ownership patterns that has occurred as many clubs have become public limited companies (plcs), has meant that they have become subject to a new regulatory framework. Although many commentators as noted above feel that this level of intervention has not been sufficient to eradicate a culture of complacency among those who govern the game. As a result of this shift to plc status many clubs have found themselves having to manage a range of publics which extend beyond their traditional fan base, resulting in clubs engaging – to various degrees – with aspects of a growing sports public relations culture (Boyle *et al.*, 2002).

Of significant interest in this particular area is the work of Greenfield and Osborn (2001) who place their analysis of the regulatory framework that has shaped the game within the wider context of the regulation of aspects of popular cultural activity. In their book they suggest that, 'The defining moments in the recent history of the game have concerned legal involvement' (Greenfield and Osborn, 2001: 198). Without doubt, the Taylor Report into the 1989 Hillsborough disaster which ushered in a new era of all seater stadia played a key role in helping to renew a game which if left in its pre-Taylor state would not have been nearly as enticing a 'product' for BSkyB in the early 1990s.

Central to this approach is an understanding of the 'different aspects of regulation [that] have evolved to confront the new challenges that the increasing economisation of football has thrown up' (Greenfield and Osborn, 2001: 195). They argue that at the core of these changes is a broad agenda that is driven by the media as it increasingly impacts on footballing culture. Significantly they also suggest that this new footballing paradigm in which television in particular takes centre stage has resulted in the concept of the 'fan' itself becoming an increasingly problematic concept.

> It is increasingly difficult to describe who, or what, a fan actually is. Traditionally this was far clearer in an age when someone turned up, rain or shine, to support his (usually his) team and regarded those who turned up only sporadically as 'fairweather'. Now supporters have become consumers, and the way in which football can be consumed and, therefore, how a team can be supported has changed.
>
> Greenfield and Osborn, 2001: 197

While we find this analysis helpful, we would also caution against the abandonment of more traditional notions of fandom. As we argue in later chapters we suggest that while aspects of the new media environment have re-shaped part of the landscape of football fandom (and indeed made it a more complex terrain to map out) it has not eradicated some of the core characteristics of fan culture. That is of course not to say that the new 'entertainment' paradigm in which football finds itself has not helped to create a new relationship with a generation of consumers who have grown up with football in its current highly mediated form (see Chapter 7).

Media systems and globalisation

One of the growing areas of interest in sport more generally as a cultural form among those from both a media studies and sociologically informed background is the issue of the impact of globalisation on the game. At its core, is an assumption that various forms of communication are playing a key role in restructuring and compressing space and time with regard in particular to cultural form and practice. In turn, these raise a range of issues around identity formation, commercialisation and the governance of the game. Of course these processes form part of a wider political and economic network which is impacting on a number of institutions and cultural forms of which sport, and more specifically football is just one (Maguire, 1999; Miller et al., 2001; Williams, 2002a).

Some scholars concerned by the evolution of a more globally oriented cultural and entertainment industry offer a pessimistic outlook with regard to the impact that the political economy of these media sectors are having on sport as a cultural entity. Law et al. (2002) map out the extent to which sport has become embedded in the corporate networks of major entertainment institutions. These organisations simply view sport as a form of product, which can generate income across a range of platforms and a variety of distribution chains. The future their analysis outlines is one in which private, commercially driven and global media corporations control the flow of top level sport available to the fan. In so doing these corporations eradicate the last vestiges of national/ cultural regulation which seeks to position sport as something other than purely 'media product'.

While clearly elements of their analysis shed light on the extent to which sections of sport appear to have been annexed by corporate media culture, the situation on the ground remains complex and at times contradictory. As Miller *et al.* argue:

> Sport is increasingly shaped by the media, spectacularized by commerce, employed to deliver audiences to sponsors, and intimately linked to the technological opportunities afforded by various media delivery forms (satellite, cable, webcast, microwave) but not in a manner that ignores dissent and resistance. As such, globalizing tendencies must always be viewed as mediated by local structures, including the nation-state.
>
> Miller *et al.*, 2001: 24

For example in the UK, legislation does exist which protects aspects of sporting culture for free-to-air television (Boyle and Haynes, 2000: 216), the relative strength of PSB in this country (although under varying levels of political attack) also acts as a check on the unbridled commercialisation of the British broadcasting market. In the case of football, an emphasis is placed on the rights holders, as custodians of the game to strike a balance between selling the sport to television and retaining something of the intrinsic value of that sport as a significant cultural entity. Certainly in the Scottish and English cases, a failure to recognise the social and cultural value of the game will ultimately lead to the sport's long-term demise as a mass spectator sport in these particular markets. There is also the issue of resistance among supporters and shareholders to the supposedly inexorable commodification of the sport by media interests. Again in the UK, the most high profile example of this in recent years was the successful lobbying which led to the blocking of the proposed takeover of one of the world's largest football clubs, Manchester United, by one of the most successful pay television operations, BSkyB. Significantly it was the 'public interest' aspect of the takeover which was given as one of the key reasons for stopping the takeover (Walsh and Brown, 1999; Greenfield and Osborn, 2001: 54–63).

Also central in any investigation into the impact of globalisation on the football industry is the extent that we appear to be shifting from a paradigm of broadcasting which primarily has been organised and regulated within national boundaries (accepting that there was always signal overspill), to a more diverse and complex communications system, where the national now operates cheek by jowl with the global. In the development of new media digital technologies

and their uneven integration into existing structures, and in particular a distribution network (the Internet) which is potentially global, a new set of dynamics
between traditional broadcasters (some of whom are attempting to transform
themselves into global players), commercial communication organisations (both
local, but increasingly global) and content providers (such as bodies like UEFA,
the FA Premier League and individual clubs) is being played out. Even public
service broadcasters who are operating within previously clearly defined internal
national markets and cultural spaces within broader political states find themselves readjusting to accommodate shifting patterns of technology and audience
expectations.

So a broadcaster such as the BBC in the UK can make a decision in 2003 to
migrate its services from an encrypted digital satellite platform (BSkyB) to an 'in
the clear' service which will enable digital viewers across the UK to access
national/regional programming, such as news and current affairs, previously
only available within clearly demarcated national/regional communicative
spaces. Thus someone in London now wishing to watch BBC Scotland's
national news broadcasts can do so. Significantly, the only area which appeared
to prove in any way problematic was the requirement that the BBC re-negotiate
its contract with the Scottish Premier League (SPL) for live rights to Scottish
football, given that these now would be beamed across the UK, freely available
to digital viewers outside of Scotland. However, as the BBC presses ahead with
its digital agenda it seems largely indifferent to the impact its expanded services
have for rights holders.

We would concur with Williams when he argues:

> This is not simply a picture of a dominant global sports culture flowing in a
> single direction to uncritical sports consumers. It is one, instead, in which
> sporting tastes, attitudes and values are regularly destabilised and reconfig-
> ured as key media interests, and corporate actors remake relationships
> through sport at local, national and global levels.
>
> Williams, 2002a: 73

Thus one of our concerns is tracking aspects of this process across both the UK
and wider European arena as it relates in particular to the football industry and
the evolving traditional and new media sectors of the economy.

Another central concern in this book is the impact, in a range of economic,
institutional and cultural spheres that evolving media technologies are having
on cultural forms such as football. For instance, the development of digital
television and the growth of the Internet, combined with the liberalisation of
the broadcasting and telecommunications markets, both in the UK and
across Europe raise a range of issues addressed throughout the book. The
impact of a growing synergy between media corporations and football clubs is
examined in the following chapters, focusing both on the UK and then the rest
of Europe (Chapters 2 and 3). Allied with this concern is an interest in the

extent to which elite football clubs have been developing new media strategies which reflect a growing awareness of the global business opportunities offered by evolving communication systems, and are symptomatic of a growing process of commercialisation within mainstream popular culture. Of particular interest here is the tensions that exist between the local and the global as football clubs attempt to re-position themselves in an environment where the elite of the sport operate as commercial institutions seeking to maximise the value they can extract from a range of media rights they now see themselves holding (Chapter 5).

We argue throughout the book that football offers us an insight into how this process is evolving, and highlights some of the wider cultural and political shifts that are taking place within the terrain of popular culture. It illustrates tensions between the local, national and global frames of reference that the sport finds itself operating within. It is also raising attendant issues around access, media influence, commercialisation and 'publicness' which are equally central in ongoing discussions about the evolving mediascape which we occupy as both citizens and consumers.

There are of course other areas in which the process of globalising forces combined with the centrality of importance of television revenues for clubs in particular is forcing change. The growing debate in Europe about the tensions between increasingly powerful elite clubs and their national associations highlight aspects of the intersection between football, media influence and national identity. There is also the changing cultural contract that exists between the game and its supporters. As football increasingly moves into the realm of television driven entertainment, to what extent does the new media age offer an acceleration of supporter alienation, or an opportunity to positively re-define that relationship for a new century?

These are areas of concern we will return to in more detail in the latter chapters of the book.

On the ground: the views of the fans

Studies on football fandom have highlighted the exploitation of the traditional fan, and the longer-term erosion of the fanbase that has sustained the game throughout the downturns in its fortunes (Brown, 1998). This – bottom up – view of the game and its relationship with television has been welcome, important and has provided much needed empirical research which has acted as a counterweight to the corporate discourse which appears to increasingly drive much of the football economy and culture.

However one needs to exercise a degree of caution in presenting a pre-television age in which football existed as a more pure form of popular cultural activity, more rooted in the local and more 'traditional' in its practices and culture. If this is the case it is more likely to be found in the game up until the 1950s, for the history of football in the age of television is one of change, tension and a democratisation of sorts. In other words, television as a form of representation has actually helped to promote the game, raise its profile and at times add to the excitement that is generated by the moments of collective identity which transcend the sport (Boyle and Haynes, 2000).

The notion of a golden age of football, which television has somehow ruined, while appealing for some when they are subjected to the rough end of the game's apparently rampant commercialisation, is in fact a myth. One could argue that the fans have always been exploited in various forms throughout the history of the game which has been run primarily by a class other than its main-stream supporters. Fans have often been the last to be consulted on change within the game. Indeed as Fynn and Guest have argued:

> Fans have always been treated with disdain. It is nothing new, only the details change. When supporters who traditionally were drawn from low-income groups, provided the chief source of income by paying to attend matches, stadia were large and facilities poor. Now that football attracts a wealthier clientele, stadia are smaller but facilities are much better. It is not television or commercialisation that are the enemies of the fans, it is the attitude of owners and administrators, and that is the same as it always has been.
>
> Fynn and Guest, 1999: 258

In addition, it could be argued that many of the processes that have eroded some of the more traditional fabric of the sport and its attendant fan culture are the result of wider social and cultural change. This is not however to dismiss the importance of the supporters (or the legitimacy of their many grievances), far from it. We would argue that it is the fans who ultimately invest in the club with much of its distinctive sense of identity, and whose passion for their team remains central in helping to give the game the unique position that it enjoys within contemporary popular and media culture. Rather it is to suggest that the game's relationship with the media and television in particular has been an uneven and at times contradictory experience for supporters. It has been partly about control, but it has also been about access and democratising the sport through its free-to-air coverage, reinforcing various local and national identities in the process.

At this point we want to turn our attention to offering a brief overview of some of the key moments in the evolutionary history of the relationship between broadcasting and the sport in Britain. This we hope will help set the historical context for the arguments we develop in the rest of the book.

Football on television: the evolution of a relationship

It is difficult for a football fan in 2004 to appreciate the degree to which extensive live football on television is a relatively recent phenomenon in Britain. Throughout the 1960s and 1970s, the relatively stable relationship between the game and television revolved around televised highlights, reflecting in part the deeply held concern among the footballing authorities about the impact that live matches would have on attendances at matches (Haynes, 1998).

The footballing authorities have always been ambiguous about the relationship they should have with television. A fear of losing match day revenue, control of the sport and supporters' loyalty has been counterbalanced by the income television has helped generate through the direct and indirect exposure it brings to the game, the clubs and the players. Horrie (2002) notes how the advent of ITV in the mid 1950s, and the appetite of the new commercially oriented regional network to secure football led to a threatened breakaway league in 1955. ITV was keen to do deals with the individual clubs involved, but the Football League threatened to expel any member clubs who entered into such arrangements with ITV companies.

Led by Newcastle United, the idea emerged of a 'TV Floodlit League' encompassing Sunderland, Arsenal and Tottenham Hotspur and the Edinburgh teams Hearts and Hibs (the Old Firm appeared more reticent about playing with English clubs in those days), with ITV prepared to pay £50,000 for the privilege of broadcasting these evening matches. Horrie argues that the idea

> was destroyed by a combination of political lobbying by the small clubs, the opposition of the FA, and vacillation on the part of ITV, which had begun to doubt that the matches would get the audiences needed to justify the massive investment. There was another decisive factor. Manchester United and Celtic came out against the idea of a British Floodlit league because it conflicted with their preoccupation with the European Cup.
>
> Horrie, 2002: 8–9

However it was clear that television and football were about to become inextricably linked as two of the central tenets of British popular culture attempted to co-habit with each other. What is significant about this incident from the mid 1950s is that it highlights the inherent built-in tensions between these two institutions as they plot the future development of the sport.

This period of turbulence existed before an established pattern of agreement emerged between football and television, which would last until the 1980s. But it does serve to remind us that from the outset, television impacted on the game, not simply in terms of its ability to re-represent the game and help create stars who became known the length and breadth of the country (and beyond in an increasingly global televised world). But that structurally the relationship would be about control of the game and its ability to exist as a distinct form of popular cultural activity in an increasingly mediated age. An age in which television, with its drive to commodify and repackage cultural forms for its own commercial and ideological ends, would become the central driver of a more global mediated popular culture.

1960s–1980s: change and consolidation

While football and television wrangled over the value to the game of live football, developments within the wider broadcasting environment began to reshape the relationship and establish the codes and conventions of televised sport which would remain, with minor alterations, until the 1980s (Whannel, 1992; Rowe, 1999; Haynes, 1998; Boyle and Haynes, 2000).

In 1962, the Telstar satellite allowed live pictures to be relayed across the Atlantic for the first time. When the link arrived early for British television, to such an extent that the US Presidential press conference was not up and running, it was to sport that the medium turned. The first live television pictures carried from the US were from Chicago and featured a baseball game. Live televised sport was about to go global.

Also during this period, developments in outside broadcast facilities and the advent of videotape meant that the editing of football matches to provide highlight packages, offered a way forward for both the game and television. The BBC's 1964 *Match of the Day* programme, initially launched on BBC2, itself a new channel that year which extended the BBC's influence in the television market, was to provide a template for television coverage of the game for almost twenty years. The Corporation paid the Football League £3,000 a season for the rights to broadcast the highlights package. Horrie (2002: 25) notes that they had to increase this to £60,000 a couple of years later in order to see off competition from ITV. It wouldn't be long before the two key broadcasters in the UK market realised that by working together, in an informal cartel, they could both benefit by securing football rights at a highly competitive rate both for the public service driven BBC and the more commercially orientated ITV network.

The perception that football had a natural home on television was enhanced by the success of the 1966 World Cup held in England, which generated some of the largest television audiences seen in the UK. By 1968, ITV had introduced regional football highlights programmes. Between 1968 and 1979, the cost of securing the rights to English league football rose from £120,000 a season to £534,000, with the money going to all league clubs, regardless of whether they had appeared at all on television that season. Despite an infamous attempt by Michael Grade at the regional ITV company, LWT, to 'snatch' the rights in 1979 and the increase that television paid for football rights rising to £2.2 million in 1980, the BBC/ITV cartel remained largely intact.

The cosy duopoly between the licence fee funded BBC and the commercial publicly regulated ITV network, represented a limited market for the selling of football rights. In many ways football on television was part of a wider cultural consensus which saw the television market in Britain across a range of programme catogeries remain relatively stable, with occasional high profile defections of light entertainment stars from the BBC to a better paying regional company which formed part of the ITV network. The advent of Channel 4 in 1982 did little in the short term to disrupt this relationship between the BBC and ITV, and given its remit as a minority PSB channel to innovate meant it made little impact on the televising of football.

Live football did of course exist, but was restricted, on the domestic front to the English and Scottish FA Cup Finals (carried by both the main channels) and the European Cup Final which alternated between them each year. In addition, the Scotland v England Home International fixture was also carried live. Throughout its relationship with television, the footballing authorities, and increasingly a growing band of club chairmen, had felt that the sport had undersold itself to the medium. There was by the early 1980s a feeling that more live football may increase the revenue streams into the game and also attract better commercial sponsorship deals.

The economists Dobson and Goddard (2001: 23–24) argue that:

> The 1960s and 1990s in particular appear to be transitional decades, when football's economic structure was subject to quite radical and fundamental change. In other decades, football's economic structure exhibited signs of much greater stability.

Clearly this pattern was closely linked to the scale of revenue flowing, in this instance to the English game, from television and the attendant commercial sponsorship opportunities that this exposure offered.

The break-up of the BBC/ITV cartel 1980–1992

When ITV's *The Big Match Live* went out in October 1983, it carried for the first time a live top flight English league game. As part of an agreement between the Football League and television, ten matches were broadcast live on a Sunday, with the League getting £2.6 million for these rights. The major clubs in England began to realise that opportunities existed for increasing the revenue streams from television. When BBC/ITV offered almost £4 million a season for nineteen live matches plus highlights in 1985, it appeared that the clubs would have little option but to agree. However, led by the media tycoon Robert Maxwell, whose footballing interests had encompassed the lower league clubs Oxford United and Derby County, the chairmen rejected this bid convinced (by Maxwell) that they could extract more value from their rights.

Wider events kicked into play however. The running sore on the English game, hooliganism, again raised its high profile head with pitch battles at Luton prompting calls for the introduction of ID cards for supporters. Within ten weeks the football industry had been blighted by two further incidents. A fire in the main stand at Bradford, killing 56 fans and the death of 42 Italian supporters at the European Cup Final, screened live on the BBC at the Heysel Stadium, following the collapse of a wall during battles between Liverpool and Juventus supporters. As a result of the latter, English clubs were banned from European competition for five years. These tragedies dramatically impacted on the image of the game, and highlighted some of the chronic structural and social issues that ran deep throughout the governance of the sport.

By August of that year no television deal was done, and six months later the Football League accepted a deal of less value from BBC/ITV than had previously been on the table.

Wider policy and structural change within the broadcasting industry were however about to reshape British television. Driven by the neo-liberal economic policy of the Conservative Government under Margaret Thatcher, the closed world of broadcasting was to be exposed to the rigours of the market, and UK broadcasting policy was to be repositioned from primarily one concerned with its cultural remit, to one driven by industrial and technological policy. This viewed the audio-visual industries as both users and drivers of new technologies such as the satellite and cable delivery systems that could now, with political sanction, challenge long established so called natural monopoly businesses, such as television and telecommunications.

The advent in 1988 of the Government sanctioned British Satellite Broadcasting saw pay-TV introduced into the UK marketplace. BSB would launch with a dedicated sports channel, and identified this area, along with movies, as the subscription driver it needed to secure its viewers. In May of that year, they audaciously offered the Football League £9 million a season for ten years for exclusive access to live English football. Up until now, the game had received less than £5 million a season, despite the substantial increases that television in other European countries such as Italy, Germany, Spain and France was now paying to cover the sport (Fynn and Guest, 1994: 61) (see Chapter 3).

Alerted to the dangers of this, Greg Dyke, later to become Director-general of the BBC, and then Chairman of ITV Sport, intervened. Initially by lobbying the big five clubs – Tottenham Hotspur, Arsenal, Manchester United, Everton and Liverpool – who had been keen since the mid 1980s to secure more revenue from television through the formation of a Super League, and then by making an offer directly to ten clubs. Eventually ITV did a deal with the whole of the Football League, paying a then staggering £11 million a season for a four-year deal. It was a landmark arrangement in the history of British televised football, because it enshrined the notion of live football as an integral part of the regular televisual diet of football supporters. The Big Match saw seventeen cameras being used to cover games for the first time in the UK, and the game was more aggressively marketed by the increasingly commercially orientated ITV network.

Dyke realised that the market was changing for commercial television in the UK. Increased competition longer term from new satellite stations would potentially eat into ITV audience share and advertising revenue. He was also aware that televised football on a Sunday could boost a traditionally 'dead' slot in the schedules, while also attracting a younger male audience that advertisers were willing to pay handsomely to reach.

The television market place in the UK commercial sector was about to become extremely competitive, and while commercial television had existed in the UK since 1955, in reality it was a form of publicly regulated commercial television, operating within a regulatory framework which extended many of the public service obligations which had shaped an organisation such as the BBC. Both the 1984 Cable and Satellite Act and the 1990 Broadcasting Act were about to lift some of these obligations and to open the market up to greater competition, with major implications for the future structure and shape of the football industry.

1992 – the move from PSB to niche viewing: from citizen to consumer

The start of the 1990s saw two competing satellite systems attempting to establish a pay-TV platform in the UK market. As we noted above, BSB, through its dedicated sports channel had been interested in football as the key content since its inception. Through an alliance with the BBC it had secured coverage of the English FA Cup and also completed deals to bring both live Scottish and Italian football to a UK pay-TV audience. However the BSB pre-launch was plagued with problems, and by the time they had launched in 1990, nine months behind schedule, a rival Sky TV was already in place, using older technology, but refocused from a pan-European operation to one keen on establishing a foothold in the embryonic UK pay-TV market.

Within a year Sky effectively took over its rival as the companies merged and a new organisation BSkyB emerged. As part of the BSB package, the new company retained two key people who would help re-shape the way football would be covered on UK television. Vic Wakeling, would later become Head of Sports at the company (and one of the most important people in British football as indicated in the *Independent*'s 2003 list quoted at the start of this chapter), but initially came on board as Head of Football, while BSB's Andy Melvin would soon become executive producer of the Premier League coverage on the newly merged channel.

Ironically given the key role that Greg Dyke had played in helping to create the climate in which the breakaway FA Premier League would be born in 1992, with the new league of course retaining all of its television revenue, it was in fact the newly formed BSkyB who would reap the benefits. Dyke in fact rejected an approach from BSkyB for a joint bid for the 1992 rights with ITV. However the BBC under John Birt were much keener to do business as they saw their ability to compete at a negotiating table diminish as the cost of live rights rose dramatically. Birt argued:

> The technology allows, for the first time, rights holders – soccer, movies, whatever – to extract more of the value of their product from the consumer. And the simple strategic analysis showed that it was impossible for the BBC to follow that.
>
> Cited in Horsman, 1997: 94–95

After some highly dramatic negotiations (Horsman, 1997: 95–100; Horrie, 2002: 93–105; Fynn and Guest, 1994) BSkyB secured the exclusive live rights for the newly created FA Premier League in a deal worth £304 million and involving the BBC securing highlights for a relaunched *Match of the Day*. While only about half a million viewers watched the first game of the new deal, they were now paying £5.99 a month for the privilege.

What the success of the deal proved was that the value placed on football by television had now dramatically changed, as had the money flowing into the game. Also, despite the accepted wisdom that the UK market could not sustain a pay-TV platform, it became clear that this was simply wrong, and that BSkyB and pay-TV were going to be an increasingly important part of a newly emerging broadcasting ecology for the remainder of that decade and beyond.

Not only would BSkyB help alter the structure of the sport through the money it would invest in the game, it also changed television coverage and how the game was represented to the viewer. Through people like Vic Wakeling, BSkyB brought aspects of both American and Australian televisual coverage of sports to the UK. They laid down a template for the way that television would cover the game in the 1990s that would be copied, if not quite emulated, by all its terrestrial rivals.

During the 1990s, many of the innovations brought to coverage by BSkyB, such as reverse angle shots of goals and incidents, the onscreen logo ident and clock would be adopted and modified by traditional broadcasters to such an extent that in 2004, football on television looks very similar regardless of whether it is free-to-air or on a pay-TV platform.

As Dobson and Goddard (2001: 69) have argued:

> Football's rehabilitation as the most popular and fashionable national sport has also been aided by skilful exploitation by the industry of selective aspects of its own 'heritage'.

There is little doubt that led by BSkyB initially, all the major broadcasters now sell sport, and football in general, in terms of the integral part that television plays in the heritage of the sport. The so called 'natural' home of the game.

To this effect it is also now clear that Premier League football has become an integral part of the BSkyB brand identity. Not only had the gamble to pay such an amount successfully helped position the company as the key player within the pay-TV market, the money that was now flowing into the game (or at the very least into the players' wage packets) was transforming the sport.

In 1996, BSkyB, mindful of the potential emergence of telecoms companies encroaching onto their market in the medium term, secured their core asset, live Premier League football for a further four seasons (1997–2001) at a cost of £670 million. It would be the last time that such a long-term deal would be secured as the pace of change within the media environment quickened towards the end of the 1990s. Bolstered by the BBC once again securing those all important free-to-air highlights which meant that key sponsors secured national exposure on terrestrial television, it appeared that the spiralling value of television rights would continue indefinitely (see impact on other leagues in Chapters 3 and 6).

This deal was also significant in that it would see BSkyB's hegemony over top flight English football consolidated and the tentative introduction of a new business model within the television industry, pay per view (PPV) football arriving for the first time in the UK. For football the honour of being the first PPV match was bestowed on the Manor Ground home to the then First Division Oxford United in their match against Sunderland in March 1999.

It would be the advent of digital technology and the harnessing of this technology to extract increasing revenues from consumers and the securing by BSkyB of the 2001–2004 rights to the elite of the English game that would set the parameters for the new battlefield that television and football was about to enter into. It is this aspect of the relationship that we look at in more detail in the following chapter.

Who has got the power?

To what extent is it accurate to depict television as the bad guy in this relationship? Is it the force that has dismantled the traditional relationship between the roots of the game and its core supporters? The issue of rights has always been a tricky one for the governing bodies of the sport and governments who seek to intervene in this aspect of national cultural activity. In effect, as Greenfield and Osborn have argued:

> The question of protecting this area of culture from the free market is problematic as any reduction in income for sports bodies raises the question of the need for increased state funding. It is not a straightforward issue,

since there is support, not based on purely ideological grounds, for a free market in sports rights. Sports are keen to maximise income and, after all, they have precious little else to sell.

Greenfield and Osborn, 2001: 175

Of course it was the ability to remove such activity from free-to-air television in Britain (always a slight misnomer as the BBC was funded by payment of a licence fee and the other channels through advertising revenue which was indirectly passed onto consumers every time they purchased a good or service), that brought into focus such arguments. A process facilitated ostensibly by developments in satellite technology in the 1990s, but in reality fostered by a changing political and economic climate that was committed to opening restricted broadcasting markets and increasing viewer choice. Television itself had become something increasingly made sense of in political circles as part of economic or industrial policy. The cultural dimension of the medium, its function as part of popular and national culture and the contribution it could make to notions of 'publicness' and civic society were largely absent from the political agenda. Minimal protectionism exists in the listed events but a strong sense that televised sport is central to a sense of cultural citizenship (Rowe, 1996) has given way to a resignation that viewers will at some point have to pay to view football.

In a relatively short period of time the issue of televised rights to football has gone from being something which the existing broadcasters could negotiate relatively quickly (in many cases operating as a cartel as we noted above). It now involves a complex tender document, and is often accompanied by a sustained media PR campaign to shift the value of the rights before the document is even sent out (the case in 2003 for example saw extensive briefings to the press as all sides involved in the 2004–2007 negotiations used media leaks to strengthen their hand). All of which has shifted the cost base of football on television considerably.

In 2003, the cost per hour of sport on BBC television was £192,000, with sport second only to drama in terms of cost and now clearly considerably more expensive than news and current affairs (*Broadcast*, 1 August 2003). In the late 1980s, sport cost the BBC £27,000 an hour and was one of the cheapest forms of programming. Central to these costs has been the increase in football rights.

We would argue that there has always been a tension between football as a carrier of cultural and social identities, something rooted in the local, but related to the national, and the game as a commercial entity, bound up with sponsorship, money and prestige. What has happened is that these tensions have become more explicit as the game has undergone a significant restructuring post Hillsborough driven by the new financial underwriter of the game – television.

Allied with this the deregulation of the broadcasting environment and the development of new media platforms have simply accelerated a process, the origins of which have been laid for some time. In other words, fans have always been exploited, the game has always been controlled primarily not by those who watch the game, and the supporters have always been the last to have a say in the fundamental shifts in the game's governance.

Conclusion: a whole new ball game?

Blain (2003) raises the issue of sport's autonomy beyond the hegemony of media culture. He argues:

> Now that observers are well past the stage of being struck by the transformation of culture into media culture we can contemplate a new phase in the interaction between culture and the media, which is in part the normalization of media culture as culture.
>
> Blain, 2003: 233

In the case of football, we would argue that any such transformation also has limitations. We might argue that while football can be viewed as primarily a media product, it also has its own culture (sometimes hidden, sometimes nasty) that can at times be resistant to the wider cultural values that the sport finds itself embued with, for example hooliganism, the traditional heavy drinking culture associated with travelling fans and such like.

As Blain has suggested:

> In a media-saturated society it has become very difficult to know what everyday values are and who produces them. It has become precisely a point of argument as to whether the media; in filling their pages with the imagined love affairs of football coaches on the bruises on Beckham's foot, are imposing an ideological or marketing agenda of their own (or both); or playing back to us, for our gratification, our own concerns.
>
> Blain, 2003: 249

This is certainly an issue in the new media age as the sheer volume of 'football chatter' (often interactive) across a range of media platforms has become substantial. This also raises issues of how globalisation is impacting on the game and its relationship with the media and the impact on the fans' relationship with the sport (see Chapter 7). In many ways this is the ideological impact of a wider process that Whannel (2002) has called 'vortextuality'. As he argues:

> The growth in the range of media outlets, and the vastly increased speed of circulation of information have combined to create the phenomenon of a 'vortex' effect, which I term here 'vortextuality'. The various media constantly feed off each other and, in the era of electronic and digital information exchange, the speed at which this happens has become very rapid.
>
> Whannel, 2002: 206

It is this digital landscape that we are particularly interested in throughout the book.

We argue that a new set of economic, technological and cultural circumstances over the past decade has impacted on the symbiotic relationship between football and the media in various ways. Put simply the rules of engagement between football and the media have changed. The media landscape looks very different. Terrestrial, free-to-air television is no longer the primary vehicle for live football; subscription and pay-per-view have increased in importance as business models to deliver audio-visual content; digital television has attempted to add value to the presentation of televised football through interactive elements including viewer editorial control (player-cam) and e-gaming; and a broader 'unbundling' of media rights to football has emerged to assist the delivery of content in various formats. The widening spectrum for new media has enabled football related rights to be leveraged across a range of different media and telecommunications platforms. While media and telecommunications companies initially invested in football clubs in order to influence future broadcasting rights negotiations and support the infrastructure of club owned media operations, this policy has been reversed in 2003–2004. This indicates how quickly and at times unpredictably the media market is changing.

The football industry have argued that these developments have led to a wider choice for football fans and consumers to enjoy the game as well as providing much needed revenue streams from various subscription and pay-per-use services. There is, however, a broader range of complications to these developments which we want to examine in the book.

This work then is not primarily focused on football as a sociological phenomenon, although it draws on the work of football sociologists such as Giulianotti (1999) where appropriate. Rather, a central theme throughout the book is a concern with the political economy of communication as well as its relationship to wider cultural and social practice. What we are attempting to track here is the importance of contemporary media developments in helping to act as a driver for wider cultural change, and often impacting quite markedly in already existing cultural forms, in this instance football. What Miller et al. (2001: 93) view as:

> A televisualization of sport and a sportification of television [with] audiences built up by national services at public expense being turned into consumers by preying capital, and new technology that has not excited customers being pegged to the sports habit.

Whannel's (1992) work developed the concept of cultural transformation when examining the aesthetic, representational, ideological and structural impact that television has had on sport. In that spirit, we would hope that in studying the evolving relationship between what we are choosing to call 'new media' (with all the caveats to this mentioned earlier in the chapter) and football, that some insight might be gained into the contemporary state of the relationship between media and popular cultural forms. We clearly place this work within a wider political economy frame of analysis, but it is one that we hope is sensitive to the key role that representation, image and audience play in generating and creating cultural practice and meaning.

The next chapter extends our examination of television's relationship with the game, as the former enters the digital era.

Chapter 2

The digital revolution
A whole new ball game?

ITV Digital was born out of the presumption that there was no limit to the amount of football that the public would watch. On BBC1 there was football, on Sky Sports there was football, on ITV1 there was football, and on ITV Digital, well, there were highlights of Wycombe versus Port Vale. There were still plenty of other things on telly, of course. There was drama about footballers' wives or quiz shows featuring retired footballers.

John O'Farrell, the *Guardian*, 27 April 2002

The banks who underwrite the clubs have looked on ever more nervously. Football has lost its lustre as an investment, and a reluctance to grant new credit is matched by a desire to call in old debt. Hence the prospect of administration hovering over so many big names.

Paul Kelso, 'Clubs face harsh facts and feel the squeeze', the *Guardian*, 12 October 2002

Introduction: enter the digital age

On a wet and gloomy November day in 1998 a new era of television was ushered in that would ultimately have a profound impact on the shape of English club football. ONdigital, the brash new digital terrestrial television (DTT) service was up and running, promising to break the stranglehold of BSkyB on the delivery of multichannel television in the UK. The £90 million launch came one month after BSkyB had begun their migration to digital television. Where Sky Digital promised over 300 channels and enhanced interactive services, ONdigital had a limited offering of up to 30 channels. Some may have observed that the Battersea headquarters at the brash Marco Polo House had previously been home to the ill-fated breakfast broadcaster GMTV. Nevertheless, ONdigital's new management were confident about its potential to loosen the grip of its established rival as the chosen route to a new era of television.

In many ways the new upstart in the UK digital, multichannel, pay-TV sector had every right to be bullish about its prospects of converting the country's households to digital television. The UK had evolved into the largest pay-TV market in Europe. In the context of televised football, if one looks at the way in which the game connected with the mushrooming television and new media services at this time it is easy to understand the optimism.

As we have already outlined in Chapter 1, the evolution of a new set of economic, technological and cultural circumstances in the mid-to-late 1990s had a profound impact on the symbiotic relationship between football and television in various ways. First, terrestrial, free-to-air television was no longer the primary vehicle for live football. Although there is arguably more live football on free-to-air television than at any time in the history of televised sport, the most important rights remain those to the key domestic competition the Premier League. As we discuss later in the chapter, regulatory pressures have opened the window for terrestrial broadcasters to share in the spectacle of what has become the most lucrative football league in the world. However, when the Premier League celebrated its tenth anniversary towards the end of the 2002/3 season it became clear that it was also a celebration of a particular relationship between football and pay-TV. As we go on to discuss in Chapter 4, it has been subscription television, and to a lesser extent pay-per-view, which has underwritten the importation of world football stars with lucrative salaries to match.

Second, it is now well established that football fans are prepared to pay for the privilege of watching live games. Football as 'dish-driver' has made the multichannel household commonplace and established BSkyB as a major force in British broadcasting. The widespread criticism of BSkyB's original deal for the newly formed Premier League in 1992 seems long forgotten, a footnote in the history of televised sport. Although attempts to introduce pay-per-view games has met resistance in some quarters and has not been taken up as enthusiastically as subscription services, the commodification of televised football is now secured.

Third, in the presentation of football, digital television has attempted to add value to its coverage through interactive elements including viewer editorial control (player-cam) and i-gaming, with, as we argue in Chapter 7, mixed success.

Fourth, UK media and telecommunications companies began in the 1990s to invest in football clubs in order to: a) influence future broadcasting rights negotiations; b) support the infrastructure of club owned media operations. While there has been a retrenchment in this process, we want to focus on this aspect of potential cultural convergence in more detail in Chapter 5. The potential direct business linkage between media and telecommunications corporations and English football has raised some of the most intriguing and politically sensitive issues in the football media nexus. Most importantly, the battle to secure rights has become far more contentious as the commercial, and indeed political, interests in such deals have become increasingly complex.

Finally, related to this point has been a broader 'unbundling' of media rights to football. The separate 'windowing' of rights has emerged to assist the delivery of content in various formats to benefit both rights holders and media outlets. In broadcasting these rights include live coverage, highlights packages, pay-per-view, sell-through video and DVD, analogue and digital radio, and VOD or video clips. In the broadly defined area of new media, rights have been leveraged for live audio-visual and audio Internet streaming, text services to mobile phones including WAP, and, in 2003 audio-visual clips to 3G devices.

The football industry have argued that these developments have led to a wider choice for football fans and consumers to enjoy the game as well as providing much needed revenue streams from various subscription and pay-per-use services. There is, however, a broader range of complications to these developments which need to be highlighted. The remainder of this chapter looks at two interrelated stories of football in the era of digital television. First, the rise and rapid fall of ONdigital, later renamed ITV Digital and the impact of its rights deal with the Football League. Second, we analyse the negotiation of the various 2004–2007 broadcasting rights to the Premier League in the context of regulatory pressures from the EU Competition Directorate.

ONdigital: the new home of football

ONdigital, a joint venture between Carlton Communication and Granada Media who held a near-monopoly in the ITV Network, represented a significant upsurge in the proliferation of new media technologies available in UK households. DTT was a more restricted service than satellite or cable digital television technologically bound by the bandwidth available to a standard aerial. Essentially, what ONdigital provided was a platform for the two ITV companies to showcase their new channels with the potential to drive new streams of revenue through the sales of additional advertising. However, the key issue for the company was whether or not it could capture enough new subscribers to warrant the levels of capital investment by Carlton and Granada who were underwriting the enterprise. The service was launched in the belief that the digital terrestrial platform could deliver affordable, accessible and easy to use multichannel television to people who had shied away from the services offered by BSkyB. For many households the reluctance to subscribe to BSkyB was either because of cost or as Banks (2002: 117) has pointed out due to 'customer antipathy towards satellite dishes'.

When the service began, the economic environment in which television was operating, was one characterised as seemingly boundless. Just one week after the service began Granada proudly announced its best ever set of annual figures to the City with a record-breaking profit of £735 million (Granada Media, 1999). Much of this was based on a buoyant advertising market, with ITV's coverage of World Cup France '98 boosting ad sales with revenues up 5 per cent. But the advertising bubble was soon to burst as the US dotcom boom in the late 1990s suddenly crashed on unfulfilled promises and inflated valuations. The whole media and communications sector would be thrown into a global recession just as Carlton and Granada were staking enormous sums of money into an untried market for digital television.

The launch and early months of the service were beset by technical, operational, managerial and public relations' problems that were to prove portents of a far greater crisis to come. The supply of set top boxes (STBs) was not meeting demand and the software that ran the boxes had a tendency to crash. Furthermore, once Sky Digital axed the £199 for their STBs, ONdigital were forced to follow suit and give away STBs free in order to entice new customers. This placed a huge financial burden on Carlton and Granada with some estimates that the free technology was costing the two companies £100 million a year (Doward, 2002).

The service was also hampered by the limited coverage of the ONdigital signal that only reached 50–60 per cent of the UK. These technical difficulties were compounded by a growing suspicion among consumers that the service was merely a second-rate alternative to Sky. BSkyB had been frozen out of the franchise to operate the DTT platform by the Independent Television Commission (ITC) and the European Commission's competition authority DG4 who feared Rupert Murdoch's unhealthy level of control of multichannel television in the UK. According to Doward (2002) this cast the terrestrial broadcasters adrift from any expertise they might have been able to draw on and made them competitors with Sky rather than partners. In this context, ONdigital was confronted with overturning the grip of an established multichannel service, having to buy in 'blue-chip' programming, principally sport and movie channels, at a cost they could ill-afford (from the outset ONdigital was paying Sky £60 million a year for these services). As the BBC later discovered on the re-launch of the DTT platform through the Freeview service, having BSkyB as a collaborative partner rather than predatory rival provided distinct advantages in getting a new service up and running.

The technical problems faced by the service were also impacting on the internal relations of the company. In a subsequent employment tribunal hearing in November 2000, Chief Executive Stuart Prebble had to admit that the much heralded launch masked internal friction and belied significant concerns by management about the delivery and technical specification of STBs. Furthermore, the operational success of the company's call centre was called into question by senior management. Prebble openly admitted that in spite of the public perception of a smooth entry into digital television, 'it was not a success internally in terms of managing the situation' (Bowers and Teather, 2000).

Prebble, who also occupied the role of Chief Executive of the ITV Network, had himself been brought into the new company in July 1999 after the much-publicised departure of ONdigital's original Chief Executive Stephen Grabiner. Grabiner resigned after initially accepting a job with News Corporation's Internet investment company e-partners, before making another about turn to join venture capital company Apax. The episode dealt a body blow to Carlton and Granada not least because Grabiner's decision was partly driven by indecision and divergent views about ONdigital's strategy to compete with BSkyB (Barrie, 1999). Other departures followed and within two years of operation the company had either dismissed or lost four out of five of its original directors.

Beset externally with pressures from consumers and commercial partners and internally with discord among senior management and between the two major shareholders, ONdigital turned to football to steady the ship. The decision to stake a claim as a serious sports channel would ultimately lead to a premature end to the company and the UK's DTT platform as a subscription service.

The Football League deal and ITV Sport

As many multichannel broadcasters across Europe have discovered, having a dedicated sports channel in their 'bouquet' of channels is an essential feature of their service in an increasingly competitive environment. As Papthanassopoulos (2002: 189) has noted, there has been an explosion of sports channels across Europe from the mid 1990s onwards with more than 60 dedicated sports channels by 2000. Not surprisingly, in August 2001 Granada and Carlton made moves to build their own sports brand with a new service ITV Sport. The channel represented a widespread faith in the industry that sports channels could drive subscription to pay-TV with other services being pulled along in their slipstream. The strategy had worked well for BSkyB throughout the 1990s and ONdigital's executives clearly believed sport, specifically football, would do the same for their service. It is instructive to analyse the rise of the sports channel and the Football League deal in some depth as it reveals some of the wider economic and political pressures that impinge on the new media environment. Our analysis also argues that a purely technology-driven explanation for the rise, and fall, of digital television in the UK, is wholly inadequate.

Digital deals

Investment in a dedicated sports channel appeared to make sense given the expanding portfolio of sports coverage on the ITV Network. ITV had poached key personnel from the BBC including presenter Des Lynam in a deal worth £5 million who was persuaded to leave by another long-standing servant of the BBC, producer Brian Barwick who had been instated as Head of Sport at the ITV Network. ITV1 had bolstered its football coverage having secured the 2001–2004 Premier League highlights from the BBC in a deal worth £183 million, which introduced a prime-time Saturday evening programme *The Premiership* fronted by Lynam.

Moreover, from its inception in 1992 the Champions League had been covered on ITV1 and throughout its first three years ONdigital had sought to leverage these rights to drive subscriptions. In 1999 UEFA increased the number of entrants to the competition from 24 to 32 and introduced a second-group phase to increase the number of matches played. The new format secured regular European football for the leading clubs as well as a regular supply of live football for television. On securing rights to the new format ITV split the coverage of games between Tuesday and Wednesday evenings. One game would be screened on the ITV Network on terrestrial television while the other evening's football would appear on ITV2 on ONdigital.

With the development of the new sports channel the digital broadcaster could promote this coverage to a far more targeted market that demanded 'live' football under a more distinct brand. The channel was heavily cross-promoted on ITV1 at every opportunity. With a single genre sports channel in place ONdigital hoped the next push to its target of 2 million subscribers would be achieved. As well as the 'spillover' of Champions League games to the subscription channel, the key to achieving a long-term strategy rested with the exclusive rights to the Nationwide League. To fully understand the collapse of the digital broadcaster it is important to review the Football League rights deal at some length.

The deal

Because of the strategic importance and financial implications of rights negotiations the story behind the tender process is rarely revealed. There are exceptions such as Matthew Horsman's (1997) investigation of BSkyB's first moves into sports broadcasting and the inpropriety of some chairmen and broadcasters during the first rights deal for the Premier League. Valuation of sports rights has become an important function within the sports media business. There are key individuals who operate in all the major sport markets around the world, the majority have legal backgrounds and act as intermediaries between rights holders and broadcasters. Usually, the auction for football rights is organised around sealed bids along with the broadcasters' presentation of how they plan to cover a particular event. These processes are rarely revealed to the public.

The Nationwide League deal was completed in June 2000. The preceding months had seen intensive negotiation and discussion between the Football League and a range of broadcasters interested in the rights tender. As much by coincidence as design, the rights for the Premier League and a package of rights for the Football Association, including England internationals and the FA Cup, were also tendered during the same period as the Nationwide League rights and sold within three days of each other. The en masse sale of rights meant the battle to secure live football was intensified. Furthermore, sports broadcasters were operating within a far more competitive broadcasting environment. Not only was ONdigital (along with the ITV Network) competing with BSkyB, but also cable companies NTL and Telewest had entered the market.

With the relatively new broadcaster Channel 5 also in the hunt for live sports rights the three governing bodies of football were in an unparalleled bargaining position. The BBC were peripheral players in terms of exclusive live rights to the Premier League, but would have been expected to have been interested in the highlights to the competition, possibly with a minor interest in the Nationwide League as well as continuing its association with the FA Cup. The environment created a sellers' market and placed intense pressure on all broadcasters, but especially ONdigital, to secure some live football to remain credible in the eyes of its viewers. Football, the crown-jewel in the BSkyB success story of pay-TV was a 'must have' content in such a competitive environment. ITV Sport had seen the blueprint of what was possible with Sky Sports and cast itself in the same mould.

This confrontational strategy would ultimately fail for a variety of reasons we shall set out later in the chapter. Before moving on to analyse the ultimate collapse of the enterprise in the Spring of 2002 it is instructive to recall the bidding process for the Football League rights and the pressure to succeed in the bidding process the management of ONdigital felt at the time. In the subsequent High Court case involving the Football League and the two shareholders of ITV Digital, Carlton and Granada, certain aspects of the initial bid period were revealed in court for the public record.

The summary judgement on the high court proceedings reveal that the Football League were concerned about the possible knock-on effect of the Premier League rights sale and that a rapid conclusion to the auction would help secure the best deal. The tender document had been released in March and the initial bids from broadcasters were discussed at the League's commercial committee meeting early in June 2000. ONdigital's bid was clearly viewed as the main contender but at an initial bid of £240 million spread over three years the League's representatives asked the broadcaster to reconsider and up their bid.

The bidding broadcasters were sent a memorandum by the League's representative Stephen Townley asking each party 'to make any adjustments they feel necessary to their previous proposal' (Langley, 2002). At this time BSkyB were heavily committed to retaining the Premier League rights and made a strategic decision to drop out of the bidding process. Nevertheless, unaware of just how many broadcasters remained interested in the rights to the League rights ONdigital upped their bid the following day to just over £96 million per year over a three-year term. The League considered the deal and pressed for more in the knowledge that ONdigital were eager to secure the rights, not wanting their proposed launch of ITV Sport to be bereft of football. Townley met Prebble to finalise the deal. Prebble had sought assurances from two directors representing both of the digital broadcasters' owners Steve Morrison (Granada) and Nigel Walmsley (Carlton). Both also acted as non-executive directors of ONdigital. That evening, a final figure of £105 million per season was agreed. From our research we are aware that Prebble had the authorisation to push the cost of the rights even higher, possibly to £130 million per season. But at this point the League would have been more than satisfied with what they had achieved and decided to call a halt to the bidding process.

The news of the rights sale for a total £315 million over three years was broken to the 72 Football League chairmen at their end-of-season Annual General Meeting held in Chester the following day. The deal was greeted with mild-shock and excitement by the chairmen not privy to the negotiations who were due to benefit from a 400 per cent hike in the global annual revenues from the new contract (the previous deal was worth £25 million per year). From the start of the contract in August 2001 the clubs benefited from an initial payment of £136.5 million with two further instalments of £89.25 million (totalling £178.5 million) due in August 2002 and August 2003.

ITV Sport channel

Once the deal was signed in June 2000 executives at ONdigital also set in motion their plans to launch the subscription sports channel. Although ONdigital in collaboration with cable operator NTL had competed with BSkyB for the Premier League rights, they were more than happy to have secured a significant amount of domestic football with the Football League, with over 100 live games per season, to fill the schedule of the dedicated channel. Andrew Marr, Head of Media and Public Affairs for ONdigital also made moves to dampen concerns that fans would have to pay even more to watch live football by stating 'Football fans are used to paying to get their football coverage. What people have to decide now is which service provides the best deal for them' (the *Mirror*, 17 June 2000).

The announcement clearly reiterated the belief among management that ONdigital's offering was more attractive to sports fans. A key aspect of ITV Digital's strategy in this respect was the decision to keep the channel exclusive to the DTT platform. BSkyB had been obliged to offer two of its premium sports channels, Sky Sports 1 and Sky Sports 3, to ONdigital from its inception due to a clause in their rights deal with the Premier League. ITV Digital had not negotiated any such clause with the Football League and believed the exclusivity of the channel would help motivate new viewers to digital television to opt for their service over their more established rivals BSkyB.

Before launching the sport channel the first strategic move by Carlton and Granada was, in July 2001, to rebrand the entire company from ONdigital to ITV Digital. The move brought the service closer to the ITV brand. To quote one analyst, 'ONdigital had no brand equity' (Day, 2002b) and therefore underplayed its association with nearly 50 years of broadcasting. Positioned alongside ITV1 and ITV2, ITV Sport would be heavily associated to the core values of both the ITV Network and the digital platform ITV Digital. On the launch of ITV Sport in August 2001 Prebble set out the rationale for the channel:

> We intend to give the Nationwide League and Worthington Cup the sort of coverage hitherto reserved for the Premier League and FA Cup. The League is the heart and soul of football and reaches some of the most dedicated football fans in the country. We'll make sure that these fans, who make up the 13 million who regularly attend League matches (more than go to the Premiership) get the very best TV service for their clubs.
>
> Quoted at http://www.mediabullet.co.uk 17 January 2001

The deal also secured 15 live games for the ITV regions in England and Wales as well as regional highlights packages. Combined with *The Premiership* on ITV1 and the Champions League spread across its free-to-air and subscription channels, ITV Sport had a potentially attractive portfolio of televised football.

The intention of Granada and Carlton was to consolidate these rights across the ITV Network and the digital service with the branded channel, ITV Sport, and a re-branded service ITV Digital. The change of nomenclature did not please everyone in the ITV Network. Management at Scottish Media Group (SMG) were unhappy that ITV Digital would benefit from its association with the ITV brand as it would not be advantageous for the whole Network, only ITV Digital's owners Granada and Carlton.

The £26 million account to re-brand the service was handled by ad agency Mother. Their task was a need to deliver a coherent message of what ITV Digital stood for. Consumers had remained confused as to what differentiated the service from BSkyB. Football played a huge part in the evolution of the marketing communications strategy. The advertising attempted to clarify the services on offer, specifically the fact that ITV Digital enabled viewers to potentially view the Premier League as well as ITV Sport's own offering of the Champions League, Nationwide League and Worthington Cup competitions as well as men's tennis from the ATP Tour.

The campaign turned to a puppet monkey and the comedian Johnny Vegas to emphasise the power of the DTT viewer to access top sports content. Not wanting to alienate the female audience, the campaign also played on a familiar domestic dispute of who controls the remote control with a battle to view sport or movies. The campaign certainly raised the profile of the service and even turned the 'Monkey' into a cult popular cultural figure. However, BSkyB also weighed in with a vociferous marketing campaign that simply displayed the number of channels available through ITV Digital and Sky digital with the slogan 'Bigger choice. Same Price. Only with a minidish'. The campaign was graphic and to the point and effectively demeaned what ITV Digital had to offer. By autumn 2001 there were signs that all was not well and the comic 'Monkey' motif soon came back to haunt the service.

The collapse

The economic downturn in the media and telecommunications markets was beginning to cause a certain amount of retrenchment in advertising spend across all media sectors. As we have highlighted in Chapter 1, the large investment in setting up new media infrastructures such as digital television and 3G telecommunications networks had left global corporations with huge debts and a decreasing amount of capital to sustain investment. By June 2001 it became common knowledge in the City that Carlton and Granada were seeking a third investor in the company to share the financial burden of developing the service, specifically the telecommunications company BT. Confidence in the company was hit further in the autumn of 2001 by City analysts Zenith Media, whose report on the ITV companies was damning on the prospects of the company making any return on its investment in the ITV Sport channel. The report concluded, 'Failing divine intervention, ITV Digital should be sold or dismantled with all despatch, because this money's not likely to come back' (Teather, 2001).

The figures for the ITV Sport channel certainly made gloomy reading. The channel had only attracted 200,000 subscribers by the start of the 2001/2 season. Consequently the viewing figures for Nationwide League games was appallingly low even for a subscription channel. Estimated figures of 1,000 viewers for games between Cambridge United versus West Bromwich Albion and Nottingham Forest versus Bradford City severely undermined the funding and razzmatazz that had gone into promoting the new channel. At a cost of £1.2 million per game in rights *The Times*, 28 March 2002 would later remark that it would have been 'cheaper to drive each viewer to the ground, put them up in a five-star hotel and give them all £500 spending money'. Figures for ITV Sport's coverage of the Champions League games faired little better. While the live games on ITV1 could attract up to 5 million viewers, games involving Deportivo la Coruña versus Manchester United and Panathinaikos versus Arsenal attracted a mere 52,000 and 15,000 respectively on ITV Digital. These low figures alarmed UEFA whose communications director Mike Lee publicly raised fears that they would 'like the games to be made available to a wider audience' (Cassy, 2001).

Aside from the fact that live Nationwide League football was proving to be less than compelling in attracting subscribers, there were two specific reasons why ITV Sport was struggling to build a substantial subscription base. First, was the intransigence of ITV Digital to open up the channel to Sky digital viewers and subsequently their inability to broker a deal with the satellite broadcaster once it was realised that the policy of exclusion was not working and subscription levels remained stagnant. In November 2001 Carlton and Granada undertook a strategic review of the company which was headed by ex-BSkyB chief executive David Chance. One outcome of the review was a move to broker a carriage deal for ITV Sport with BSkyB with the hope of opening up access and driving up subscriptions. At the same time, BSkyB had also received pressure from the Football League urging them to seek a carriage agreement for ITV Sport. In an official statement the League chairmen felt it was 'unacceptable to the many football fans who subscribe to Sky that they are currently denied the opportunity to watch their teams and the Nationwide Football League'. Fears that BSkyB were simply hoping to drive out a competitor increasingly appeared to be grounded in reality.

Negotiations broke down due to the refusal of BSkyB to pay the £80 million licence to carry the channel. Earlier indecision about carriage on the digital satellite platform among the ITV Digital board had delayed the talks and by this time BSkyB realised it had nothing to gain from supporting the channel by possibly undermining subscriptions to its own sports channels.

The second major issue slowing the rate of new subscriptions was piracy of 'smart cards' that activated the ITV Digital STBs. A long standing fear of the media industry in the digital age has always been the ability of consumers to illicitly copy digital media or circumnavigate the conditional access system that acts as the gateway to subscription TV channels (a problem which we note in the following chapter is particulary endemic in television markets such as the Italian). Encrypted signals that enable access to subscription and pay-per-view content are the bedrock of leveraging revenue from digital multichannel television. Take away the ability of broadcasters to secure content behind encrypted signals and the whole business model is effectively undermined. From the outset ITV Digital faced a massive problem of piracy. Some estimates put the level of pirated cards at 100,000 (the *Guardian*, 13 March 2002) but it is likely the number could have been twice that. Consumers would receive their STB from ITV Digital, subscribe to the minimum subscription service (for £6.99 a month) and substitute their 'standard' smart card for one enabling access to all the premium channels. Pirated cards were distributed via age-old black market networks in pubs and street markets. News that ITV Digital was facing a huge piracy problem surfaced in March 2002 when its main supplier of smart cards (a subsidiary of Vivendi Universal, Canal Plus Technologies, that supplied smart cards to 12.5 million STBs worldwide, including ITV Digital) filed a $1 billion lawsuit in the US courts regarding the piracy of their technology by rival manufacturer NDS. NDS was a subsidiary of News Corporation and had Lachlan Murdoch, son of mogul Rupert on its board.

Canal Plus claimed NDS had paid hackers to break the encryption code of their smart cards by reverse engineering and then posted the details of the code on the Internet. This enabled card pirates to re-code cards to provide access to all premium channels without payment. The claim of corporate espionage was refuted heavily by NDS and their owners News Corporation. But the levels of piracy of ITV Digital STBs was enormous and seriously damaging the levels of new subscribers to the ITV Sport channel and the rate of 'churn' of existing viewers renewing their subscriptions.

Unfortunately for ITV Digital the legal action taken by Canal Plus was too late in the day to save the digital platform. The litigation against NDS was eventually dropped in appeasement a year later after News Corporation acquired a controlling share of Italian pay-TV platform Telepui from debt-laden Vivendi Universal. Within the space of 12 months Murdoch's Sky Global brand had bolstered its position as the leading pay-TV provider across Europe (see Chapter 3).

The downturn in the UK advertising market was continuing to hit Granada and Carlton who saw their capital investment shrinking. It appeared to many at ITV headquarters that the cumulative effect of technological problems, the exit of senior management, the undermining influence of 'smart card' piracy and perhaps most importantly in the words of Stuart Prebble the 'ferocious' competition from BSkyB meant that the company had no realistic chance of survival. The debt to the Football League was a noose around ITV Digital's neck. Something would have to give.

When is a contract not a contract?

In December 2001 Granada and Carlton sought to substantially cut the cost of supporting ITV Digital. They began negotiations with the platform's main programme suppliers in an attempt to renegotiate contracts. Top of the list was the two outstanding payments of £89 million due to the Football League. News of ITV Digital's crisis was filling the pages of the financial and media press and the League sought parent company guarantees that the rights fee would be paid should ITV Digital become insolvent. The issue of guarantees from Granada and Carlton and the failure of the League to complete the long form agreement for the rights contract were to be at the heart of the subsequent court case.

ITV Digital emphatically refused to sign any agreement regarding guarantees. Instead, the broadcaster made moves to restructure the deal by offering the League two reduced payments of £25 million for the two remaining years on the contract. On 21 March 2001 the League Board met to discuss the restructured offer. The response was quick and emphatic in the belief that the contract signed in June 2000 would be honoured by the platforms owners. Chairman of the Football League Keith Harris announced:

> The media speculation whipped up by ITV companies about this contract has, of course, been very unsettling for our clubs and their supporters. Nobody should be in any doubt that if this contract is not honoured, there will be widespread bankruptcies in many local communities and our national game will be left devastated. In such circumstances, Carlton, Granada and ITV Digital will bear a heavy financial and social responsibility.
>
> The Football League, 2002

The statement from Harris clearly alluded to the wider social and economic impact any loss of revenue would cause the League clubs. The war of words had begun and the League stuck to its task of recouping the £178 million due. The one concession it made was to accept the second instalment of £89 million in August 2002 with the view to renegotiating the third instalment in 2003.

ITV Digital went into administration on 27 March 2002. Publicly, the company made a commitment to emerge from administration with a more robust business to carry forward the DTT platform. The key issue was whether or not the League deal could be renegotiated. The League, deeply upset and angered that the company had moved into administration against all the promises to the contrary made threats to take Granada and Carlton to court in a £500 million lawsuit. The two parties were given six weeks to meet a settlement with the administrator to provide a progress report for the court on 15 April.

The League drafted in a range of consultants to help with issues of administration and finance, legal protection and public relations and lobbying. A key strategy was to gain public sympathy for the plight of the League and in particular for the clubs to try and build pressure on the television company to honour its contract. Leading lobbying firm, GPC International were brought in to ensure the issue was politicised and advised all League chairmen to seek face-to-face meetings with their local MPs. Financial pressure came from public relations firm Holborn PR who were used to get the League's point of view across to the City. The League was quick to publicly castigate ITV Digital regarding the turn of events claiming that executives had been saying one thing while preparing for another. One League spokesman was reported as saying:

> One minute, it's a rosy picture, the next they need insolvency experts. We think they started casting around for administrators on 14 February.
>
> Quoted in Shah, 2002

The League threatened to lodge a complaint with the Financial Standards Agency regarding the underhand behaviour of ITV Digital and its owners. The League had also brought in the vice-chairman of Tottenham Hotspur, David Buchler, who was also chairman of Kroll Buchler Philips, a leading corporate recovery firm. Offering his services as a favour to the League, Buchler was known to champion the argument that companies that agree contracts with third parties through joint ventures should be subject to greater scrutiny. With this in mind the League applied for the full disclosure of information from the board minutes of ITV Digital to ascertain how the decision to move into administration had evolved and how much money Granada and Carlton had put aside to keep the flagging service going. The League was also concerned that there was a conflict of interest over the appointment of the administrator Deloitte and Touche. The City accountants had undertaken consulting work for both the League and ITV Digital in the past and it was thought that this implicit knowledge of the two organisations could compromise fairness in the administration process.

The whole affair became an embittered and messy public relations battle between the League, and its club chairmen, and the ITV companies. The League began to draw on the support of the whole football community but were initially unhappy that the FA had remained silent on the issue. Prompted by the mounting pressure from the 72 League chairmen, the FA's then chief Adam Crozier joined the mounting war of words against the ITV companies:

> There is no doubt that the dispute has already harmed the ITV brand in the eyes of the City, the consumer and indeed the sports industry. There is now a perceived lack of trust in ITV which could undoubtedly have a long-term effect on the network's ability to build relationships in the future.
>
> Cited in Carrick, 2002

Support for the League also came from a constituency of fans who rallied to form their own pressure group called the Football Fans Union whose slogan 'Can the Commercials' asked fans to boycott the ITV channels and avoid watching any commercial breaks. The campaign received the full support of the League's Chief Executive, Burns, whose own members subsequently started a campaign of direct action against ITV Digital under the banner 'Save Our Clubs'. The campaign included a march on the headquarters of Carlton and Granada in an unprecedented public display of political protestation by the hierarchy of English club football.

The slurs and mud-slinging began to irk executives at both Granada and Carlton who railed against the claim that they were responsible for the League's financial plight. The Granada Chief Executive, Steve Morrison, was seen to hold talks with the League's advisor, David Buchler (both friends of Arsenal vice-chairman David Dein) at the north London derby between Arsenal and Spurs (Garrahan, 2002).

Morrison was keen to deflect direct criticism from within football of Granada's role in the affair. As major stakeholders in the ITV Network Morrison felt the reputation of ITV Sport who had contracts for the Premier League, the FIFA World Cup and UEFA Champions League could be damaged. Upset by Burns' negative publicity campaign Prebble and his team withdrew their final conciliatory offer of £74 million and refused to negotiate any further. In a public statement the ITV Digital board announced that:

> The Football League has overplayed its hand. We wanted a constructive dialogue all we got was a tirade of abuse.
>
> The *Guardian*, 18 April 2002

The following day League chairmen met in Manchester to discuss where to go next. Up to 30 of the 72 League clubs were in deep financial crisis and the loss of television revenues, money which had been ploughed into the salaries of players on inflated contracts, was threatening to push many of them over the financial abyss. In the same month, the League had announced their highest attendances at League grounds for 33 years with 14,791,689 fans visiting grounds during the 2001/2 season. The pride in raising attendances proved cold comfort to many clubs facing a huge hole in their finances. Confirmation that ITV Digital had been liquidated on 27 April 2002 served to intensify the reality that a number of clubs faced administration as costs far outweighed income.

Anticipating the move by the Football League to legally pursue the outstanding rights fee from the parent companies Carlton and Granada, the two broadcasters began High Court proceedings claiming relief on any liability under the original rights contract. The League submitted a counterclaim for £178.5 million plus another claim for damages declaring that 'Carlton and Granada were jointly and severely liable as guarantors of ONdigital's obligations under the June Contract' (Langley, 2002: 1). The case centred on the contract signed by ITV Digital for the Football League rights and the extent, if at all, the two ITV companies had underwritten the payment of the rights fee with parent company guarantees.

The League representatives argued that Carlton and Granada had given guarantees of payment during the initial bidding phase and that this, by implication, was part of the eventual contract to license the rights to ONdigital (ITV Digital). The broadcasters denied any such agreement and indeed pointed to the League's late scramble to have a long-form agreement of the contract agreed and signed with guarantees included immediately prior to ITV Digital moving into administration as evidence that no guarantee actually existed. Reviewing the original bidding process for the rights, including the initial discussions and the final June contract, the judge had little option but to side with the television companies.

As Justice Langley (2002: 15) concluded the League's case fell at the 'first and fundamental hurdle'. No guarantee was written into the June contract, neither did ONdigital have the authority to offer guarantees from its two parent companies. The League's claim that the negotiating process included a 'unilateral offer' of guarantee by the parent companies, was dismissed by the judge as 'inventive but misconceived'. Crucially, the judge was damning of the way the whole business of football rights was handled. The League executives, its legal representatives and chief negotiators were all viewed as culpable in the way the contractual licence was poorly assigned. Summarising the judge argued:

> It is all the more unpromising when the relevant negotiations are conducted in a major commercial context between two companies with the benefit of the professional advice of experienced management and lawyers. In my judgement the Football League's case remains just as unpromising at the finish as it looked at the start.
>
> Langley, 2002: 12

The outcome of the High Court case not only paid to the monies owed by the liquidated company but also severely damaged reputations within the League and its associates. Although Burns was installed as Chief Executive of the League after the deal had been negotiated, his failure to reclaim any of the outstanding rights fee and the loss of the court case led to mounting pressure for him to step down. In August 2002 both Burns and League Chairman Keith Harris resigned.

Top executives at ITV also lost their jobs over the collapse of the digital broadcaster. Stuart Prebble resigned as Chief Executive of the ITV Network and Steve Morrison, Chief Executive of Granada, left the company to appease shareholders over the huge losses incurred by the company as it attempted to keep ITV Digital afloat. By the time the liquidation process had been completed in the autumn of 2002 a mere 2 per cent of the total debt had been raised from the

sale of assets (£27.3 million) (Gibson, 2002c) and to save face Granada and
Carlton were forced to donate any rented STB's to their owners free of charge.

'The clock is ticking': the Government shows its hand

Reflecting on the events that led up to the demise of ITV Digital it is instructive
to review the position of the UK Labour Government regarding the impact
of the collapse on both digital television and the football industry. Towards
the end of 2001 the Government began to keep a close eye on ITV Digital
once City analysts became concerned about the company's ability to stem the
haemorrhaging of Carlton's and Granada's cash and stay afloat. Prime Minister
Tony Blair's special advisor on media matters, Ed Richards, began sounding-out
executives across the media sector. By the autumn of 2001 the Government
were clearly getting nervous about their aim to switch-off the analogue signal by
2006–to–2010. One remedy was to boost the signal for ITV Digital to promote
the platform with greater reach and reliability. This was a bone of contention
for the Chief Executive of ITV Digital Stuart Prebble, who later blamed the
demise of the enterprise on the Government's sluggishness in supporting the
DTT multiplexes.

As rumour began to spread about the floundering business the Government's
plans for the future of digital television looked increasingly compromised.
Once ITV Digital had moved into administration the Government attempted to
distance itself from the failed service. The Secretary for Culture, Media and
Sport, Tessa Jowell MP, made a statement in the House of Commons to
dampen any blame being apportioned to the Government. Jowell proclaimed:

> The hard truth is that this is a failure of a company not a technology [fur-
> thermore] Digital TV and the promise it holds is more than ITV Digital.
>
> BBC, 2002

One month earlier Jowell had enforced the point that 'the clock is ticking' in
respect of the Government's 'switch-over'. Reports that the Government had
sounded-out other broadcasters with the hope of bailing out the platform
clearly rankled executives at Carlton and Granada and may even have hastened
their decision to pull the plug on the enterprise.

One year on from the collapse of the company Prebble attacked the Government's role in the whole fiasco claiming that it had undermined the position of
ITV Digital by not ensuring a strong enough signal for the three multiplexes
the DTT ran on. Moreover, the success of the re-launched DTT platform Freeview backed by the BBC, BSkyB and Crown Castle was viewed as a political
decision that reflected the dominance of BSkyB in the UK pay-TV market.

> The truth is the Government were terrified of doing anything that would
> irritate Sky. I absolutely think that. News International owns the *Sun*. I

think this Government is uncomfortably close to Murdoch, and the communications bill demonstrates that. I think it is all politics: the Government's wish to save the platform, the power of the BBC, and because Sky was not opposed to it, the problems fell away.

Stuart Prebble, quoted in Brown, 2003

Prebble's complaint about the weakened signal were rebuffed by Gary Tonge, director of engineering at the ITC who clarified the matter in a letter to the *Guardian*:

The ITC got the technical rules changed in 2001 to allow the increases, and with the Government we applied continuous pressure to the broadcasters to implement them. They finally agreed to do it in March 2002, but by the time the work was done ITV Digital had collapsed.

The *Guardian*, 9 June 2003

Whichever argument was correct, the final outcome remained and BSkyB now had ensured a near-monopoly position in the pay-TV market, using football to bolster its position in the process. ITV digital had taken on the satellite broadcaster at its own game and lost heavily. Unfortunately for the Football League it had been caught up in the cross-fire of a highly competitive new industry and had not secured its own liability enough to protect it against the consequences.

If Prebble and the ITV companies were smarting from the lack of support from the Government, the Football League did not fair any better. The Government's official line on the plight of League clubs during the weeks leading up to the insolvency of ITV Digital was sympathetic but strictly non-interventionist. The Government were particularly cool on the many calls from club chairmen, the Professional Footballers' Association (PFA), supporters' groups and a selection of back-bench MPs calling for the Culture Secretary to put pressure on Carlton and Granada to secure payment of the television rights.

In March 2002 League Chief Executive David Burns had made a presentation to the All-Party Football Group of MPs chaired by Alan Keen. The group of MPs were known to have taken the opinion that Carlton and Granada had a 'moral obligation' to solve the League's predicament but their lobbying did little to persuade Jowell. The Government held the view that football clubs were responsible for their own finances and had brought the problem on themselves by accepting inflated players' salaries. This position echoed a similar line taken by the Conservative Government in the mid 1980s when Prime Minister Margaret Thatcher could not understand the call for Government support to assist the modernisation of the game after the Heysel and Bradford disasters in an era of £1 million transfers.

The only recompense from Government was the establishment of Supporters Direct which had been set up with the assistance of the Government to enable fans to get involved in the running of clubs through supporters' trusts. Jowell suggested clubs would have to turn to their communities to find alternative sources of finance to sustain their activities. And, in an address to the House of Commons, she commented that 'We expect that Supporters Direct will take a prominent role in helping to secure the future of clubs over the coming months' (Jowell, 2002). The Government's response was cold comfort for the Football League clubs and their fans. The League faced a bleak future having been at the centre of a process that would damage confidence in the game's finances and its ability to woo broadcasters and new media services to invest huge sums of money in the sport.

The ITV Digital collapse ultimately hurt football more than the media corporations with many clubs threatened with bankruptcy and administration (Banks, 2002). The clubs did manage to redeem some revenue from their television rights with a much depleted offer from BSkyB in July 2002 worth £95 million over four years but much of the financial damage had already been done. The ITV Digital fiasco led many media sports commentators to conclude that the boom in television sports rights had reached a ceiling. Indeed, as we shall go on to discuss, the football authorities and clubs began to brace themselves for significant reductions in the amount of rights fees they could leverage as negotiations for the next round of broadcasting rights got underway.

The changing regulatory context for broadcast rights to football

> The restrictive effects of collective selling agreements (namely, that they amount to a price fixing mechanism, limit the availability of the rights of sport events and strengthen the market position of the most important broadcasters) limit both competition between broadcasters and consumer choice. The effect on competition has to be evaluated in its economic and legal context, taking into account, for example, the feasibility of participants selling rights individually.
>
> Mario Monti, 2001

With the rapid expansion of dedicated sports channels during the 1990s and the related competition for the rights to football, regulators have begun to investigate the collective sale of rights in the belief that they may not be in the public's interest. Digitalisation of the pay-TV sector has broadened the capacity to deliver multiple sports channels and the potential, for example, for every Premier League game to be screened live.

In December 2002, the European Commission competition directorate DG4 opened proceedings against the English Premier League regarding the restrictive nature of the live television agreements it had with BSkyB. The football industry had already been rocked by EC competition law in the wake of the Bosman rulings that freed up the movement of players out of contract. Now, the spotlight turned to the collective sale of rights, exclusive agreements and its negative implications for broadcast markets and consumers. The EC argued that collective agreements restrict the number of games available to subscribers, and were keen to explore the possibility of all games being opened up to the multi-channel broadcasting environment, including the Internet. As we shall discuss in Chapter 3 a similar process had already taken place regarding the sale of rights to the UEFA Champions League and now the EC's focus shifted to the domestic markets of top-flight football in England and Germany.

The basis of the EC's interest in television rights to football lies in European Union competition policy. The general criteria for competition policy are the prevention of abuse of market power and remedies to counter the misallocation of resources (Doyle, 2002: 168). European legislation has primarily focused on regulating the behaviour of dominant firms rather than intervening to alter the structural make up of a particular market. This is particularly true in the media industries where the liberalisation of markets to encourage the growth of new media businesses has in turn enabled the concentration of ownership across the sector. In terms of television rights to football, the Commission believes that the joint sale of rights represents a 'horizontal restriction of competition' (Toft, 2003: 8). Central to this debate is the ability of clubs to trade some of their media rights individually. The issue was made clear by one DG4 official Torben Toft in a paper delivered to delegates at an EC conference on Broadcasting Competition Law in January 2003:

> [T]he concentration of rights in the hands of sports federations reduces the number of rights available. Moreover, availability of rights is reduced still further by an increasing number of TV rights contracts being concluded on an exclusive basis for a long duration, or covering a large number of events. This strengthens the market position of the most important broadcasters they are the only operators who are able to bid for all the TV rights sold in large packages.
>
> Toft, 2003: 7

Another EC official is reported as saying the Premier League deal with BSkyB is like 'one supermarket doing a deal with beer manufacturers to become the exclusive outlet in the UK' (Gibson, 2003a).

As we discuss in Chapter 5, in an era when football clubs can establish their own channels and Internet sites with the potential to deliver audio-visual content via broadband the EC's policy began to have a significant implication for the prospective sale of any rights. In the context of the English Premier League and its near entrenched relationship with BSkyB, the issue of exclusivity across the main rights package for live football was also in the firing line for EC competition regulators.

The Premier League deal with BSkyB had been scrutinised before by the Office of Fair Trading in 1999. The OFT believed the deal to be anti-competitive at a time when multichannel television was beginning to establish itself and the prospect of digital television with even more channels was around the corner. The Restrictive Practices Court ultimately ruled that the collective sale of broadcast rights to the Premier League were pro-competitive largely because they benefited consumers. The court argued that money was spent on players and stadiums in the late 1990s due to equal sharing of money through the League. The investigation was also the backdrop to the planned takeover of Manchester United by BSkyB in 1998 (Walsh and Brown, 1999). BSkyB saw a competitive advantage in controlling not only the richest club in the Premier League but also the potential of controlling the broadcast rights of the club should the OFT investigation rule against collective selling. In the event the merger was blocked by the Department of Trade and Industry after an investigation by the Monopolies and Mergers Commission (now the Competition Commission) on the grounds of public interest. But the seeds were sown in the minds of the major clubs that certain rights could be retained and exploited.

The move by clubs to develop their own television and broadband channels has awoken the competition authorities to the restrictive practices of sports federations in the sale of rights. For instance, between 2001–2004 the Premier League sold rights to 106 live games per season when 380 games were potentially available. This restriction of output has been viewed as detrimental to consumer choice and new media markets. In particular the global sales of secondary rights to Premier League games in markets outside the UK have been largely undervalued. At the very least, the deals brokered under a collective system have not been as favourable to those clubs such as Manchester United who have global brand appeal and could potentially earn far greater commercial revenue through the promotion of live football on their own channel. In April 2003 United's then Chief Executive Peter Kenyon infuriated other Premier League chairmen when he announced that he had conducted unilateral talks with EC officials regarding the sale of overseas rights. Clubs without the global cache of United were vehemently opposed to changes in the collective agreement that had previously brought £178 million between 2001–2004. It was in this context that the sale of rights to the Premier League from 2004–2007 were conducted.

The price is (not?) right

The collapse of ITV Digital led to a re-evaluation of rights fees throughout football. Leading those who were now sceptical about the prices being paid for sports rights were the Chief Executive of BSkyB Tony Ball and the head of Sky Sports Vic Wakeling. Throughout 2002 Sky Sports had shed some of its key sports rights including the England Rugby Union games in the Six Nations tournament, Scottish Premier League football and UEFA Cup football. BSkyB had picked up the Football League contract on the cheap and would add its joint rights to the Champions League to its impressive portfolio of football coverage.

Premier League football remains a central driver of subscribers to BSkyB. Through bundling its channels, with Sky Sports at its pinnacle, the company had successfully achieved its target of capturing seven million subscribers by the end of 2003. Added to its impressive market performance and dogged competitiveness was the potential of saving money in the downturn in the value of sports rights. BSkyBs dominant and bullish position was bolstered by a decline in competition for rights. It had seen off rival ITV Digital, had out-flanked cable companies NTL and Telewest who were both burdened with significant debt, leaving the satellite broadcaster with a far stronger hand in the negotiating process for the 2004–2007 rights. Commenting on the renewal of Premier League rights Ball also hinted at the importance of exclusivity to the value of the rights:

> The Premier League are now wrestling with the EU. They have a statement of objections from the EU competition authorities which they have to answer concerning collective bargaining ... The key with the Premier League is the level of exclusivity and if it gets it or if they're made to change their packages to reduce exclusivity, then clearly that's going to have a big effect on the value of the product.
>
> Interview with Cantos.com, 14 January 2003

For its part the Premier League had begun to make moves to leverage as much value as possible from the new rights from the start of the 2002/3 season. Much emphasis was placed on the global appeal of the Premier League with matches screened live to 152 countries. The global expanse of the League's popularity led Chief Executive Richard Scudamore to proclaim that 'a sixth of the world's population sees a game at some point during a year' (Campbell, 2002b). In April 2003 the Premier League also drafted in a new rights negotiator, lawyer Simon Johnson, who had previously been ITV Network's director of rights and business affairs, to handle the next round of rights (Gibson, 2003a). The public relations battle to either play up or mark down the value of the rights had begun in earnest. It showed the important role that the sporting and financial press play in helping to create climates of opinion with regard to the true value of Premier League rights (Boyle *et al.*, 2002).

The key to the whole negotiation and bidding process was the EC investigation and its 'guiding hand' in the structure of the deal. While not prescriptive, the EC edict that collective selling could only exist where the consumer ultimately benefited from wider choice and no broadcaster could exclusively sew up all the rights clearly influenced the initial tender document issued by the Premier League in June 2003. The newly structured package of rights initially consisted of three main tranches of live games. The so-called 'gold' package consisted of 38 matches on Sunday afternoon at 4.00pm. The 'silver' package also consisted of 38 matches on Monday evenings, midweek and Sunday at 2.00pm. The 'bronze' package consisted of a further 62 matches on Saturday afternoon with kick-offs at 1.00pm and 5.15pm. The three packages were designed to create more competition among broadcasters and increase choice to the viewer who would now have 138 games to watch rather than the 106 of the previous deal. Further, by increasing the volume of games available the Premier League were more likely to maintain their gross income from television rights even though the unit price of each live game would have decreased.

The invitation to tender also included the traditional highlights package as well as a new package of rights that enabled a broadcaster, or club channel, to screen 'near-live' matches available from midnight on the match day. Finally, all 380 matches were available in clip form to mobile phones to transmit merely five minutes after the game had ended. These new rights were an attempt to appease the EC regulators who had complained that the majority of the Premier League games were not screened in their entirety or even within extended highlights. It also met demands from the EC to help promote new technologies such as 3G phones, rights that had largely remained dormant as telecommunications companies rolled out new services.

In breaking up the rights into more 'windows' and increasing the number of games available the Premier League attempted to dampen any further demands from the competition authorities. The invitation to bid for rights had followed a series of lengthy consultations between the Premier League and the DG4 officials. The Premier League reiterated their fears that if clubs were allowed to sell the premium television rights it would create greater imbalance in the League and may push some clubs into administration. Such fears touched on the declaration regarding the specificity of sport adopted by the European Council in Nice that provided some exemption from the competition rules of the EC Treaty. The Football League and the FA also made representations to the EC in the hope of persuading the Commissioner Mario Monti that collective selling of television rights under the 'solidarity principle' was legitimate and necessary for the football industry.

The waters were muddied somewhat when a delegation of MPs from the All-party working group on football made their representation to the Commission with the notion that collective bargaining could continue as long as more of the Premier League revenues were redistributed to the lower leagues. The collapse of ITV Digital and the resulting financial meltdown of the Nationwide League clearly prompted the idea. Although the Premier League already made contributions from its television rights fee outside the League to the Football Foundation and the PFA nearly 90 per cent of the revenues stayed with its members. The intervention by the group of MPs was smartly rebuffed by the Premier League who thought the MPs' approach was 'naïve' (Soccer365.com, 2003), their 'solidarity principles' clearly ending with the 20 Premier League clubs.

Broadcasters had remained publicly silent on the impact of the EC intervention, but the Premier League's response to the regulators' pressure had a direct influence on their approach to the bidding process. BSkyB were unlikely to favour any dissolution of their exclusive contract and would seek to maintain their position or dramatically drop the value of their bid. Rumours that BSkyB had made a move to acquire all three packages of live rights for the same price as the previous deal sparked fears that the EC regulators would mount a further challenge to the rights sale. Less than two weeks after the initial bid process the League increased the rights packages from three to four, breaking up the 'bronze' package of 62 games into two separate licences. The move lessened any possibility of BSkyB controlling all the live rights and increased the chances that a terrestrial broadcaster, either the BBC, ITV or even Channel 5, might be able to introduce live Premier League football free-to-air for the first time since its inception in 1992.

The belief that terrestrial broadcasters or one of the cable companies could snatch any of the live rights was ill founded. In August 2003 the Premier League announced the winners of its rights tender. All four live packages were bought by BSkyB for a total of £1.024 billion giving the satellite broadcaster more games for less money when compared to the previous deal. ITV's sensitivity to paying inflated rights fees for football post ITV Digital meant that they massively undershot the BBC's bid for the highlights package that the corporation comfortably won for £105 million. This meant the return of Premier League highlights to *Match of the Day* in 2004. All the major deals reflected a deflation in the value of rights to televised football, although the collapse was not as great as some predicted.

However, the thorny issue of a fair and transparent tender for the rights loomed over the deals. Although the Premier League insisted that all four live rights packages had been marketed and bid for individually the financial might of BSkyB meant that realistically there would only be one winner. With BSkyB consolidating its position as the exclusive broadcaster of live Premier League football the EC once again expressed concern at the tender process. In September 2003 a renewed 'statement of objections' was raised and the threat of a 'negative anti-trust finding' again seemed likely (Hodgson, 2003). An agreement late in 2003 to allow eight matches to be screened live on terrestrial television has not seriously dented BSkyB's dominant position.

Conclusion

What the story of football rights and the dawning of the digital television era reveal is the blind faith many television executives place in the game to deliver audiences. ITV Digital got it wrong because the expectations of what football could do for its subscription base were wildly optimistic. When allied to the managerial problems of developing a new service with all the associated technical problems it is little wonder that the entire enterprise collapsed. Conversely, football authorities have also had to shoulder the responsibility of ensuring rights fees are maximised in order for their member clubs to survive. In the late 1990s television revenue became an increasingly high proportion of football club revenue. When that financial crutch was dramatically taken away with the collapse of ITV Digital many League clubs were left floundering for their very survival. Premier League clubs have faired better and with a renewed three-year deal the top Premiership clubs are assured a handsome pay day when they appear on Sky Sports. The renewed contract has come at a price. More games to be screened with more disruption to the fixture list away from the traditional Saturday 3.00pm kick-off. Moreover, the deal may yet be derailed by regulators, with £30 million wiped from the value of rights as BSkyB loses its exclusivity.

Many of these new pressures have been brought about by rapid changes to the media environment. Technology has certainly opened up the horizon of televised football, but in the UK context this has seen a fiercely competitive global media corporation face off any competition to reign supreme in the digital pay-TV sector. As we shall discover in the next chapter, similar processes across Europe have disrupted the harmony between football and television in the new media age.

Chapter 3

The European dimension

Power and influence in new media football markets

> As the history of European television has shown us, the successful development of any new technology and form of television has to do with the content and the perceived value added that they offer to the viewers.
>
> Papathanassopoulos, 2002: 32

Introduction

This chapter places developments in the UK against the backdrop of wider shifts in the European media and footballing landscape. The previous chapter outlined how key factors in the development of a digital broadcasting environment in the UK have shaped and impacted on the football industry in the UK. In this part of the book we want to focus on the wider European dimension and examine how the particular evolution of the digital TV market has directly influenced the relationship between television and football across a number of European countries. Here we want to examine the dynamics influencing the changing relationship between rights holders and media corporations across the Continent and focus on the wider implications of these shifts for the governance of the game.

Rather than simply list the current arrangements between rights holders and media organisations – a process that as we have noted in the previous chapter is continually evolving and shifting – we want to identify wider shifts and trends in the marketplace and highlight some of the more specific social and cultural implications of such a process. We begin by analysing the emergence of a European digital television market and the impact this has had on the value of football rights.

The digital television market in Europe

A combination of economic, political and technological factors have all shaped the European television market over the last few decades. Despite repeated threats to intervene directly, the European Union has broadly left the market to drive developments in this sector. Where it has intervened it has often been to

reinforce the centrality of the market as the best mechanism for delivering cultural diversity and choice in the broadcasting sector. Some such as Murdock (2000. 55) have argued that in reality this has been at the expense of defending the traditional public service notion of broadcasting and in particular the centrality that universal access has in such a model.

We concur with Murdock (2000: 39) who argues that too much writing about the impact of digitalisation is driven by a form of technological determinism. A view which identifies digital technology itself as the prime agency driving change across the broadcasting market in particular. As we have argued already in Chapter 2, the advent of the digital age is really part of a wider structural process of marketisation; as the market has become the central frame of reference for cultural activity. Murdock argues that there are five areas which have driven this process: 'privatisation; liberalisation; the reorientation of regulation; corporatisation, and commodification' (Murdock, 2000: 39–43).

In particular the 1990s have seen a distinctive new stage in the longer process of opening up previously closed or restricted broadcasting markets to increased competition. It is however worth noting that, unlike the UK television market discussed in the previous chapter, countries such as Italy, Spain and Germany had already seen the hegemony of state financed broadcasters broken in the 1980s with the rise of private sector broadcasters such as Mediaset in Italy and RTL/Bertelsmann in Germany. The advent of digital technology has heralded an intensification of this longer process of deregulation, or, perhaps more accurately a re-regulation of broadcasting within a more commercial and market driven frame of reference.

While there may be specific characteristics associated with particular television markets across Europe, Papathanassopoulos (2002: 2) has argued that there are a set of common issues which are being faced in all these distinctive markets. He argues that these include:

> The increasinging commercialisation of the media, the fragmentation of both audiences and advertising expenditure and the reliance on new methods of funding, such as subscriptions and PPV.

To this list one might add the growing challenge faced by public service broadcasters to retain rights to sporting events (and indeed define a role for themselves) in an increasingly competitive marketplace. There is also the public struggle to define the cultural and social role of television in the digital age in an era where the language of the market and the litmus test of 'consumer sovereignty' enjoys prominence. Also of significance is the emerging relationship between previously rather distinctive areas of the broader media landscape such as media companies, telecoms and the information technology sectors of the economy. This process raises wider concerns about patterns of ownership and genuine plurality and diversity of choice in the market. As we argued in the previous chapter and examine in more detail below, it is partly this process of consolidation and concentration which has been occurring since 2002 in the pay-TV sector that has significantly depressed the value of football rights across a range of distinctive European markets.

Since 1996, when Canal Plus, the French pay-TV service became the first European broadcaster to launch a digital service (Canalsatellite Numererque), there has been a steady growth in the digital television market. Recent industry estimates suggest 80 million European households will have digital TV by 2007 (Research and Markets, 2003). At present, the digital television market accounts for over a third of all TV homes across Europe. It is worth noting that across the European markets, digital television is being delivered across a range of platforms including satellite (the dominant player in the French market for example), cable and terrestrial delivery systems. The high level of competition within the digital marketplace, dominated by private commercial pay-TV stations, during the late 1990s and early part of this century was crucial in initially pushing up the value of the rights to football in markets such as France, Italy and Spain in particular.

The advent of a digital televisual landscape marks an intensification of the pressures on public broadcasting which have been developing since the late 1980s. In most markets, the initial drive to introduce a digital platform has come from the private television sector, which as we discuss below has used the acquisition of football rights as part of their strategy to establish a foothold in this market. The dominant model for many of these platforms is primarily subscription based. One of the issues for public broadcasters has been the impact of increased competition on an already diminishing audience share as the impact of the previous wave of satellite and cable delivery systems of the 1990s consolidates. Murdock (2000: 55–56) argues that one challenge for public broadcasters in this new digital age is to forge new public networks. He suggests they 'need to see themselves not as free-standing pillars of cultural enterprise but as (digital) nodes in a network of public institutions'. Such a view echoes the more optimistic view of a network society envisaged by Castells (2000). Murdock's vision, however, places more emphasis on new media networks such as the Internet as a public good.

The success of digital uptake varies from market to market, with specific issues coming into play. For example the strength of free-to-air television, with up to thirty channels available, has inhibited the uptake of pay-TV in the German market (Papathanassopoulos, 2002: 42). Whereas in the UK, Freeview, the BBC-led digital free-to-air offering, complements a well established pay-TV sector providing an alternative route to multichannel television.

Ultimately, Papathanassopoulos (2002: 104) argues that the central content for digital services will be traditional television content such as sports and films. However this ostensibly good news for sports (and football viewers in particular) is tempered when he adds a note of caution and suggests, 'In fact, television will become much more expensive for all, operators and viewers'.

For many media executives across Europe, the success of Canal Plus as a subscription based service offering exclusive sports and film content, appeared to be the business model required to become profitable in the emerging European pay-TV market. As we noted in earlier chapters, the BSkyB business model in the UK revolved around exclusive football content in particular. Given this, it is largely unsurprising that in the fledgling digital television culture that channels should also look to football as the key driver in establishing a presence and subscription base in this new era. As we have seen in the UK, this was a process that provided short-term excess for the sport as competition from digital platforms in Germany, Italy and Spain helped to spiral the value of football rights. This land grab frenzy among both established media players and the new entrants to the market (often telecoms corporations) would prove to be costly in the longer term for both media corporations and the game alike.

The case of football in European television markets

Perhaps one of the most significant changes in the relationship between football and television over the last 20 years has been the migration of the game from public service broadcasters to commercial free-to-air and private pay-TV platforms. As we have argued elsewhere (Boyle and Haynes, 2000) sport has been an important driver of audiences and subscribers across differing television markets. Yet, in reality it appears that it has been football which is the key sport in helping to forge and sustain new television channels. The rise in satellite and cable delivery systems in the 1980s and early 1990s, helped facilitate the launch of a range of dedicated themed channels such as those dedicated to sports.

The oldest pan-European sports channel Eurosport available in 54 countries worldwide has undergone a number of changes since its launch in the 1980s (Collins, 1998). Co-owned by TF1 and Canal Plus, it depends on advertising and sponsorship revenue streams, rather than subscription fees, and broke even as far back as 1996 (Papathanassopoulos, 2002: 190). The rise of the dedicated sports channel across European television markets has been marked over the last decade or so. Koranteng (2000: 16) noted that at the highpoint of the sports right land grab in 2000, there were up to 60 sports channels in the European market, in 1995 there had been three (including Sky Sports in the UK). Yet for all the relative success of Eurosport, which saw a dedicated localised British version being launched in 1999 (there are also French and German versions), it is the specific nationally based sports channels, often driven by exclusive live football content, that have been the focus for the explosion in coverage of the sport that has taken place across European markets in the last decade. As Blain *et al.* (1993) argued in their study of sport and national identity in the early 1990s, it is the national dimension of sports culture and markets which remain important in driving advertisers and subscribers to channels rather than a more general pan-European sporting diet.

The gradual erosion in the power of the European Broadcast Union (EBU) the traditional cartel of public service broadcasters which helped to secure many international sporting events for national public service broadcasters has been ongoing since the 1970s, when the rise of a more commercially driven television network in Italy first seriously challenged the dominant public service model of national broadcasting in Europe.

There is also little doubt that while sports such as motor racing have been important, it is football which has been the key sport in helping to establish new pay-TV stations across the main European markets. In fact no digital pay-TV package has been launched which did not include live football as part of its content. In March 2003, for example, the leading European markets in terms of digital television uptake were the UK (34 per cent of homes) Spain (18 per cent) and France (17 per cent) (Screen Digest, 2003). In all these markets the key platform has been satellite digital, which has used football as one of its key drivers to attract subscribers.

In many ways the advent of digital television appears to be the latest – and most intense – stage in the ongoing commercialisation of European television. The spiralling in the value of football rights across Europe pre-dates this current stage in the evolution of television. The rise in the 1990s of increased competition in the television markets across Europe and the erosion of the public service cultures which had dominated the sector pushed the value of football rights ever upwards. While we examined the UK case in previous chapters it is worth noting that the general percentage rise in the value of sports rights in other markets was even greater than the UK experience, with both Spain and Germany seeing percentage growth in the value of sports rights between 1992–1998 of 140 per cent and 168 per cent respectively (the UK growth was 126 per cent) (Molskey, 1999: 20).

The advent of digital technology, with its ability to allow even more channels to be broadcast, simply accelerated this commercial process. In addition it offered the promise of additional revenue streams through a range of services which digital could offer, including the potential to gamble on matches as they happen (see Chapter 7 for more discussion on this and the range of interactive services being offered). It initially appeared to signal an epoch defining moment in the long relationship between sport and television; football rights holders had finally achieved what they had always wanted, which was a competitive and multi-layered media market which viewed the acquisition of football rights as absolutely central to the growth strategies of companies in that market. The digital era appeared to offer the prospect of finally allowing the full implementation of PPV television on a commercially sound basis. In fact a digital PPV service had been launched by CSN – the digital arm of Europe's first and then biggest analogue pay-TV service – in France as far back as 1996 (Koranteng, 2001: 82; Papathanassopoulos, 2002: 203).

Digital football: a new dawn?

A combination of factors including attempts by governments to leverage additional income from the traditional analogue spectrum and the enticing commercial returns that a fully functioning digital television market could offer for manufacturers and both new and existing media organisations, helped propel the emergance of digital television in the main European television markets. Different nations faced specific issues. For example, in Germany as we have noted the strength of free to air television, and the amount of football carried on this platform meant that by the time Kirch merged their digital platform DF1 with their rival Bertelsmann's Premiere platform it was already clear that the £972 million the company was paying the Bundesliga for live PPV and Internet rights for 2001–2005 was a financial burden. Ironically, one of the free-to-air channels, SAT 1, carrying highlights of the Bundesliga was actually owned by another part of the Kirch empire. In spite of moving the scheduling of the SAT 1 Bundesliga summary from 6.30pm to 8.15pm in an attempt to draw new customers to Premiere's live coverage, the pay-TV channel continued to lose viewers to the free to air channel (Hesbrugge and Wipperfurth, 2001).

Kirch's digital and PPV strategy had seen it aggressively use sports rights, and football in particular, to leverage additional income from existing television channels. This included its controversial brokerage of the 2002 and 2006 FIFA World Cup rights for which it paid £1.17 billion, and by using football to drive its digital uptake. However, a combination of poor take up for the digital services and the over payment for film and football rights ultimately led to the collapse of the KirchMedia empire after building bank debts of £850 million. Moreover, BSkyB, the second largest shareholder in KirchPayTV had become increasingly nervous of the company's perilous state and exercised a 'put option' to force KirchMedia to buy back its £1.1 billion stake in the pay-TV operator. Unable to pay, the Kirch empire began to crumble.

The parent company of Premiere, KirchPayTV eventually went bankrupt in May 2002, plunging the Bundesliga into a financial crisis. In marked contrast to the UK experience where political intervention to help ease the financial crisis among the Nationwide football clubs in England following the collapse of ITV Digital was non-existent (see Chapter 2), German politicians and banks put together a £200 million football contract which saved the league from financial meltdown. While this represented a 20 per cent cut on the Kirch deal, it also signified the political importance that the country's premier football league has in wider public German culture. Within the political sphere it was viewed as a matter of national pride and esteem that the Bundesliga should be able to continue to function.

The general re-alignment downwards in the value of football rights is well illustrated by the German situation. Here, the combination of free-to-air and pay-TV rights to the Champions League (marketed by the UEFA company

TEAM) were secured for £90 million a season in the deal struck for the 2003–2006 rights. This was a decrease of about 70 per cent on the previous deal (*Soccer Investor Weekly*, 17 July 2003).

The launch of digital platforms in both Spain and Italy in the late 1990s had PPV sport, and football in particular, as central tenets of their business models. It was envisaged that it would be exclusive football content involving La Liga and Serie A and B clubs that would drive business towards these new digital platforms.

Yet despite particular market differences the broader picture of there being too much competition in an embryonic digital market and companies significantly overpaying for football rights (either for league or individual club's rights) remains remarkably consistent across the main European television markets. Despite the threats by governments to switch off the analogue signal (as impossibly early as 2006 in Italy and 2012 in Spain) the digital market (often with three different distinct platforms of delivery) remains complex and confusing for the consumer. Some countries such as the UK and Germany have seen the role out of free-to-air digital services from public service broadcasters such as the BBC, competing with a mixture of free-to-air and pay digital satellite and cable channels, while others such as France have only recently (2003) seen the launch of terrestrial digital services.

There are also a number of wider issues that will impact on the growth of this market. Among them include the role of the EU in any attempt to intervene to prohibit the expansion of the public media sector. Not least as commercial rivals argue (often with a substantial degree of self-interest) that unregulated public media growth in the digital economy acts as a disincentive to private sector development. In reality, this is a mixed picture, with for example public sector media (the BBC) helping to drive the expansion of the digital radio market in the UK, with clear benefits for the commercial sector.

Papathanassopoulos (2002: 210) argues that what we are seeing in a European context is in fact a process which extends beyond the issue of football rights.

> This development simply indicates a deeper transformation of some main aspects of the public sphere, at least, in Europe. Both television, as a public service, and soccer, as a field of public expression that was not for profit, used to be regarded as expressions of civil society, but nowadays, with the deregulation and commercialisation of television, globalisation and technological diffusion have started to become the main profit tools of large corporations.

In addition to this analysis, we would argue that how this process is being played out across Europe is substantially influenced by particular national patterns of media development. As the case of Italy, which we look at below, serves to illustrate.

The case of Italy: football, media and politics

As broadcaster and journalist Gabriel Marcotti has argued, historically it was only in extreme circumstances that Serie A football was shown live on RAI the state owned broadcaster. In other words, unlike the UK market of the 1980s, there was no established culture of live league football on television emerging which would aid the development of new players to the media market. Marcotti points out that until 1991 and the advent of DigaPu, a digital/analogue station (free-to-air, but requiring a digital decoder to view), which began broadcasting a live match on a Sunday night, live top flight Italian football was almost absent from the televisual landscape in that country (Interview with authors, 3 April 2003).

The Italian football rights market is interesting, not least because it has pioneered a more commercial and aggressive relationship between television and football rights. As Tunstall and Machin argue, as far back as 1996:

> the Milan based Media Partners negotiated Europe's first pay-per-view football contract for the Italian league. In 1998 four top Italian football clubs (AC Milan, Inter Milan, Juventus and Napoli) made an exclusive pay-TV deal with Canal Plus. It was also the Milan trio of Media Partners and the big two Milan football clubs (plus Juventus) which took the lead in the proposed European football league that would include three teams from each of the big countries.
>
> Tunstall and Machin, 1999: 232–233

Thus the selling by individual clubs of their television rights is part of Italian media culture, and has allowed the larger clubs to generate substantial revenues from television. However even in this context media analysts such as Alex Fynn, the architect of the FA Premier League and someone who worked closely with the Milan Media Partners in the 1980s, argues that the top two divisions in Italy are important to television. As a result the money flow extends beyond the elite and allows some element of competition to be extended across a wider range of teams, facilitating the real possibility of clubs being promoted and having a realistic chance of remaining in the top league (Interview with authors, 3 April 2003).

It would however be the 1990s before the selling of individual rights for live matches would really take hold, and again, as in other media markets, it would be the competition from digital platforms, keen to secure subscribers which would act as a catalyst for the latest stage in the evolution of the relationship between football and television in that country.

Football also occupies a different cultural space in Italian society certainly in contrast to the UK. As Tobias Jones has noted:

> To understand Italian football, and therefore its politics and media, it's useless to use British terms of reference. In Italy the equivalent of British

monopolist, or American anti-trust, laws don't exist. There's no notion that there are areas of objectivity that must be observed, be it in refereeing or in news reporting. There's no central state that acts as a check on the various Citizen Kane characters. Their most obvious example of that 'strapotere' outside football is media ownership. In Italy there is no fourth estate; newspapers, with a few exceptions, are divided amongst the oligarchies. It's called 'lottizzazione', 'sharing the spoils'.

Jones, 2003: 76–77

Thus someone like Silvio Berlusconi can be both the owner of AC Milan and have extensive media interests, as well as being Prime Minister, without apparently being called to account for the blatant conflict of interests which exist.

In 1998–1999 part of the response of RAI, the state public service broadcaster, to the advent of the digital age, was to begin to move to a post analogue era with the launch of three digital satellite channels, including RAI Sports (Murdock, 2000: 54). However RAI has always viewed its match and goal highlights programmes as central to its football portfolio, rather than live games from Serie A, which as we noted above only developed in the early 1990s, much later than many other media markets around Europe.

The particular evolution of the pay-TV football market in Italy meant, that by season 2001/2, football fans in that country wishing to watch live matches needed to be subscribing to either Stream or Telepui (or if they wanted to watch extensive coverage both platforms). Each station carried a live match on their digital platform on a Saturday and Sunday night, with the other games being made available through a series of PPV season ticket packages. Stream had exclusive access to seven teams, while their media rival had 11 Serie A teams. Crucial in this arrangement is the fact that football rights were being sold individually by clubs and not centrally by the league. In addition, as was the case in other European media markets, both these channels were on competing digital platforms, thus making it potentially confusing and expensive for the consumer to subscribe to both decoding systems.

Which brings us to one of the central problems any company in the Italian market has in attempting to make a subscription television model work – the high level of piracy that exists in that market. Journalist Gabriele Marcotti has argued that up to 60 per cent of the public were using 'dodgy cards' to decode many of these matches and it could even have been as few as a third of dish owners who were actually paying for the services (Interview with authors, 3 April 2003).

By 2002 both Telepui and Stream were both losing substantial amounts of money from over investing in an inflated rights market. Despite small subscription uptake, in particular for the smaller Italian teams, clubs, even clubs at the bottom end of the league were getting paid up to 15 million Euro by the competing digital stations.

The crisis came to a head with the delay in the 2002/3 Italian league season. In order to protect the smaller teams, in a system where clubs sold their rights individually and the big clubs clearly benefited from this process, there were attempts to put some checks in place to avoid the competitive imbalance that such vast discrepancies in television income will generate within a league structure. One of these included all the teams having to have a PPV television deal in place before the season started. In September 2002, against a backdrop of a dramatic re-negotiation downwards of football rights across media markets in Europe, Stream and Telepiu would only offer £3.4 million per club for the PPV rights to eight Serie A teams. This compared to the £31 million being offered to the top clubs such as Juventus.

The Italian season failed to kick off on schedule, with the eight clubs forming a consortium called Plus Media Trading (PMT) in an attempt to leverage more money from television. A compromise eventually saw the top six clubs forgo some of their income so it could be redistrubuted to the lower clubs. However even in the Serie A highlights market, RAI secured their package paying almost 40 per cent less than they had done in previous seasons. Selling individual clubs' rights may have appeared profitable for the clubs when the market was booming and there was competition from competing digital broadcasters, however by 2002, market conditions had changed.

As noted above, a key element of the Italian situation has been the ability of clubs to negotiate individually with the competing companies for live rights to matches. A situation which enhances the position of the larger clubs, with Juventus for example able to secure in the region of £31 million a season in 2002 for its PPV rights. In contrast, some of the smaller clubs in Seria A saw the value of their PPV rights being worth just over £3 million a season.

A similar situation exists in Spain, where Pedro Tomas, the President of the Spanish Football Federation (LFP), has been urging clubs to return to the pooling of rights and their collective selling. He argues that the move to the individual selling of rights over the last six years in Spain is helping to create a long-term imbalance in top flight football as large clubs secure more and more television income (*Soccer Investor Weekly*, 5 June 2003). The top 12 clubs in La Liga have set up a G12 grouping, which some fear ultimately want to break away from La Liga and set up an English style Premier League. A number of the top teams in Spain, such as Valencia, are striking deals with regional broadcasters which will last until 2006, while others, such as Real Madrid, are selling rights to a pay-TV digital platform. Those clubs outside of the elite G12 in Spain are then attempting to sell a collective package. This mixed economy of rights selling is extremely divisive within the Spanish game and symptomatic of the tensions over rights between clubs and governing bodies of football which characterise the digital age of the game.

In Italy by April 2003, Rupert Murdoch was able to extend his BSkyB brand into the Italian pay-TV market when News Corporation finally secured a majority stake in Telepui. A new company Sky Italia would see Telepui merge with Stream (owned by News Corporation and Telecom Italia) creating a business with 2.3 million subscribers. As part of the European Union's five month investigation into the deal – concern was raised about the monopoly position of the company within the Italian pay-TV sector – among the conditions imposed by the EU was that no deal with football clubs could run longer than two years. While Murdoch would have liked to reproduce the UK Sky model of exclusive football rights helping to drive subscribers, the new company, under Italian regulation, will not be allowed to have exclusive access to football rights. A factor which may inhibit the stated objective of the company to eventually secure 10 million subscribers, something which would bring it into competition with the Italian Prime Minister Silvio Berlusconi, whose family run Mediaset and is a major player in the free-to-air media market in that country (the *Guardian*, 13 May 2003).

The existing deals with ten Serie A clubs such as Juventus mentioned above will continue to run until the end of the 2004/5 season. However such is the scale of change in the Italian market that the 2003/4 season was also delayed. In this instance the problem was synergising the newly created Gioco Calcio (the league's satellite channel covering second tier Serie A and Serie B matches) with the Sky Italia platform which would carry this channel.

What the Italian case highlights is the extent to which football finance is being shaped and moulded by the wider ebbs and flows of an increasingly complex and unstable media market. In Italy some clubs are dependent on television income for almost 60 per cent of their financial income. Add to this a specific market where the roll out of new technologies will always be subject to wider cultural and social influences and you have a recipe for calamity. Thus, even in football-mad Italy, a combination of extensive piracy and poor policing of this aspect of the market, and two competing digital platforms overestimating the allure of live football in a market with a strong free-to-air football highlights culture, simply emphasises that football and television continue to operate in an uneasy and increasingly unstable alliance.

The evolution of the UEFA Champions League

Given the situation we have just outlined in the Italian market it should be no surprise to learn that Milan and Berlusconi has been among some of the key agitators for change within the wider European game. This of course predates the digital age but is still important as it has put in place various models and templates for the game's development which are still being used and adapted today.

The UEFA Champions League is now one of the foremost club competitions in world football. While its origins predate the current 'new media age' the development of the competition has been heavily influenced by the evolving media markets across Europe, in particular the establishment in the 1980s of pay television systems in a number of countries. The roll out of digital technologies, allied with a wider opening up of television markets in Europe have all shaped the context within which the Champions League has operated.

The drivers for change in European football, have, more often than not, been the big clubs, such as AC Milan, often with strong links to media companies (something which until recently British clubs have not had), who have been keen to either extend their influence and revenues or consolidate their elite status. Banks (2002: 125–129) has looked in detail at the factors which drove the formation of the Champions League in 1992, which emerged from the knockout competition of the European Champions Cup, to a larger extended format in which every opportunity was afforded the bigger European clubs to maximise revenues from television by extending the length of time they were involved in the competition.

For the purposes of this chapter we want to identify some of the key implications of the emerging elite football landscape that has been increasingly shaped by money from television since the early 1990s. One of the key characteristics of the evolving relationship between football and television in the new media age is the increasing pace of change. The European Champions Cup remained largely unchanged since its inception in 1955 until the early 1990s (Glanville, 1991). Yet over the last number of years the competition has undergone a series of structural changes in both its format and its relationship to media, sponsors and advertisers, including regular appearances in the competition of teams other than the domestic champions of European leagues (Banks, 2002: 125–142).

The process and practice of selling a media sporting product into various European media markets has been driven in a more aggressive and commercial manner than previously imaginable. From the presence of on screen corporate sponsors, to the embedding of commercial partners into the television production context, UEFA, in part responding to threats of a breakaway league, have to all intents and purposes reinvented a competition for a more commercial market-driven and competitive European television sector. In the process UEFA has created a competition which generates substantial income for the organisation (about 25 per cent of revenue is retained by UEFA) with it also retaining the rights to distribute the bulk of the income generated via a complex system based on merit, domestic performance and the size of the television market within which a club operates. The anomalies this can throw up include the Champions League winners often not earning the most money from the competition. Thus in 2002, the champions Real Madrid earned £21.5 million, with six clubs above them earning more, including FC Nantes, who were eliminated in the second group stage, but still earning £31.8 million (Morrow, 2003: 25).

Battle for control: G14, UEFA and the European Commission

Part of the wider power struggle in the digital age of football has seen the more powerful clubs in Europe attempting to strengthen their collective position with regard to UEFA. As the chairmen and executives of Europe's leading clubs informally met on a regular basis during their forays across the Continent it became apparent that they shared common interests. Working in unison they would have a powerful lobby within the game in order to influence the governance of the sport. To this end, the G14 group of elite clubs was officially established in November 2000 as a European Economic Interest Grouping with its main base in Brussels. While originally comprising solely of a selection of previous European Cup winners, the group has since expanded to 18 clubs and seeks to promote greater co-operation between these elite clubs. As Simon Banks argues:

> While the founding principles of G14 seem innocuous enough, it is obvious that the main reason for its existence is to promote the interests of Europe's top clubs, even if that is to the detriment of smaller clubs.
>
> Banks, 2002: 131

As the interests of the G14 converge, the latent threat of a breakaway league is ever present. Such political manoeuvring has been denied by G14 members who state their aim as operating within the present structures of the sport. Rather Genevieve Berti, the Communications Manager for G14, argues that:

> Football is a strange world. Football is not about having markets or selling products or trying to move towards reforming any law. It is not really from that. Football is about winning games, winning competitions and it is a sport. Right from the start the intention or the real actual objectives of the founding members was not to engage in any lobbying activity or trying to infiltrate structures. It was not really focussed on that. [...] They tried to give a certain spirit to the grouping. Which is first, to defend and safeguard the interests of the members. Which is obviously a way to say that whenever we think that there is a danger, or there is a matter of concern, the joint position should help us to safeguard or to defend the matter that we don't want to be challenged on. [...] They would ensure that the grouping takes all the necessary actions to build a better future and foster co-operation.
>
> Interview with authors, 25 April 2003

What is clear, is that these clubs seek to maximise the revenues they can derive from their clubs and take a view that their collective pulling of influence will help them shape the agenda of European football in the new century. The motives of the G14 are usually couched in a managerial ideology that espouses 'best practice' in the economics and governance of football. But it is also clear that their commercial power has been leveraged with significant effect. Pressures to change the distribution of media rights, instigating discussions on salary capping and battles with FIFA and UEFA over compensation payments to clubs for the release of players on international duty are illustrative of their influence.

Thus the issue of various battle lines of power between clubs and organising associations (be they national or international) and the wider issue of the game's governance has become more pronounced in the digital age. While power struggles are of course not new to the game (Sugden and Tomlinson, 1998), in more recent times they have been more focused around the value and ownership of the image rights to the game. Alex Fynn, one of the original architects of the Berlusconi inspired European Super League proposal of the late 1980s, which helped to force UEFA to set up the original Champions League, argues that despite the seemingly cyclical challenges to the authority of UEFA that appears to come from the larger clubs, that in reality, by 2003, UEFA is in a more powerful position than it has been for decades. He suggests that UEFA:

> Now recognise that through control of sponsorship, advertising, TV rights, that they have the power. While UEFA has ascended to some of the demands (of the larger clubs), they have been guided by what has been best for all of their members and they are in a stronger position now, than they were when the Champions League was conceived.
>
> Interview with authors, 3 April 2003

A point reiterated when UEFA flexed its muscles in 2003 and decided to shorten the Champions League format from a possible 17 matches to 13 matches from season 2003/4 by dropping the second phase group stage. A move not supported by many of the elite G14 clubs, who despite protestations that their players were playing too much football, saw the potential loss of television revenue from a reduced Champions League format as something they would like to resist. UEFA, while making all the right public relations pronunciations, ignored these concerns for what they saw was the greater good of the competition.

In addition, Fynn argues that while television revenues are key to the clubs, what is of fundamental importance in shaping the patterns of power and dominance in the European game in the new media age is the distribution and redistribution of this income and the league structures which underpin this. Fynn argues that both the English and Scottish leagues provide good examples where only the top elite teams are viewed as important (Interview with authors, 3 April 2003). For example in the Premier League in England, the top twenty

teams are all that apparently matter to television in this country, with a corresponding allocation of the television revenue focused on these clubs. However
elsewhere in Europe, such as in Germany, Spain and France, up to 40 teams
matter, in the sense that serious money moves further down the footballing
food chain. Why this is important is that it helps to eradicate elements of
competitive imbalance within any league structure, something increasingly
endemic in both the English and Scottish games where a handful of clubs
dominate (see Morrow, 2003: 5–6). Thus teams such as Alavas, Deportivo
La Coruna and Malaga in Spain, Bologna in Italy and Kaiserslautern in
Germany can enjoy some domestic and indeed European success in a manner
which is becoming increasingly rare in the British game. Despite this, some feel
that the flow of money in the digital age to the elite clubs across Europe is one
of the main challenges facing football across the Continent as it seeks to retain
elements of competition in both domestic and European leagues (Morrow,
2003).

The issue of rights has been around for some time within various European
markets. In 1996 in the Netherlands, Sport 7, a joint venture sports channel
between the Dutch footballing authorities (KNVB) and the electronics
company Philips paid $450 million to secure exclusive rights to Dutch top flight
football. However following disputes with cable distributors, the Dutch government, the EC and the top clubs such as Ajax and Feyenoord, who disputed the
right of the KNVB to sell their rights for home matches, the company collapsed
within a year.

At a broader European wide level, there is an apparent contradiction at the
heart of the EC's dealing with sport and television. In recognition of the cultural role of sport in society, and the potential threats to public access to televised sporting events of a strong pay-TV market, the 1997 Television Without
Frontiers Directive allows member states to protect certain events from exclusively migrating to pay-TV platforms. However, on another front, the EC
Competition Commission is keen to apply competition law across European
media markets by limiting restrictive practices (which some in the sports industry view the Television Without Frontiers Directive as being an example of).
From 2000 in particular, the EC, and in particular its Competition Commissioner Mario Monti, has been keen to investigate the selling of football rights in
a range of media markets across Europe. In applying classic competition theory,
he has argued that while more football matches are now shown on a range of
platforms than at any other time in the history of the sport, this still means that
a large number of games are not shown. Central in this argument has been the
roll out of digital technology and the erosion of the scarcity of spectrum argument, which has helped frame the regulation of television for many years. In
other words, in the digital age, the technology exists to broadcast many more
matches simultaneously than ever before.

As we noted in the previous chapter and discuss further in Chapter 5, the
Commission appears keen to promote and strengthen competition in the new

media markets of the Internet and 3G mobile telephony and views more rights being retained by individual football clubs as central in this process. While the Commission accepts the declaration on the specific characteristic of sport adopted by the European Council at Nice in 2000 (Toft, 2003), it also views sport increasingly as a business. Crucially, the EC seems relatively uninterested in whether anyone actually wants to watch these matches, something which previous media analysts have failed to take into account with their overly optimistic predictions of uptake for pay-per-view televised football. As we will see in Chapter 5, the EC, like so many other new media companies, views sports content as vital in driving subscribers to these new technologies (Toft, 2003: 6).

The EC investigation into the 'anti-competitive joint selling' by UEFA of Champions League rights resulted in no single national broadcaster being given sole live rights to the competition from 2003. Crucially for UEFA however, in July 2003 the Commission accepted the wider case for the 'joint selling' of some core rights. By this they mean the ability of an organisation, such as UEFA, to sell the collective rights for a competition, rather than those rights reverting back to individual clubs. Of course the 2003–2006 deal meant that UEFA could no longer sell to a single broadcaster, and a range of specific media rights windows were created, which in theory could facilitate more broadcasters to secure Champions League rights.

The rights were broken up into 14 different categories, some to be centrally marketed by UEFA, some to be jointly marketed by clubs and UEFA, and some to be exploited solely by the clubs. This latter category of rights represented a major victory for the clubs and confirmed the emerging power of the G14 to get its voice heard beyond football's established corridors of power. The G14 had commissioned a report on rights windowing and the recommendations of the consultant's report formed the basis for the EC's settlement with UEFA.

Also of interest was the selling of 3G rights which gave mobile users (with the appropriate handset) the opportunity to pay to watch goal clips five minutes after the match had ended (see Chapter 5). Clubs are now able to retain and exploit their Champions League matches on a deferred basis, and crucially retain the archive rights to matches. This content can be distributed via digital television, the Internet and through 3G mobile telephony. Significantly, UEFA, through UEFA New Media and its website Uefa.com, has been building its online presence for a number of years. The 2003/4 Champions League campaign also saw UEFA, in partnership with Real Networks, offer a subscription based online package to view a highlights/goals and footage package from midnight on Champions League match days. In the UK, they entered a partnership with BSkyB, who as the pay-TV holders of Champions League matches were able to help drive traffic to the UEFA website.

Such developments suggest that UEFA is keen to mobilise the rights it holds to drive revenues through the Internet, at a time when they now feel the broadband market in Europe is at a stage to support such a development. This core issue of the viability of football on the Internet as a revenue driver, and the complex issues it raises about the relationships between clubs, governing bodies of the sport and media corporations is the focus of Chapter 5.

Of the Champions League deal, the EC, through Competition Commissioner Mario Monti, clearly saw a vindication of the Commission's interest in the selling of football rights. He argued:

> The Commission's action will provide a broader and more varied offer of football on television. It will allow clubs to develop the rights for their own fan base and will give an impulse for the emerging new media markets such as UMTS services [...] This positive outcome shows that the marketing of football rights can be made compatible with EU competition rules without calling into question their sale by a central body to the benefit of all stakeholders in the game.
>
> European Commission, Press Release, Brussels, 24 July 2003

Unlike the rest of Europe, the UK had not had a pay-TV platform carrying Champions League football until the migration of some matches by ITV to ITV Digital in 2001 (see previous chapter). Most other European markets have had a mixture of free-to-air and pay-TV packages carrying the competition since the mid 1990s. As a result of this new UEFA deal, the 2003/4 season saw BSkyB and ITV in the UK sharing games in a manner more in keeping with the main European television markets for the first time.

As we noted in the previous chapter when looking at the UK market, the intervention of the EU into rights issues is one of the characteristics of the more complex media landscape in the digital age. However there remains a fundamental paradox in the EC's competition thinking on football. Put simply, it is not always in the long-term interest of the sport to have it over exposed on television, a situation that some may feel has already been reached, certainly in the UK market. While in the UEFA Champions League, the growth of meaningless second phase matches (and correspondingly poor television ratings) has been, in part, one of the reasons for the restructuring of the competition which took place in 2003. Also, while some football supporters as television viewers may benefit from increased access (at a price) to football, this may also be to the detriment of the football supporter who attends matches (a lot do both of course) as games are scheduled for the benefit of a range of television platforms.

Conclusion

While the economic downturn in the value of football rights across Europe, driven by an advertising downturn and a consolidation in a range of digital television markets, may mean a narrowing of the wealth gap between the elite and the rest of football, this is by no means guaranteed. Such now is the centrality of the market and the ability of clubs and leagues to attract a substantial television audience that as Morrow (2003: 30) argues:

> Reducing rights income may be inescapable, but awareness of this new economic reality may in fact reinforce the gap by encouraging bigger leagues and bigger clubs to seek a larger share of a dwindling cake. The market will dictate that a bigger share of reduced rights income will flow to the higher quality leagues.

What remains central in the evolving landscape of European football, and its relationship with the media, is the centrality of television, albeit increasingly digital in nature, as the de facto delivery system of live football content.

Despite the moves to build a European broadband market for Champions League footage discussed above, it is the broadcasters, rather than the new media operators such as BT, AOL, Yahoo! and MSN, who remain the key financial drivers of the game in Europe. The more optimistic predictions of migration of content to the Internet simply has not happened, for a range of reasons, some technical, but most social and cultural, which we want to examine in more detail in Chapters 5 and 7.

While we would argue that television, and not the Internet, will remain at the core of any rights issue over the next decade, this is not to suggest that the media landscape will not continue to evolve and develop, often in unpredictable ways. Rather, that we underestimate the resilience of television as a cultural and social form with which people engage at a variety of levels and social contexts (be it in the home, or in a pub with friends and supporters) to remain a core element of the mediated experience of football for many years to come.

There is another significant issue which has underpinned much of the developments we have discussed in this chapter. For many key media players and for many involved in the business hinterland with which football has become associated in the last decade or so, the game has increasingly become viewed solely in economic terms. With the liberalisation of television markets across Europe, there has also been a migration of the game to niche pay-TV markets. This connects to a wider argument being made by media analysts such as Murdock, who has argued that:

> By reinforcing the fragmentation and dispersal of the television audience set in motion by the first wave of multichannel television it prompts us to ask: what is likely to happen to the quality of the communal life if the shared symbolic spaces that national broadcasting has traditionally provided through its coverage of great civic and sporting occasions are only available in the future on specialised subscription channels.
>
> Murdock, 2000: 46

As noted above, central in this process has been the wider erosion of the position of public service broadcasters across Europe as carriers of elite European football competition. The range of free-to-air games varies in different nations. These differences are influenced by a range of wider cultural factors which sees the game occupying differing public spaces in countries such as Italy as opposed to Britain. While a mixture of platforms now exists in most European countries, football is viewed in these markets less in cultural terms and rather more in terms of the size and nature of the audiences it can deliver to advertisers or increasingly subscribers to pay-TV platforms. On rare occasions such battles can be won in the public interest, as with England's crucial 2003 qualifying game in Turkey. Here, free-to-air television coverage of the England game was enforced in spite of the fact broadcast rights were held by a pay-TV channel. BSkyB released 'as live' rights to ITV, in order to assist the FA's attempt to persuade England fans not to travel to the game where trouble was predicted.

We would concur with Gardiner and Gray (2003) who argue that EU intervention to protect certain sporting events remains vital for the long-term well-being of sports such as football. One of the challenges is reconciling the evolving media competition regimes with an interventionist outlook which highlights the cultural and social dimension of televised sport. Gardiner and Gray suggest:

> Indeed, it is in the interests of sport that certain events are not shown exclusively live to a pay-TV audience. The public have a right to view the major specific national and world sporting events. Media giants may want to gain near-exclusive rights and allow the market to operate unfettered, but their claims need to be vigorously deterred.
>
> Gardiner and Gray, 2003: 52

To this, we would add that much of the burden of this responsibility falls on the governing bodies of sports such as football, who often have in their gift the rights to sell.

What is clearly emerging across European markets is that any uptake in digital television to such an extent that the analogue signal can be switched off, will clearly require a substantial development of the free-to-air digital market. As in the UK, this has been in part driven by PSB broadcasters such as the BBC, with other markets such as France and Spain looking to establish similar scenarios; a mixture of free-to-air and pay digital platforms driving a wider migration from analogue. While football remains a key element of any pay-TV package, it cannot be viewed in isolation from what is on offer across any given television market. The case of Germany for example, which in 2003 saw only 6 per cent of households in that country taking pay digital television, suggests that the drive to move to these platforms is simply not compelling enough for viewers, given the range of material available across other free-to-air platforms (Screen Digest, 2003).

However the battle for control for the image (and imaging) of the game is not simply one between private and public media systems. It is also about the

players and the clubs that employ them and how they seek to control and interact with the wave of opportunities that the advent of digitalisation seemingly
offers them. Some in the game see the Internet and the advent of mobile telephony and communications systems as the next phase in the ongoing battle for
control. One dimension of this shifting football media nexus is how new media
content is exploited and how commercial rights are licensed. Who stands to
gain from these new circumstances is the theme of the next two chapters.

Chapter 4

Commercialising celebrity
Player power and image rights

È arrivato ama un re, e parte come un ladro.
Corriere dello Sport, on the transfer of Ronaldo from Internationale to Real
Madrid, 31 August 2002

Image rights will be the fastest-growing revenue line for football clubs in the future.
Jose Angel Sanchez, marketing director of Real Madrid after the
Ronaldo deal

I loathe everything Beckham stands for: the cultivation of mediocrity, the celebration of kitsch, the veneration of the trivial, the manipulation of everybody and everything for personal gain, the naked lust for fame, for its own sake. But more than that, I loathe the way in which the rest of us are complicit in this blatant act of empire-building. I loathe the way in which this ghastly couple have come to speak on behalf of all of us, as if they had anything to say.
Michael Henderson, commenting amid the mounting media hysteria
surrounding the proposed transfer of David Beckham, the *Daily Mail*,
16 June 2003

Introduction

A new legal term has entered the lexicon of football fans. Image rights, broadly defined as the commercial appropriation of someone's personality, including indices of their image, voice, name and signature, entered football consciousness during the 2000/1 season. For many football fans, a community that have long scrutinised the contractual negotiations of professional footballers, image rights must seem just another stage in the ongoing commercialism that characterises the modern game. Although footballers have been exploiting their fame and notoriety for commercial ends for many years, with George Best arguably the starting point of a new generation of modern marketable players, image rights present a new departure in the economics of the sport.

In this chapter we plan to analyse the growing concern of football clubs, players and their agents with the control and commercial exploitation of their media images. We trace the reasons for the increased activity in this area that pulls together a variety of commercial, legal and political concerns, some related to media freedom, and others with deeper impacts on the relationships between football as cultural industry and its fans. As we have argued throughout this book, the framing of fans as consumers is at the heart of many of the changes undergone in professional football in the 'new media age'. Image rights, however broadly defined, offer a symptomatic signpost to many of these transformations.

The definition and meaning of image rights is by no means absolute, either legally or in its common use. With this in mind the chapter first outlines the rising use of 'image rights' and what they actually mean. From a media perspective, the market for celebrity images is certainly important in this respect. Analysing the alchemy involved in turning fame and notoriety through sport into money presents an interesting avenue for understanding the growing importance of image rights for certain players. We then focus on recent cases in the wider sporting world that have set the legal precedents for players and football clubs as they pursue their 'rights' via the courts by recourse to the various laws protecting intellectual property. In the context of football, we relate this to what might be called the Europeanisation of UK player contracts, from 'Bosman' onwards.

The heart of our argument lies with the analyses of the reasons for image rights clauses in player contracts. Here we present two inter-related accounts: first the centrality of stars, if not mega-stars, to the rising popularity of the English Premier League; second, the financial necessities of finding new and imaginative sources of revenue to sustain the mega-star economy of contemporary football. The chapter then turns to some of the emerging conflicts in player contracts, principally between club and country, but also between conflicts of interest in the worlds of sport sponsorship and advertising. We then return to specific legal concerns regarding player websites and the computer games industry leading on to our final media and cultural analysis of the commercial, legal and technical enclosure of football as popular culture in the digital age.

The rise of image rights

UK press reports on the importance of image rights in a player's contract first surfaced in July 2000 in the wake of the then record breaking signing of Luis Figo from Spanish rivals Barcelona to Real Madrid for £38 million. Key to the deal was a contractual clause over the licensing of image rights from the player to the club. A similar deal was struck one year later with a further world record signing of French international and World Player of the Year Zinadine Zidane for £46.2 million from Juventus, and again in 2002 with the signing of Brazilian World Cup hero Ronaldo for £29.8 million from Italian club Internationale. All the deals enabled Real to capitalise on the commercial value of their new acquisitions, specifically in the sale of replica shirts bearing the players' names.

The reason for Real incorporating image rights into the contracts was simple. In 2001, Real Madrid sold more replica shirts than any other club in Europe with revenues from direct sales in excess of £27 million. With the names Figo, Zidane and Ronaldo, Real could expect rich pickings from future replica shirt sales as well as income from other merchandising and sponsorship activities. As we shall go on to discuss below, the nature of these contracts represents a new phase in the commodification of football, with leading European clubs such as Real Madrid at the forefront of this hyper-commercialism.

Image rights gained further recognition during 2001–2002 in the UK during the protracted negotiations of England captain and the then Manchester United player David Beckham who has been used to spearhead the club's merchandising drive. Beckham's licensing of certain image rights to Manchester United is indicative of the changing economic position of star players at Premier League clubs. As we have argued elsewhere in this book, football in the age of global, multichannel television has generated massive wealth for certain clubs, passed on to a select group of players through inflated salaries. The global nature of the English Premier League, in particular, has opened new vistas and marketing opportunities. In Beckham's case this includes a new groundswell of devoted fans in South East Asia, a persuasive reason for Manchester United to get their 'blue-eyed boy' to sign on the dotted line.

Beckham's protracted negotiations over image rights were followed with intrigue by the UK media and set a benchmark for future contracts by fellow professionals. Image rights featured strongly in the reporting of Everton teenage striker Wayne Rooney who in January 2003 agreed his first professional contract after a month long dispute over the value, not of his football ability, but his potential to be marketed as a 'brand'. We analyse these developments more closely below and suggest that they are a symptom of a wider enclosure of intellectual property rights across the entertainment industries. Football, proclaimed the 'new rock-'n'-roll' at the turn of the century (see Redhead, 1993 and 1997), has conjoined with other areas of the entertainment field to shore up the value of its prized assets, the player as star. As we shall see, for some in the game a footballer is as much a performer as an actor or pop singer. We can certainly agree in this context that David Beckham, the star, has probably got more in common with singer Robbie Williams than he does with fellow professional Robbie Fowler.

These developments are interesting for the media study of sport along several axes. Principally, image rights represent a process of turning cultural or symbolic value into economic or capital value. The process of this exchange is therefore an interesting case study in the commodification of culture. In the context of football, the inter-relationships between footballers, agents and football clubs is worth scrutinising, not least because players are often pulled in two directions motivated by both personal interest (supervised by their agents) and their role as a member of a team (or national representative). As we shall discuss, the tension between these two forces driven by the interests of corporate sponsors and advertisers has become politically sensitive, not only in football, but also across various team sports. The media plays an important role here as the conduit for marketing the player as a 'brand' and sustaining their status as a sporting celebrity. But quite often the player as individual comes into conflict with the player as part of broader team interests.

Of related interest, are the centrality of contracts, licensing and the controlling force of intellectual property in the organising principles of cultural industries: in this case professional football. In particular, the premise for part of this chapter is the argument that new media, and the cultural industries more generally, are subject to increasing constraints from expanded and increasingly punitive policing of intellectual property rights. New statutes introduced to shore up copyright in the digital environment, in particular the implementation of the EC Directive (2002/29/EC) on the 'harmonisation of certain rights and related rights in the Information Society', have further compounded this regulatory zeal to protect digital media assets.

Paradoxically, from a legal perspective, a further point of interest is that in the UK there is no specific law protecting 'image rights'. While rights of personality exist in other European jurisdictions and the US, football clubs in the UK have had to turn to alternative legal devices to control image rights (including the registration of player names as trademarks).

One of the problems in the general discussion of image rights is the continual confusion as to what it means. The confusion stems from a lack of understanding the two dimensions of legal protection used by players and their clubs, as sports lawyer Nic Couchman explains:

> On the one hand there are proprietary rights, and on the other there are contractual rights. A proprietary right is something that basically means I can stop anybody using my property. A contractual right is more about what I am expressly authorising a third party to do and what I am expressly saying to them what I won't do.
>
> Interview with the authors, 16 July 2003

Consequently, image rights in the UK context have become a contractual agreement above and beyond the 'standard form agreement' set out in accordance with the Professional Footballers' Association. These individual agreements extend the ability of clubs to exploit a player's image in a group context – such as squad photos or promotion of club sponsors – to licensing such rights for various commercial purposes exploiting the player's distinctive 'brand'. In this way, argues media lawyer Nic Couchman, 'international image rights are being harmonised in the dressing room' (quoted in Day, 2002a).

As the potential conflicts of interest between individual players and clubs has grown regarding their promotional activities the Premier League and PFA introduced a new set of image rights clauses in the standard player contract effective from the start of the 2003/4 season. Clubs have moved to incorporate image rights in contracts in order to maximise the value of players as brands to help boost their merchandising revenue. However, as we shall go on to discuss in more detail, elite players may wish to opt out of the contract and replace with their own image rights clauses. Players such as Beckham demand further remuneration for their status as global stars and the media coverage they draw and may wish to negotiate further contractual clauses to shore up and clarify their commercial value to a club.

As we shall discuss, the influx of international players into the domestic English Premier League has been crucial to this process. The European influence on the British game on the pitch has increasingly been mirrored by emerging practices off it including attention to the health and fitness of player finance and contracts. Understanding the globalisation of the labour market for football and the enforced harmonisation of European legislation on the industry are key factors in this respect.

Finally, broader issues regarding media coverage of sport and whether or not information about players including images and names are in the public domain or not are increasingly important. As journalist Julia Day has noted in respect of negotiations over image rights: 'To a great extent, celebrity names and images are, by definition, in the public domain. That is why they are famous and therefore valuable' (Day, 2002a).

This suggests that any attempt to monopolise the sporting names and images raises questions of press freedom and potentially threatens freedom of expression. Paradoxically, the attempt to commercially control images and other information about football is happening at a time of expansion in the communication of all things related to the game. More broadly, legal critics such as Lawrence Lessig (2001) have argued that innovations in new media are potentially being undermined by the enclosure of intellectual property rights.

Football has been one of the most vociferous industries in protecting domain names and has been involved in a significant number of disputes taken to the World Intellectual Property Organisation and their domain name Arbitration and Mediation Centre. Furthermore, as we shall argue, new technologies of control are also being introduced to make sure that no unlicensed or illegitimate uses of football's commodity is being literally 'ripped-off'. The implications for a vibrant, creative football culture in the digital age can be seen in parallel entertainment industries such as music, where attempts to ring fence the distribution of digital content have polarised the industry against millions of people downloading MP3 files through peer-to-peer networks. Before moving on to our analysis of player contracts and image rights, we shall briefly review two prescient cases concerning the protection of sporting celebrity images and also landmark rulings on the use of club trademarks that provide a wider context for understanding new legal practices in the football industry.

Not for sale: disputes in sports image rights

As we have stated above, there is no specific image or personality right covered by UK law. Any legal entitlement in an individual's characteristics has been denied because of a general suspicion that 'property in personality' is 'a commodification too far' (Cornish, 1999: 31). However, this has not prevented sport stars from attempting to prevent others using their images for commercial purposes without their permission. In general, advertisers and sponsors will always seek prior consent from the individual concerned, either directly, through an agent, a club or governing body. For this reason, the market for global sports endorsements is very lucrative.

In 2003 the value of global sports endorsements by leading sports manufacturer Nike reached $1.4 billion, much of which were investments in English football clubs such as Manchester United and Arsenal (CNN, 2003). Such massive investments in football indicate the scale of the media sports economy and the financial rewards at stake. In the global sports economy, British sports stars will also be more than aware of protection in other legal territories, in particular the US, where the right of personality is vehemently policed by celebrities and their agents. Nevertheless, because of relatively weak protection in UK law, confusion often arises as to what is and is not a legitimate use of a star's image and what can be done about it. Therefore, when a sports star's image is illegitimately used, various legal remedies are drawn upon to recompense lack of consent and any resulting injury (financial or otherwise).

Lawyers have increasingly turned to innovative interpretations of law to protect celebrity names and likenesses. Trademarks as a 'badge of origin', nascent regulations on privacy and Human Rights, and damages brought against goodwill and misrepresentation under the common law tort of 'passing off', have all been used in recent court cases where well known personalities have complained against the illegitimate use of their image. Well publicised cases that failed in their attempt to block the commercial use of photographs of Diana Princess of Wales and the name Elvis brought attention to the problems faced by celebrities in their attempts to control personality merchandising. Case law had only contemplated damage where there was some common connection in the business activity of the two parties. Quite often monopoly rights in a celebrity image or name cannot be given due to their very popularity in the media and general ubiquitous coverage. As Lane (1999: 34) suggests: 'To be known to everyone is not to be known for everything.'

False endorsement of sports stars

However, in the case of *Eddie Irvine* v. *Talksport* in March 2002, the Formula One racing driver won a groundbreaking High Court action that effectively recognised the value of sports celebrity image rights and affording protection on them. Irvine brought the case after the UK commercial radio station (then Talk Radio) used a doctored photograph of the racing driver on a promotional leaflet distributed to 1,000 potential advertising agents. Irvine heard of the illegitimate use of his image after Ian Phillips, the director of business affairs for the Jordan F1 team, called Irvine's manager to congratulate him on having negotiated a sponsorship deal with Talk Radio. The leaflet showed a digitally manipulated image of Irvine holding a mobile phone replaced with a portable radio carrying the logo of Talk Radio. The impression given, that Irvine had endorsed the promotion and the radio station.

Mr Justice Laddie held that the manipulation of the image for commercial gain clearly represented false endorsement affecting the goodwill of Irvine's reputation and name. The ruling recognises that the name and image of a sports star can effectively constitute a brand, with all the various economic rights associated with that status. In the field of 'passing off', it also confirmed that defence no longer rested on the two parties sharing a common field of activity. Although the case afforded protection to Irvine's image rights it proved something of a hollow victory. Irvine only received £2,000 in damages (the estimated worth of the endorsement concerned) and having rejected an out-of-court settlement of £5,000 was ordered to pay his own legal fees which were reported at £300,000.

The protection of image rights were further solidified by a subsequent out-of-court settlement following court action taken by ex-England cricketer Ian Botham and Diageo, the owners of brewers Guinness. Guinness had used archive footage of Botham's famous heroic exploits during the 1981 Ashes series. The advert juxtaposed images of Botham with a voiceover of another cricket legend, Fred Trueman, who exclaims 'he couldn't bowl a hoop downhill'. The rhetoric of the advert aims to suggest overcoming adversity with the generic Guinness campaign slogan 'believe'. The advert, run throughout the period of the 2002 World Cup, therefore linked Botham's great sporting moment with the Guinness brand without his permission. The case rested on damage to Botham's reputation as an enduring sports celebrity and the false attribution of any endorsement of the Guinness brand in the public's eye. Botham settled for an undisclosed sum, but the efficacy of the case was to shore up the concept that sports stars had 'image rights' that could be protected through the courts. According to intellectual property lawyer Alison Willis the settlement would 'provide celebrities with increased bargaining power when negotiating their future contracts' (*Birmingham Post*, 23 September 2002). This has certainly been the case in the football context where new contractual relationships have emerged that clearly accept the ownership of certain image rights by some of the Premier League's star players.

Football trademarks

Premier League football clubs and their players have not, however, been given monopoly rights over the control of particular images and club indicia. In a related and relevant court case, Arsenal challenged the right of a street trader, Matthew Reed, to sell club related souvenirs and memorabilia. Arsenal claimed the unofficial merchandise contravened a series of trademarks they had registered in 1989 including the name Arsenal, their nickname 'the Gunners', and the club crest bearing the distinctive shield and cannon. Even though Reed had posted a sign prominently stating that his goods were not official merchandise of the club, Arsenal's lawyers argued that the street vendor was guilty of 'passing off' the goods as being authorised by the club. The case went to the High Court in April 2002 where the judge accepted Reed's defence that the use of the Arsenal crest worked as a 'badge of allegiance' or loyalty rather than an unauthorised use of trademarks. The ruling suggested that club crests were in the public domain, many of them having existed for more than 100 years.

Arsenal challenged the ruling and the case was referred to the European Court of Justice for guidance and clarification on Trademark law. In November 2002, Arsenal appeared to have gained a significant victory. The judges overturned the High Court ruling to conclude that 'it was immaterial that, in the context of that use, the sign was perceived as a badge of support for or loyalty of affiliation to the trademark proprietor' (*The Times*, 18 November 2002). Commenting on the ruling, John Williams (2002a) noted that the European Court's ruling potentially brought to an end a long history of small-scale businesses focused around match days providing ancillary services many fans found an essential part of the football experience. Williams connected the ruling to a broader shift in the policing of intellectual property rights in the game:

> This development also fits with a wider pattern of assertiveness from the bigger clubs and their powerful sponsors over image rights – control over how they are portrayed and their images sold via the mass media.
>
> Williams, 2002a

The value of this historical tie was ultimately not lost on Justice Laddie when the European Court ruling was referred back to the High Court in December 2002. In another twist to the case the judge considered the European Court ruling to have found fresh findings of fact, something which it had no jurisdiction to do. On the strict guidance on trademark law, Justice Laddie concluded that Arsenal did not have a case and that Reed's products did indeed represent 'a "badge of allegiance" by which fans declared support for their team and was not being used as a trademark' (Kelso, 2002). However, in May 2003 the European Court's ruling was finally ratified on appeal and Reed's operation was closed down.

As the case went through the courts other football clubs and sports manufacturers were closely monitoring its outcome in their bid to clamp down on 'unofficial' merchandise. Arsenal's North London rivals Tottenham Hotspur won a battle to register the word Tottenham to protect its range of merchandise sold officially through the club. The registration had been challenged by local traders who claimed that Spurs should not be allowed to claim rights to a place name used by many to signify a London borough not a football club. The legal picture on football brands was complicated further by a ruling against Spanish club Barcelona. The club had a European trademark on the club nickname 'Barca'. They attempted to gain an injunction on a London restaurant that had also used the name. However the court ruled in the UK context that Barcelona had no connection with the name Barca beyond sport and therefore could not claim a trademark in the generic area of 'entertainment' (Singh and Carter, 2003).

What these cases help illustrate is a need for football clubs to set legal parameters for their commercial operations. All major clubs in Europe, even those on the fringes of success in the Premier League and the wannabe's of the Football League, recognise the importance of building brands for their commercial prosperity. But, as we have consistently argued throughout this book, although football can generate huge income in some quarters' it is not like any other business. The images and names in football are not merely economic assets to be exploited, but are embedded more generally in the cultures of football, from fan-driven websites to the posters that adorn the bedrooms of teenage boys and girls up and down the country. Arguably, what might be called the cultural contract between football and its fans is changing (something we return to later in the book). Football, the oft-cited 'people's game', is rewriting the bond it has with its fans and this is primarily along commercial lines protected under the sign of law, including all the property rights that are generated from the core value of the game, its stars. Television has certainly been an important driver of these changes, but there are also other interrelated processes that have placed footballers in an unparalleled.

Cash, celebrity and contracts

To fully understand how processes of enclosure of intellectual property rights have been imposed on football – referred to by Samualson (1996) as a 'copyright grab' much like a land grab – it is important to focus on specific economic and organisational changes in the football industry itself. As we have outlined in previous chapters, the television-led transformations that have impacted on the football industry throughout the 1990s and into the twenty-first century have had a profound effect on the professional lives of leading footballers and their material wealth. Three inter related processes are responsible for this change: salary inflation fuelled by the aspirations of leading clubs, increased visibility of star players in the media, and changes in the contractual relationships between players and clubs after the Bosman cases.

Salary inflation

The influx of huge sums of money from television rights has underwritten an inflationary spiral in player wages. Salaries account for 50 to 80 per cent of the annual turnover of a Premier League football club. For example, Manchester United's wage bill leapt 40 per cent in 2001–2002 to £70 million after rene-gotiating contracts with some of its key players (the *Evening Standard*, 30 September 2002). Fuelled by a mixture of fear and greed, Premier League clubs, and those with aspirations of joining the likes of Manchester United, Arsenal and Liverpool, have invested heavily in football talent. In an environ-ment where large squads are considered essential for success this has meant that even fringe players have benefited from the influx of cash into the game. A reserve team player for a Premier League club could realistically earn £20,000 per week, where the average salary of Second and Third Division players is in the region of £30,000–£40,000 a year. This has led some club chairmen, such as Bryan Richardson, Chairman of Coventry City, to argue that football clubs are experiencing a form of 'financial diarrhoea' where TV revenues fall straight through into the pockets of the players (Greenfield and Osborn, 2001: 73).

The financial risks of such a strategy have begun to take their toll on some of the country's most established clubs. Midland clubs Derby County and Leices-ter City had invested heavily in overseas players during the 1990s in order to maintain Premier League status. John Williams in his *Leicester Mercury* column states clearly the pull of this strategy for club and fans alike:

> Even in an era when the championship race is so narrowed down, the simple challenge of merely surviving in the FA Premier League, among the Bergkamps, Verons and the Zolas, seems motivation and stimulation enough for most fans. The remarkable success of the Premiership has been to mark out this kind of distinction from the bread-and-butter fare of the Football League.
>
> Williams, 2002c

However both hit the financial rocks once they slid into the Nationwide League, with Leicester ultimately ending up in administration just into the 2002/3 season.

The lure of television riches from Champions League football and associated commercial benefits has also burnt clubs that borrowed heavily to buy players with the attraction of high salaries. Leeds United enjoyed relative success in 1999/2000 reaching the semi-final of the Champions League that led to a £90 million spending spree by the then manager David O'Leary in an attempt to sustain that level of success. The club then failed to qualify for the Champions League in the following season instantly reducing revenues by £15 million. In spite of the failure to reach the Champions League in 2002, the club's wage bill was £53.6 million, £10 million more than the previous year.

From the summer of 2002 to the mid-season transfer window in January 2003 the club offloaded six of its star players to bring in transfer fees and cut the wage burden. The sale of the defender Rio Ferdinand (£29.5 million to Manchester United), followed closely by Robbie Keane (£6 million to Tottenham Hotspur), Robbie Fowler (£3 million to Manchester City), Lee Bowyer (£200,000 to West Ham), Olivier Dacourt (loan deal to Internationale) and Jonathan Woodgate (£9 million to Newcastle United) were designed to offset the spiralling debt of nearly £80 million. In March 2003 both manager Terry Venables and Chairman Peter Ridsdale were pressured out of their jobs and the team fell into a relegation dog-fight to avoid further financial insecurity and possible administration. By July 2003 the list of departures would include United's talisman Harry Kewell who joined Liverpool for a vastly reduced fee of £5 million, of which £2 million went to the player and his agent Bernie Mandic.

On the publication of the clubs' half-yearly financial figures, recording an operating loss of £17.2 million, Bill Gerrard, Reader in Economics at the Leeds University Business School lambasted the financial negligence of the club. In a comment to the *Guardian* (2003) website Gerrard argued 'Decisions were made which will hang over the club and its supporters for the next 20 years and, without significant investment, it is difficult to see how Leeds will be anything other than a selling club for the foreseeable future'.

After the club's £60 million securitisation on future gate receipts to pay for transfers and wages, Gerrard, a Leeds fan himself, was quoted as saying it was 'like mortgaging your house and then blowing all the money on a holiday'. Leeds were left with the daunting task of clawing back some of its debt by cutting costs while at the same time sustaining a squad that lived up to the expectations of its increasingly disgruntled fan base.

The cost of retaining star talent has given the G14 European clubs the motive to pursue new policies to control and reduce the wage burden they currently face. One solution has been the move to introduce wage capping where salaries are bound by a percentage of turnover. The leading clubs have agreed a nominal figure of 70 per cent from 2005 but this remains a gentleman's agreement and may also be under scrutiny by the European Commission as a restrictive practice. A more immediate response has been to distinguish between the two main roles in a player's professional activities: performance (training and playing the game) and promotion (including merchandising and sponsorship).

Significantly, clubs have begun to negotiate payment for a player's 'image rights' to enable them to use a player's value as a celebrity to develop new commercial opportunities through a range of licensed products and services. The control and management of image rights not only provides a stream of income for clubs, but also provides a way of lessening the wage burden through various tax incentives.

Players are also encouraged to set up offshore venture capital companies to house income from image rights and gain beneficial tax incentives. The Inland Revenue had been keeping a close eye on the flow of income to these accounts and in the late 1990s had investigated the transfer of two Arsenal players, Dennis Bergkamp and David Platt, from Italian clubs Internationale and Sampdoria respectively. Arsenal had set up offshore accounts for 'image rights' revenues for both players as a mechanism to offset the costs of signing the two players. The Revenue were suspicious but dropped any action when it became clear that under EU law any player moving to the UK from another member country was eligible for tax exemption on income accrued in accounts held in the former territory. Again, as Couchman outlines:

> What is new is that some footballers, increasingly conscious of their value in terms of image and brand building, are looking to capture this value through a harder-nosed attitude to negotiation of the rights attached to their images.
>
> Couchman, 2002a

However, certain distinctions need to be made. Image rights contracts are limited to the higher echelons of the game. The ability to pay players' image rights will not only differ across clubs, but also within them, as Manchester United director and solicitor Maurice Watkins has pointed out:

> Clubs and players are redefining their relationships ... There is a different approach for players whose image is known worldwide and those who are just required to appear in team photographs and on the club's Internet site and TV station.
>
> Maurice Watkins, speaking at the International Football Congress at the Planet Futbol trade fair in Barcelona (Reuters, 2002)

None of the negotiations with the elite cohort of players for image rights would have evolved without the constant and pervasive attention of the media.

Smile, you're on TV

The second key process in the changing relations between players and clubs has been the blanket coverage and promotion of Europe's top leagues across all media that has increased the visibility of star footballers and raised their celebrity status to new levels. Although footballers have been equated with pop star status since the 1960s, it is arguable that the current generation of players' symbolic value as household names is greater than ever before. Football merchandising is a significant aspect of this mega-stardom and is a contemporary adjunct to the new levels of celebrity in the game. When Real Madrid signed Brazilian striker Ronaldo from Inter Milan in September 2002 the club president Florentino Perez could not overstate the player's value to the club:

> This is a great day for Real Madrid ... The mixture of Real Madrid and Ronaldo is perfect because of the universal appeal that both possess ... One of the most important things for Real is its image. We all know that Ronaldo is one of the best players in the world, but he is also one of the most universal images in the world ... We will begin selling shirts bearing the player's name immediately and we are sure there will be a massive demand. In five years we want to be in every country in the world.
>
> *Shanghai Star*, 5 September 2002

The global nature of Real's and Ronaldo's popularity would not have been possible without television. Equally, both club and player benefit from the association each provides the other. In Europe, the Champions League has done much to amalgamate the economic axis that conjoins the interests of star players and star clubs such as Real Madrid. When Real's Portuguese midfielder Luis Figo signed a three year sponsorship deal with Coca-Cola in December 2001, Real picked up 50 per cent of the £1.2 million deal for the transfer of 'image use rights'. As we discussed in the previous chapter, the format of the Champions League is entirely driven by the needs of the leading clubs to showcase their stars with the commercial benefits that spin out from it.

The logos of sponsors for all competitions are paraded at every opportunity in post match interviews and press conferences. The amount of money television and sponsors have paid to football means that players are expected to make themselves available for comment whether they want to or not. All players have contractual duties to help promote the club they play for which includes a certain level of public relations activity.

Under standard form agreements devised by the Professional Footballers' Association with clubs and the Football Association players are duty-bound to engage in this activity and sign away any 'rights' they might have in the televising or promotion of the game. More recently, new image rights clauses have been built into the standard contract to accommodate the increasing marketing demands of clubs and the Premier League. Historically, the players' union had long argued that players forego their 'image rights' or, more correctly, rights in performance, in order that the clubs and the leagues can benefit from the television revenue. When televised games began in the 1950s the players' union received 'appearance money', a nominal payment that could be used for benevolence, insurance, education and training of their members. This 'gentleman's agreement' was later replaced by contractual regulations between the PFA and the governing bodies that ensured the union a 10 per cent cut of any television revenues with the provision that players would not demand appearance money in front of the cameras.

However, during the 1990s and the start of the Premier League, two conflicting pressures began to undermine this agreement. First, clubs saw a huge rise in their television income and refused to concede 10 per cent of the revenue to the PFA. The level of contribution from television revenues was decreased to the region of 5 per cent by the time of the second Premier League deal starting in 1997. The second pressure came from the players themselves, particularly the new cohort of stars who were increasingly seen as key to the commercial success of the Premier League. As the marketing demands on players increased with wider exposure for sponsors and the media, so the pressure mounted for players to receive a greater slice of the money flowing into the game.

Things came to a head after the third Premier League television deal in 2001. The clubs, concerned with increased costs, were looking to reduce the proportion of money redistributed to the PFA by offering the same amount as the 1997 deal. As new television rights deals kicked in for the 2002/3 season, including the £1.1 billion paid by Sky, the authorities offered the PFA £6.5 million. The figure was less than 1 per cent of the annual revenue from rights (£675 million) and less than the net figure offered the previous year. The PFA were enraged and in the context of the football authorities' intransigence held a ballot for industrial action. By withdrawing their labour from the games scheduled for television the players sent a direct message to their paymasters.

The PFA did not get an immediate victory and were drawn into an ugly public relations battle in which the players were blamed by the clubs for the inflationary wage bill faced by many clubs. The PFA chairman Gordon Taylor also received severe criticism for threatening the strike by players, some among the highest earners in the country. Taylor also received criticism for his 'fat cat' salary and unsubstantiated accusations over 'missing millions'. Many of the reports glossed over the fact that the PFA annually submitted its accounts to the Charities Commission and The Registrar of Trade Unions, and had also been audited by the FA. At the eleventh hour the PFA struck a deal with the Premier League who were also acting on behalf of the FA and Football League.

The new deal ensured an annual payment of £17.5 million (£12.9 million from the Premier League) which made up the bulk of the PFA's entire budget. In an interview with Taylor he reflected that he almost wanted the matter to go to court in order to validate the PFA's position which he held to be legally water-tight given the precedent of previous agreements. Taylor was also quick to praise his members for their solidarity over the case, with a 99 per cent vote for action with 93 per cent of the ballot returned. When asked why some of the top players have not demanded individual appearance money or even repeat fees for video releases and the like, as performers in the film and music industries do, Taylor argued:

> Players haven't done that because it is a team game. But they have shown a lot of solidarity. They have recognised a particular right and are comfortable not to pursue their individual right with regards to images, with regards to matches, so long as their association has a share.
>
> Interview with authors, 6 May 2003

However, individual image rights clauses by players with their clubs and agents do add further levels of complexity to the collective agreements.

Taylor himself was happy to concede that the whole issue of image rights 'is a bit of a minefield' (Interview with authors, 6 May 2003). For example, one dimension of these tensions is the conflict of interest between sponsors of the buying club and any previous contracts held by the player at their former club. In the case of Ronaldo he already had lucrative deals signed with Nike through Inter and the Brazilian national team. In moving to Real he came under the 'sign of adidas'. Delays to the transfer were centred on this issue rather than his worth as a player. One report by Ian Hawkey (2002) suggested Ronaldo would have lost £1.6 million in endorsements in a renegotiated contract with Nike. However, at a basic salary of £3.8 million the Brazilian striker, who ceded his image rights to the club, would not have noticed any major dent to his bank balance.

Free agents: doing a 'Bosman'

The legal challenge to the transfer system in the mid 1990s by Jean-Marc Bosman and the resulting changes to player contracts has given footballers far more power in their negotiations with clubs. The competition among leading clubs to acquire and retain star footballers, who have much more freedom to find new employment, has undoubtedly contributed to the inflationary spiral mentioned above. A further consequence of a settlement between UEFA and the EC over footballers' contracts has been the shortening of player contracts, the days of a player being tied into a club for the rest of his playing days are long gone. This means a continual process of re-negotiation in a three-to-five year cycle and an opportunity to reassess the value of the player's 'brand' to the club. While the market for players has been dampened somewhat as the finances of clubs have suffered from mismanagement and overspending the price of the game's elite players continues to rise.

The changes to the transfer system have also introduced some complex legal issues regarding player contracts. Although players have the freedom to leave a club once their contract expires, the increasing use of image rights clauses potentially provides clubs with extended control of the player's affairs. If a player were to leave Club A as a free agent to Club B once his playing contract expired, would it be possible for Club A to maintain the licences associated with a player's image rights? A situation like this would no doubt be resolved, but it remains a potential deterrent for players to leave a club where they have assigned the commercial exploitation of image rights to their original employer.

The player will receive his regular professional salary, but the company (in which the player will have a substantial stake) will earn a licence fee for the club's use of the player's image rights, with inherent tax advantages. It has even been suggested that this arrangement will give clubs some measure of protection on their transfer outlay in the post Bosman climate. While a player can move freely at the end of his contract as a matter of European employment law, could the selling club require the purchasing club to buy out the licensing rights to the player's image?

This issue was raised during the mounting speculation in the spring of 2003 that England skipper David Beckham would be joining Real Madrid. Beckham, at the age of 28 with two years remaining on his contract before becoming a free agent, was viewed as ripe for picking by the Spanish club. The proposed deal appeared to make economic sense to both clubs, with Beckham's value as a footballer arguably at its peak, but more importantly his value as a marketing figurehead potentially greater. Real, eager to push ahead with globalising their brand, particularly in South-East Asia, saw Beckham as an ideal icon to drive new merchandising and sponsorship revenues. However, as Conal Walsh (2003) noted, Beckham's decision to move would be a fine balancing act between his football aspirations and his finances. 'If Beckham's star shines less brightly amid the galaxy of talent at Madrid, how might that affect the money-spinning endorsements?' Just how David Beckham's image rights are so valuable is the subject of the next section.

Worth his weight in gold: Beckham

The most publicised settlement over the use of image rights concerns the Manchester United and England player David Beckham. Beckham's celebrity extends far beyond sport, particularly after his marriage to Spice Girl Victoria, and his image is universally recognised making him a potent celebrity. Beckham the 'brand' even warranted a special feature in the *Creative Business* supplement of the *Financial Times* in which Matthew Garraham suggested that:

> He is one of a few players to transcend football and achieve popularity among non-fans as well as die-hard followers of the sport – his face adorns magazine covers worldwide: there are 120,000 websites dedicated to him; teenage girls adore him. In short, he is a marketing person's dream.
>
> Garraham, 2002

That Beckham was the first man to appear on the front cover of leading women's magazine *Marie Claire* in May 2002 is testament to his wider celebrity status. The media spotlight would intensify in the spring and summer of 2003 when speculation grew that Beckham would be joining one of the Spanish giants, Barcelona or Real Madrid. The ultimate transfer to Madrid followed a much-publicised spat between Beckham and Sir Alex Ferguson with the United manager insinuating that the player's fame and notoriety had reached a point where it was affecting the club.

In a recent academic analysis of the Beckham phenomenon, Ellis Cashmore (2003) suggests that the universal success of Beckham as a contemporary superstar rests in the values placed upon him by those that analyse and capture his image. Beckham simply plays football, and does little else. But, Cashmore argues, the media coverage he attracts and the varied narratives that constantly attempt to retell his life reveal more about the contemporary culture we live in than about the player himself. As the media coverage of football intensified during the 1990s, Beckham was ideally positioned to benefit from what Whannel has called the 'vortextual' effect of sports celebrity (Whannel, 2002: 206). It is the speed in the circulation of information and the constant reinterpretation across all media that enhances the wider cultural capital of Beckham. Stories become inflated so quickly that there is a 'short-term compression of the media agenda' (Whannel 2002: 206) where Beckham may occupy the front, back and even the centre pages of daily tabloid newspapers. Cashmore (2003: 165) again notes that this intensity of coverage is heavily monitored and managed by a 'formidable assembly of agents, publicists, lawyers, managers and miscellaneous other advisors'.

Given this media environment where football stars become all pervasive, the potency of Beckham as a brand for Real to exploit is undeniable. His contract with Real includes the signing over of 50 per cent of his personal sponsorship which was seen as key to the negotiation of his £4.2 million salary. The importance of Beckham's image had also been central to the renewal of Beckham's final contract with Manchester United just a year before leaving the club. After protracted negotiations spanning the 2000/1 and 2001/2 seasons he eventually settled for a new deal worth £90,000 a week, £20,000 of which were for the assignment of his image rights. In entering negotiations Beckham and his advisors would have been acutely aware of the contractual wrangles faced by a former club icon Eric Cantona. The Frenchman left the club and professional football bitter at the way in which his fame and reputation had been exploited by Manchester United's merchandising arm. Cantona publicly criticised his former club for using his name and associated number 7 shirt to boost sales of replica kits without fair remuneration for exploiting his name. When he abruptly retired from the game in 1997 Cantona made a point of requesting his number 7 shirt being removed from the Manchester United shop. There is some irony in the fact that Beckham took on the Frenchman's squad number the following season and ultimately registered the trademark 'BECKHAM 7' to make full use of its commercial value.

The era of Cantona stands in stark contrast to the contemporary commercialisation of the sport. Players have expanded the range of areas in which they can commercialise their celebrity. In particular, new media have provided players with new ways to leverage income from image rights and add to their promotional activities. For example, Beckham had licensed his voice to telecoms giant Vodafone for £1 million providing personalised voicemail for Manchester United fans. The deal also provides the club and Vodafone with further synergies following their £30 million sponsorship deal struck in 1999. In the lead-up to Christmas 2002 Beckham spearheaded Vodafones' campaign to roll-out its multimedia handsets with games and photo-messaging.

Lord Tim Bell, chairman of Chime Communications and former advisor to Baroness Thatcher during the 1980s, recognised the importance of making a distinction between press coverage of sports stars and the commercial value of image rights as an aspect of a player's income and worth:

> David Beckham is happy to allow a picture of him scoring a goal being used by the papers, but if he's pictured with new boots or new clothes, then those are sponsored and he's getting paid for the images being used. There is now a growing commercial exploitation of celebrities and celebrities are beginning to realise that there is an opportunity to get money which will provide them their pension and running costs.
>
> Quoted in Bose, 2002

As well as the joint image rights deal with Manchester United, covering commercial activities on behalf of the club and its sponsors, Beckham also has a string of sponsorship deals with global brands including adidas (worth £7 million over five years), Brylcreem, Marks and Spencer and Pepsi (worth £1 million per year). Interestingly, Beckham's endorsement with the soft drinks brand clashed heavily with his commercial responsibilities as England captain during the 2002 World Cup. Beckham's image adorned one of four limited edition bottles of Coca-Cola, the market leader and deadly rival of Pepsi, his personal sponsor. Interestingly, the FA would later switch their soft drinks partnership to Pepsi, possibly driven by the England captain's high profile presence in the national side. Beckham's dilution of his exclusiveness due to Team England's £6 million sponsorship deal with Coca-Cola is an example of the many conflicts beginning to surface in the increasingly complex and convoluted contractual licensing of players and their image.

Premier League clubs had become increasingly agitated by the way in which their players had been exploited by the FA and used in the commercialisation of the England national team. The conflict came to a head in October 2002 when the FA unveiled a new sponsorship initiative with five main sponsors (Pepsi, McDonald's, Umbro, Nationwide and Carlsberg) who paid £20 million each.

Part of the deal included access to England players, Beckham included, to undertake several days' promotional activity on behalf of the FA. The players agreed to share a pool of £5 million from the deal but the autocratic way in which the FA deals had been brokered, under the guidance of Chief Executive Adam Crozier, led to pressure for the Scot to resign. Premier League clubs were furious that players were spending further time away from clubs without any remuneration to them, key commercial decisions having been taken without their consent. The power of the Premier League won-out and in October 2002 Crozier resigned.

As with any global brand, Beckham is not restricted to one territorial market. His move to Real Madrid has emphasised his global appeal that he and his associates have manipulated with immense skill. In a two-year deal with BP, he was used to promote Castrol Oil in the Asia-Pacific region. In market research the oil-company discovered that 80 per cent of consumers in Thailand, Vietnam and China said a link with Beckham would be a positive reason to buy Castrol. Certainly, Beckham's money-making enterprise from the sale of his name and image is a well oiled machine. Beckham's ability to woo the media for his own ends has reached monumental proportions. On joining Real the England captain had to relinquish his favoured number 7 shirt for the less prestigious number 23. His misfortune was soon turned into a marketing opportunity when it was rumoured that he was a lifelong fan of basketball superstar Michael Jordan, who just happened to wear the number 23. In the post Jordan era of global sport it was perhaps no coincidence that Beckham's first game for Real Madrid was in a pre-season tour of Japan scoring his first goal for the club with a trademark freekick!

Player websites, cybersquatting and the 'virtual footballer'

If players and their agents have bargained hard to commercially appropriate their image rights, they have pursued the enclosure of intellectual property rights in the digital domain with even greater veracity. The Internet and the video gaming industries have opened new vistas for the exploitation of player names and images, through for example, websites and computer games.

As we have noted throughout the book the new media age has presented wider opportunities for players and clubs alike to enter the media marketplace. One of the boom areas has of course been websites dedicated to individual players, many of them run by their agents. One of the early adopters of a website was Dutch winger Mark Overmaars who famously used his website to announce his move from Arsenal to Barcelona in 1999 before the London club could make its own public announcement.

The increasing visibility and power of information delivered by player websites has also increased the value of domain names associated with star players. The value of domain names has also made their registration a potentially lucrative business. Cybersquatting, described as a parasitic and predatory practice, is invariably designed to extort money from the owner of a well-known trademark. Associated with 'bad faith' in the registration of domain names the aim is to direct consumers away from the mark's owner's online location; or offer to sell, transfer or otherwise assign domain names to another person. Given the global status of many footballers and the ability of star names to attract readers to a website, there have been several cases of cybersquatting around the world.

In August 2000 another Dutch international Pierre van Hooijdonk and his agents Sport-Promotion B.V. brought action against a young Scottish fan for registering the URL <pierrevanhooijdonk.com>. Hooijdonk had registered his name as a BENELUX trademark including the activity of publicity services that covered the domain name of a website. In November 2000, the World Intellectual Property Organisation (WIPO) Arbitration Panel on Domain Names ruled that the fan had no right registering the domain name that was identical or confusingly similar to van Hooijdonk's trademark. The case illustrated the power of rich and famous footballers and their agents to use the law in their favour in order to protect their economic interests. The imbalance of power in this respect was particularly evident in the only correspondence from the Scottish fan to the WIPO panel:

> I do not have the money to pay to defend. I think it is totally out of order that someone with lots of money can come along and take the domain name that I paid for. All I have asked for is that if the other party pay my cost to date (payment for web design) then I would be willing to transfer the domain name to their client. They say that their client is world famous, I would dispute that very much. I may not be going about this in the proper manner but as I said before I cannot afford to contact a lawyer and pay for his/her advice. Yours Sam B. Tait.
> WIPO Arbitration Panel on Domain Names, 2000

In a new media environment where electronic fanzines abound the case also highlighted whether or not it is unfair to expand trademark law into such areas. The website was established as a tribute to the player after his period of playing for Celtic in Scotland. The case also brought attention for the need to consider the actual content of websites in such cases. Are they defamatory? Are they exploiting the name for commercial ends? Arguably on each count the fan website was not a threat either way. As a further ruling on another international star Franscesco Totti of AS Roma and Italy confirmed, the high stakes involved and the damage to secondary rights sold to sponsors (Nike in Totti's case) more or less ensures victory for any player that wants to reclaim his domain name. As the WIPO panel argued:

> There is no reason why famous sportspeople should not have a similar ability to achieve a common law mark arising out of their fame in an area of

life which attracts great interest – if not extreme enthusiasm – in those many countries of the world where 'soccer' is part of the way of life.

WIPO Arbitration Panel on Domain Names, 2002

Where player names and images are used for commercial gain without their consent or without full licence agreements the issues of financial damages do arise. This has been particularly so in the portrayal of players in the lucrative industry of computer games.

In Belgium, a group of players, including Romanian international Gheorghe Hagi and three clubs (Feyenoord, Slavia Prague and Vincenza) took five software companies to court over the unlicensed use of their names and likenesses in a range of computer games. Sony, Electronic Arts, Rage Games, Infogrammes and Eidos (all based in the UK), who had manufactured licensed games from governing bodies FIFA and UEFA, were sued in a Belgian court. The players claimed their names, images and even playing styles had been used without consent by the games' designers. Hagi was quoted as saying that, 'It is a crime that they can use name and styles without any payment or even asking permission' (Couchman, 2002b). Leading the case was Jean-Louis Dupont who had previously acted for Jean-Marc Bosman in the groundbreaking case at the European Court of Justice. The lawyer claimed a need to readdress the law in the 'new economy' of computer games and new media claiming that:

> The professional player must accept that his image be retransmitted in his work, that is, when he is on the football field or in the locker room ... But there is no reason to make use of his name or his image outside of his professional activities. However these games companies do so without authorisation.
>
> Reported at http://www.briffa.com/personality/games.htm

In a similar case, German and Bayern Munich goalkeeper Oliver Kahn sued leading computer games manufacturer EA Sports for unlicensed use of his image in the best selling game FIFA 2002. In April 2003 a court in Hamburg ordered the firm Electronic Arts not to market the game in Germany, in spite of the fact that it already had sold 180,000 units in the country. Kahn's lawyer, Matthias Pinz, claimed a new victory for footballers wanting to prevent the unsolicited use of their 'personality rights' in video games. In spite of the fact that EA Sports had signed rights agreements with international players' union FIFPro, as well as a licence agreement with the German Bundesliga permitting the use of character likenesses and names, the ruling suggests games manufacturers would need to seek permission from every player it portrays.

In an interview with the commercial director of FIFPro, former Wolves player George Berry revealed to us that players needed to understand the harm such recourse to the courts might cause. FIFPro had stepped into the market to tidy up the use of players' names in games licensed by the likes of FIFA and the Premier League. The money accrued from licensing the use of players' names within interactive computer games is used to help fund the benevolent funds of all the associated player unions in different territories. However, in Kahn's case, the player, prompted by his agent and legal advisors, had approached the issue with a different mentality. Berry argues:

> When you get players who decide that they want to go beyond (existing agreements) the problem we've got is collectively everybody gets hurt. If you get players that say 'I want X', then let me tell you all the other players will say 'well I want X as well'. What happens then is that nobody gets anything because the industry is killed.
>
> Interview with authors, 6 May 2003

Berry argued that of the 38,000 players in the FIFPro territories only a minority, around 10 per cent, are commercially marketable as individuals. However, these players, such as Kahn, would be worth nothing without their position in the broader community of football, the clubs, the national teams and the wider pool of players. FIFPro's claim is that without the 'also-rans' the game would be unsustainable and if every player pursued their commercial interest for the use of image rights in computer games and other similar uses then the market would ultimately disappear. It was this argument that ultimately persuaded Hagi and the other players involved in the Belgian case to drop their legal action for the wider good of the playing community. However, in an age when commercial contracts between players, clubs, national federations and agents become increasingly complex, conflicts of interest of this type will continue to occur for the foreseeable future.

Conclusion: balancing freedom of expression and press freedom

There are worrying signs, that the ring fencing of footballers' image rights might stifle the ability of the media to adequately cover the game. As far back as September 2002, the *Daily Telegraph* exposed secret trials of new proprietary technology by Manchester United that would effectively enable the club to control the production and distribution of all images from their Old Trafford stadium. One strategy would be to restrict access of photographic agencies after the cessation of Premier League press accreditation clearing the way for the club to set up its own photo agency via a dedicated website for the rapid distribution of photographs. Something the club would indeed implement a year later. The consequences for press freedom were clearly stated by Simon Hart in the *Daily Telegraph*:

The suspicion is that such shots would be 'sanitised' and that controversial images, such as the infamous photograph of Roy Keane remonstrating furiously with referee Andy D'Urso two seasons ago, would never see the light of day.

Hart, 2002

Image rights management at this level clearly offers new areas of commercial activity for leading football clubs with large fan bases like Manchester United which are becoming increasingly active as multimedia companies. However, the stringent legal and corporate enclosure of image rights threatens broader rights of access to information and images of the game, denying fans any connection with their heroes outside of the commercial operations of the clubs. The problem for fans and media outlets alike is the basic fact that football clubs wield incredible power over the access to their stadia. As Fitzpatrick (2001) has noted regarding the ownership of rights, whether it is connected to photographers, broadcasters or use of statistical data, 'what counts is the power of the person who can allow access to cameras and data capture equipment on their land'.

A good example of the confusion that can arise from a player or club that attempts to control media access via image rights clauses is revealed by the BBC's Head of Football, Niall Sloane:

We first heard of 'image rights', I think in Atlanta doing the Olympic Games. We were trying to shoot a new set of *Match of the Day* titles and we wanted to go up and film Juninho at the Boro. We got a fax back from somebody saying you can't do this because it infringes Juninho's 'image rights'. We thought, 'What in the name of god are image rights?' And we just picked up the phone and rang Bryan Robson, 'What's this all about?' And Bryan said don't worry we'll sort it.

Interview with the authors, 22 April 2003

Sloane's account reveals the fine balance between football using television as a medium to promote itself, in a mutually beneficial way, and the game's attempt to distinguish and commercialise the range of activities and services it now recognises it provides.

It also raises issues of the relationship between clubs, players and their agents. In the case above, Middlesbrough would have seen the benefits of their star player being paraded in the *Match of the Day* titles effectively enhancing the popularity of the player and the club. However, Juninho and his advisors would clearly have seen it as a marketing activity above and beyond his contractual obligations to the club. Time is money in the image conscious environment of contemporary professional football. Again, as Sloane observes from his encounters with players and their agents:

It's easy to do if you work with a good club, a sensible player and a sensible agent. Now in the latter category there is not many, I have to say. I think there is an awful lot of 'give me the money now' and there are very few agents that look at the long-term picture.

Interview with the authors, 22 April 2003

As we have noted above the issue of rights in the new media age is an increasingly central concern for clubs and indeed journalists. While we have looked at the emerging battle lines involving players and image rights, another arena sees media outlets embroiled with the elite clubs as the latter seek to use the global distribution system of the Internet to exploit their assets. It is to this battleground which we now focus our attention.

Chapter 5

Battle for control

Football clubs and new media strategy

> The Internet is not a community antenna. It is not simply a system for delivering a given kind of content more efficiently. The critical feature of the Internet that sets it apart from every other network before is that it could be a platform upon which a whole world of activity might be built.
>
> Lessig, 2001: 174

Introduction

The battle lines of control extend well beyond those we have just looked at between club and player. The football club in the new media age is keen to extend its control on a range of areas associated with the image and imaging of the club and extract value from them using the delivery systems which a digital environment offer. The Internet has undoubtedly had a dramatic impact on the global media environment in which the sports-media industry now operates. The degree of engagement with new media clearly varies, but there is general consensus among footballing organisations that the Internet presents a range of new possibilities for communicating with various publics.

It is becoming clear that clubs require a multimedia capacity to be in a position to exploit the online rights and image rights that will become more important over the next decade. What is evident is that every major club is keen to develop their media capacity for fear of being left behind when the projected revenues (and like a lot of dotcom financial analysis, projected, is all they are at present) begin to materialise.

This chapter develops earlier versions of this work (Boyle and Haynes, 2003) and focuses on football clubs in the UK and Europe and examines if a generic model for media development is emerging. To what extent does the business of football act at a pan-European level or are there specific cultural factors that influence patterns of development?

Some of the issues this chapter addresses include: To what extent is a footballing new media business model emerging? What are some of the implications for clubs, their communities, shareholders and supporters of these new media developments? What are footballing organisations and media companies doing to accommodate such radical paradigm shifts in communications? What implications do global, networked multimedia driven communications have for our experience and understanding of football and mediated coverage of the sport?

New media sport: a false dawn?

After the initial furore over the boom in e-commerce and the dotcom hype of the mid-to-late 1990s (Cassidy, 2002) sports rights holders have become increasingly cautious in their approach to exploiting new media technologies and digital distribution platforms. As we have argued elsewhere (Boyle and Haynes, 2004) the promotional rhetoric of the 'anytime, anywhere, anyplace' new media age has fallen well short of its potential and has largely represented an unrealistic promise.

There have been various reasons for this unfulfilled potential which are analysed below, but central to the chequered development of new media sport has undoubtedly been the age old problem of technological determinism in attempts to drive sports content through new media platforms. Rather than the culture of sport influencing the architecture of new media services, the technology often drives the delivery of content. The mistake is to believe that just because football fans like to read about the game on the back pages of newspapers they will also want to read about it on their mobile phones or interactively through their TV sets. How sports content conjoins with the architecture or physics of new media and television technologies is therefore central to understanding how fans appropriate this media into their everyday consumption of sport.

As we discussed in Chapter 2, the collapse in the UK of ITV Digital also suggests the marriage of football and new media at an industry level is in a state of crisis, or at least a critical conjuncture (Banks, 2002). The promise of new audiences for digital television platforms and lucrative streams of income for football have fallen well short of expectations. In hindsight it is clear that ITV Digital paid too much money for an inferior product when compared to BSkyB's successful coverage of the Premier League. In its drive to become a significant competitor to BSkyB the DTT platform rushed to secure live Nationwide League football seemingly without asking a fundamental question of who would watch and be willing to pay for second-string action.

As for the clubs, many are in more debt than ever before as player salaries have escalated in an inflationary spiral, pulled upwards by money from television. Despite the optimism expressed in the 2003 *Deloitte & Touche Annual Review of Football Finance*, it remains the case that while the Premier League enjoyed revenues of 1.7 billion Euro in 2001/2, the operating profit was only 130 million Euro, while players' wages rose by 26 per cent to represent on average 62 per cent of a club's turnover (Deloitte & Touche, 2003). At the same time pay-TV channels are struggling to sustain their investment in the sport in the wake of a major advertising slump and a slowdown in new subscribers. Added to these economic conditions is a general uncertainty with regard to how new media technologies can be utilised to provide profitable services that fans are willing to pay for.

Given the uncertain malaise surrounding new media and football it is interesting to focus on specific club strategies to exploit new media technologies and investigate why and how they plan to develop such services. One of the key dimensions of the Internet and multichannel digital television environment is that it broadens the spectrum of possible audio-visual services and, at the same stroke, lowers the barriers to entry for producers of mass media. Although the costs of digital production are significant, both in terms of financial investment and human resources, they do provide incentives for football clubs to vertically integrate their sporting, media and commercial activities. The reason for this is that access to new media distribution networks enables clubs to have closer control and leverage of their broadcast rights and other associated intellectual property (IP) as we discussed in the previous chapter with regard to players.

In effect, the football industry of the twenty-first century offers far more opportunities to commercialise aspects of the daily operations and running of the football club than ever before. The phrase 'access all areas' aptly describes the contemporary relationship between football and the media. The one caveat to this freedom of information being that coverage of the daily activities of a club and its players is now delivered from within the organisation itself, operating as a public relations and branding exercise rather than a journalistic account of what is really going on. Furthermore, in an environment where clubs manage their media relations through PR officers and communications managers information about football becomes more like a commodity (Boyle et al., 2002).

In this instance contract discussions over image or personality rights and rights in databases take on new commercial significance for top football clubs. We noted in the previous chapter that the delay in 2002 over the signing of 17 year old Wayne Rooney's contract with Everton appeared to be over, among other things, settling a value on the player's future image rights. Football clubs have come to realise that they have certain proprietary rights as part of the entertainment industry and have sought to commercially exploit these rights across various new media platforms.

Before moving on to discuss the specific new media strategies of football clubs in both England and Scotland, we want to briefly analyse three central contextual factors that are influencing new media strategies of football clubs. These focus on issues related to technology, market failure and regulation.

Limitations of technology

In the mid-to-late 1990s the media sports sector was in buoyant mood. This was reflected in the social, economic and cultural hopes of technological change – the so called 'Information Society' – and the potential of new delivery methods and platforms. The general signifiers of a revolution in the use of ICTs are there for all to see: the increase in mobile telephony, especially the phenomenon of text messaging; the increase in households with access to the Internet and PCs; the increase in DTH satellite and cable services since the early 1990s and subsequently digital television at the turn of the millennium. However, as recent sceptical commentators of the 'Information Society' have correctly pointed out there are more continuities with established cultural patterns and media use than there are distinctively new ones (May, 2002).

In spite of the advances in the adoption and appropriation of new media technologies into people's everyday lives the question of how sports content can be creatively adapted to new media formats in imaginative and engaging ways has largely been found wanting. The classic example here has been the failure of Wireless Application Protocol (WAP), initially launched in the UK in 1999. WAP was heavily marketed by all the major telecommunications providers as being a revolution in mobile telephony with the potential to deliver original content including sport. However, what users got was an inferior service compared to the Internet, which was one-dimensional and took an age to download.

As Professor Patrick Barwise of the Future Media Research programme at the London Business School has argued more generally about the adoption and use of new media:

> On the consumption side, consumers have not stopped watching TV and switched to the Internet. Nor have they shown much tendency to interact with TV programmes or commercials, nor to buy things via their TVs, nor to buy pay-per-view or video-on-demand content. This is not to say that interactive digital TV has no potential, only that – like so much else – it was overhyped.
>
> Barwise, 2002

According to Crabtree, Nathan and Roberts (2003) the gap between what users may want, and what is available, remains wide, the only exception here may be the rapidly expanding catalogue of ringtones (including the theme to *Match of the Day*). The massive investment by telecommunications companies for 3G licences in the UK, that heavily undermined any confidence of the financial markets in the performance of the whole sector, has set some unavoidable problems for the network operators as they launched in 2003. Namely, how to entice enough customers to make such investments viable. Sports related content again appears to be crucial in this equation. As we shall see below in our case study of Manchester United, strategic alliances between telecommunications companies and football (the carrot for adopting services you did not realise you wanted) represent the latest attempts to bridge the divide between technology and content providers with a ready-made audience. However, this would mean a significant proportion of the current 70 per cent of the population who use mobile phones in the UK trading their GSM phones for the new technology. One of the commercial difficulties faced by telecom companies remains convincing consumers to upgrade technology. Initially the 3G companies indicated that they would compete on the quality of the services they would offer consumers, rather than on price. However by late 2003, given relatively poor uptake, price cutting in this sector has began to develop, suggesting that this will prove to be a difficult market for companies who have invested heavily in licences and backing up research (Crabtree *et al.*, 2003) which indicated that cost was more important to mobile users than previously thought.

Market failure

The economic downturn in the media and telecommunications markets over the past couple of years has led to a certain amount of retrenchment in new media activity. As we have highlighted above, huge investment in setting up new media infrastructures such as 3G networks have proven too costly and left global corporations with huge debts that cannot be realistically recouped in the short to medium term. The pessimism that has followed the boom years of e-commerce and multichannel television has also impacted on sport, in particular football.

In the UK, the ITV Digital collapse ultimately hurt football more than the media corporations with many clubs threatened with bankruptcy and administration (Banks, 2002). The clubs did manage to redeem some revenue from their television rights with a much depleted offer from BSkyB in July 2002 worth £95 million over four years but much of the financial damage had already been done. The ITV Digital scenario indicated that the boom in television sports rights had reached a ceiling, this despite the substantial value from television that was secured by the Premier League for the 2004–2007 rights.

A further ramification of the ITV Digital collapse is the emergent monopoly of BSkyB in the coverage of live subscription based football in the UK. The process of consolidation in the televising of football is a growing feature of the European pay-TV environment, particularly among the newly formed digital platforms. As we noted in Chapter 3, 2002 saw Italy's two key pay-TV platforms Telepui and Stream both merging and being sold to Rupert Murdoch's News Corporation, creating Sky Italia. Thus offering a clear signal that Murdoch's ongoing attempt to dominate the European pay-TV market remains on track. Since 1999 rights to Serie A games have been divided between the two digital platforms however both have struggled to turn the appeal of football into subscribers. As a special report in the *Observer Sports Magazine* by Denis Campbell on European football rights highlights with regard to the Italian pay-TV sports market:

> The trouble is far fewer fans are paying to view than was expected: Stream has 800,000 subscribers and is close to collapse with a debt of £253m,

while Telepui has about 1.5m and is £223m in the red. A major problem is somewhere between a million and a half and two million Italians are thought to be using pirated smart cards to tune in illegally.

Campbell, 2002a

As we have noted, the inflated cost of football rights has also impacted on other leading football markets. In Germany, the insolvency of Kirch media group was based largely on the poor levels of subscription to their pay-TV platform Premier World (including Premier Sport that paid £960 million for the rights to the Bundesliga from 2000–2004). Interestingly the deal also included transmission rights for mobile phones and the Internet which the administrator UBS Bank passed on to Deutsch Telecom who launched their 3G mobile services in 2003. Again, the investment by Kirch in WAP and the Internet appeared to be a huge gamble that did not pay off once the height of the dotcom boom subsided.

It is worth noting that even established and successful companies such as BSkyB have also had their fingers burnt in the Internet 'land grab' rush of 2000. This was the year BSkyB paid £300 million for the company Sports Internet giving them access to a number of football club websites. By spring 2001, the company had written down this investment to £60 million (Cellan-Jones, 2001: 233).

There is also another impact of the general downturn in media revenues for corporations and their linkage with clubs. By 2003, the synergising opportunities offered by media corporations buying into football clubs in the UK had been dramatically reduced. When Russian billionaire Roman Abramovich took over Chelsea in the summer of that year, he not only heralded the beginning of a new era at the club. He also called a halt to the trend of media companies buying into football clubs. For all the high profile transfers which Chelsea were involved in during these summer months, of more interest was the way in which BSkyB was happy to sell its 9.9 per cent stake in the club to Abramovich and effectively write off an investment of £40 million which they made in 2000. In October 2003 BSkyB would also sell its 9.9 per cent share in Manchester United to Irish racehorse owners J.P. McManus and John Magnier for £62 million further confirming their withdrawal from future direct investment in clubs. Since the high point in the value of sports rights, BSkyB have written off almost £80 million of investment in clubs.

At the same time the debt ridden cable company NTL was also keen to shed some of the shares it had secured in a range of clubs at a time when the football bubble looked like it would continue to expand. In addition, in some of the clubs which NTL did not buy into, they did secure a position as media partners, paying clubs in the late 1990s such as Rangers, for example, £31 million to run its website operation. An investment which they can never hope to recoup given the changes in the new media marketplace since then.

By 2004 a strategic re-positing was taking place, which saw football clubs as increasingly peripheral to the core business activities of media companies. This however, as we argue below, does not of course mean that relationships, particularly around new media development would not be important – BSkyB remains a key media partner of Chelsea for example. But rather that this synergy between media and football clubs would not be as simple, or as pre-determined as many fans and analysts had predicted at the turn of the century.

UK regulatory context

With the rapid expansion of dedicated sports channels during the 1990s and the related competition for the rights to football, regulators have begun to investigate the collective sale of rights in the belief that they may not be in the public's interest. The football industry had already been rocked by EC competition law in the wake of the Bosman case that freed up the movement of players out of contract. As we discussed in Chapter 2, the spotlight has turned to the collective sale of rights and its negative implications for broadcast markets.

We noted that in December 2002 the European Commission asked the English Premier League to respond to concerns about the restrictive nature of the live television agreements it has with BskyB. The EC argue that collective agreements restrict the number of games available to subscribers, and appear keen to explore the possibility of all games being opened up to the multichannel broadcasting environment, including the Internet.

One immediate impact of this process was the opening up of UEFA Champions League rights from 2003 that were sold to a number of networks in the same country. One aspect of this is the ability of clubs to trade some of their broadcast rights individually. In the age when football clubs are able to develop club specific digital television channels and broadband Internet sites the EC edict has significant implications for future rights negotiations. The OFT inquiry into BSkyB's deal with the Premier League we discussed in Chapter 2 is of significance here. While media companies were looking to offload their stakes in football clubs by the 2003/4 season, it remains the case that the seeds were sown in the minds of the major clubs that certain rights could be retained and exploited. In spite of the fact the OFT lost its case, the top Premiership clubs have been left in no doubt that they have a future role to play in the direct transmission of televised football.

Manchester United's then Director of Communications Patrick Harverson clearly felt that this issue is set to be a long running debate within the game:

> The one thing that a lot of people look forward to or predict is the day when for example MUTV might be the main distribution platform for live Man United games in the Premier League to overseas viewers. So at the moment, instead of going through collective deals through the Premier League and then the Premier League rights marketing company selling

those to broadcasters around the world, if you wanted to watch Man United live you subscribe to MUTV whether you're in Scandinavia, whether you're in Singapore or whether you're in New York. So clearly MUTV is a very important platform for us ultimately because what we're trying to do here is build businesses around the club for the growing subscriptions by offering fantastic content to dedicated Manchester United fans.

Interview with author, 25 April, 2002

The loss of collective rights would not necessarily affect BSkyB as they would be the carrier of channels on their digital platform. What we outline below is how clubs such as Manchester United are strategically gearing up for a possible change in the pay-TV sports market and the growing importance of the Internet in the exploitation of other ancillary rights.

A business model for new media development: the case of Manchester United

Our challenge is to be more targeted, build databases and relationships and convert fans into customers.

Peter Kenyon, the then Chief Executive, Manchester United,
the Guardian, 30 March 2002

From free to fee

As has been noted earlier in the book despite the problems across Europe associated with the overpricing of football rights and the difficulty some broadcasters have had in recouping their outlay, football still matters to television.

It is also true to say that while we are looking at the strategic developments that clubs are undertaking to maximise revenue streams from a range of new media platforms, money from traditional broadcast sources remains vital, at least in the short term, but more likely the long term as well. Season 2001/2 for example saw Manchester United earn £25.82 million from television exposure for the season, while the lowest earner in the English Premier League, Leicester City, received just under £11 million (*Soccer Investor*, 6 June 2002). Figures for 2003 revealed the club's revenue from all media outlets was £56 million representing 36 per cent of the club's annual turnover, only 3 per cent less than revenue from match day receipts.

Broadcasting is vital in exposing and developing their global brand identity and with that its partnerships to high profile global sponsors such as Vodafone, Nike and Pepsi. Indeed Manchester United has a clear strategy in partnering with media experts. As their then Director of Communications, Paddy Harverson argued:

Our strategy across most of our businesses now is to partner with experts, what we call best of breeding in each area and get them to bear the brunt of the investment, the cost of the burden because of the owner investment and what we bring to it is the brand. What they bring to it is the knowledge, expertise and the funding because as a football club we're still really a relatively modest business and we're not the size of BSkyB or Nike or Vodafone so they can support the investment that with a combination of our brand produces the income for both of us, the showing, which is the model for MUTV, as it is for the Nike deal, as it is for increasingly more of our sponsorship.

Interview with author, 25 April 2002

Elite clubs such as Manchester United, Liverpool and Arsenal in England view the new platforms as a potential important way of expanding their revenues from the pay-TV market, to which over 40 per cent of homes in the UK have access.

The desire for clubs to retain greater control over what they view as their intellectual property (IP) remains undiminished despite the spectacular failures of online sports companies to generate profits. In the UK on the day the 2002 FIFA World Cup started, the UK arm of Sports.Com, one of the biggest online providers of sports content, went into administration (with 6.8 million unique users across Europe), while Teamtalk, another large online sports company, agreed to be sold to the betting group ukbetting at a knockdown price.

In a market already considerably consolidated from the heady days of dotcom mania these failures are hugely significant indicators of the future direction of the online sports market. As has been noted:

> There's doubtless an audience for sports content online, but it may be left to the survivors such as BSkyB and big football brands themselves to reap the benefits.
>
> *Revolution*, Editorial, 12 June 2002

Significantly these changes were happening at a time when Manchester United were busy signing a two-year £2 million deal with the Internet company Lycos UK giving high profile access to sponsors and editorial material associated with the club. Among other things, the deal links Manchester United to Lycos Europe and Lycos Asia with the latter developing a Chinese language site as the club seek to generate content for its non English speaking Asian fan base.

This marks another step in the strategic development of the club's media strategy. In 1998 they launched MUTV which was the first football television station to broadcast on a daily basis. This joint venture with broadcasters Granada Media Group and BSkyB was delivered on a subscription basis to fans via satellite and cable platforms. More recently these have migrated exclusively to digital platforms such as Sky Digital and NTL Digital.

Given the restrictive state (in the eyes of the clubs) of UK television rights it has meant that the key 'killer' content of showing live first team matches has been absent from this service. The loosening of restrictions for delayed live rights at the start of the most recent BSkyB deal in 2004, following the retention of more rights to clubs in the 2003 UEFA Champions League deal, have aided the development of club channels such as MUTV. As the club's then Director of Communications Paddy Harverson outlines:

> Probably the biggest event in MUTV's short history was at the beginning of the season when for the first time the Premier League rights, a portion of them became available for the clubs and you began to see what the possibilities were for someone like MUTV, where we've always had the inside scoop on the club for viewers' access, interviews, magazine programmes, features, etc. But really what people want to watch are games and all the stuff around the games so in MUTV's case where it's really starting to hit its drive now is, while we can't show live games, we've got the delayed rights to games now so you can show them in their entirety within anything between a few hours of them finishing and 48 hours and in many cases what people don't realise is that the majority of our games are not shown live on TV.
>
> It may seem like it is, certainly in the Premier League, it's not, so there are a lot of games that are neither seen live on TV nor in any great detail through highlights on *The Premiership* on ITV and there is the real value there to the content and you can see further forward when we might get more control over our content to be able to deliver more Manchester United programming for a subscription fee to more viewers at home or abroad.
>
> Interview with author, 25 April 2002

Manchester United have been distinctive in their particular business model which has evolved and adopted a twin strand through its digital TV and Internet based approach.

In other words, unlike other clubs, such as Arsenal, it does not view the Internet as the best medium for delivering its broadcasting output. Arsenal, the 2002 English champions, have invested heavily with their media partners Granada (who secured a 5 per cent stake in the club in 1999) in developing their website and layering in various subscription sections. Peter Smith, their then Sponsorship and Broadband Manager argued:

> We haven't done for example a full blown TV channel like Manchester United and Chelsea have, they lose money and the amount of content that you have to find for it and the amount of rules there are because of the Sky deal and the overseas TV deals, they have to be on an encrypted channel, there has to be four hours of new content a week which doesn't sound a lot

but you try and generate four hours with what you're not allowed to show
... it's so very, very difficult.

Interview with author, 8 April 2002

Other clubs such as both Celtic and Rangers also felt that the costs involved in running a full service television platform made it simply economically unworkable (see Chapter 6). However, the increasing emergence of the Irish based pay sports channel Setanta TV in 2002–2003, and its plans to run and bundle a number of club channels including the Old Firm, and Everton and Liverpool on the Sky platform for the 2004/5 season mean that television club channels, for a group of clubs is almost certain to evolve.

At Manchester United their strategy has been formulated on a perception that there are two ways in which supporters engage with the visual media; the lean back and lean forward view of how football fans interact with their televisions and computers. The evidence remains that fans prefer to watch live matches on television, often in the company of friends or in the pub. However there may be a market for short web-based packages consisting of goal clips, news and interviews for which fans make a micropayment.

This is a relatively new system rolled out by mobile phone companies, such as Vodafone's m-pay digital content micropayment system used for example on the Manchester United website. Users can charge anything from 5p to £5 direct to their mobile phone bill, and the pricing structure is such that users make small payments (currently from £1–£4) for a selection of reports, interviews, goals and archive material. Thus Manchester United's website has a subscription section The Red, in which additional payments are made for such material.

While revenues are slowly building, clubs such as Arsenal and Manchester United view this as a lucrative market, particularly in the case of overseas fans that access subscription sections through the Internet. Our research indicated that one problem clubs faced when charging for content on the web is that so much football material has been previously free to access. When Arsenal revamped their website in 2002 to include free sections, but also introduced subscription elements for new content, fans complained that it previously had been free. In fact what had been free to access was still there and 'premium content' had been added, it does however demonstrate one of the barriers to creating an online football pay market.[1]

But like most of the positioning being taken up by the clubs, this is a process of slowly building an infrastructure and testing what works and what does not. Harverson is in no doubt that a club such as Manchester United is in this development for long-term gain and recognises that:

I think it will take several years for just ordinary sports fans to get used to paying for things. Sports fans seem to be particularly resistant to paying for content over the Internet because there is so much of it and its all been free and obviously this is now a quality video content so there is clearly a step up and if you're sitting in your bedroom or office in Singapore and United have just beaten Chelsea 3–0 you wouldn't mind tuning in to see three great goals and a three minute review of that put together by Sky, it would be great.

Interview with author, 25 April 2002

The three central areas through which income on online sports websites is generated is subscription, advertising and sponsorship. In America it appears that those online sports websites (such as Rivals.com and NHL.com the national hockey league's official website) that are proving profitable have built their business models around subscription charging for exclusive video content (Gerlis, 2002). They view this as the key way of extracting income from traffic to the sites. Those US sports sites that have failed have tended to focus their revenue generation on online advertising. Popular American sites such as ESPN.com have developed layered subscription sections to drive income.

This comes at a time when some in the UK (Bell, 2002) are arguing that it is the advertisers' and marketeers' inability to keep pace with the web based sporting communities being developed that is preventing advertising becoming a major revenue generator for these sites. The success in the UK of the 2002 FIFA World Cup in driving traffic to particular football sites was marked. The BBC had its busiest monthly traffic ever in June, while the *Guardian*'s football website enjoyed a new one day traffic record of 4 million impressions and during June had ten days of 2.8 million page impressions (compared to 2.4 million and 2.7 million on 11 and 12 September for example). However it appears that until there is a greater shift from offline to online advertising investment (not helped by the wider downturn in media ad spend more generally in the UK over the last two to three years) then subscription based football web based business models will continue to develop.

Linked with these developments has been the decision of Manchester United, in late 2003, to set up its own online picture agency (*Soccer Investor Weekly*, 28 August 2003). This service will charge for the use of pictures, while the club will control the number of photographers who have access to Old Trafford. The club expect the in-house picture agency to service fans and publications around the globe, via the Internet, and is another example of the ways in which elite football clubs want to gain commercial value from activities related to the club which in the past have been either underdeveloped, or in this case provided commercial value for outside agencies and freelancers. Our research has indicated that there is a widespread view among top clubs that the media have been extracting commercial value on the back of club activities for too long, and that new media delivery systems offer an opportunity for clubs to redress this perceived imbalance (see Chapter 6).

There is also the issue of clubs protecting their image rights not simply from traditional media usage. Throughout 2003, a number of Italian Serie A clubs and telecom companies battled it out inconclusively in court over the issues of sending still pictures of Italian matches via mobile phones. On the one hand it was argued (and agreed by a court in Milan) that still images during a game constituted news coverage (with no fee payable to those involved), while on the other hand, clubs argued that such activity constituted an infringement of club IP, and any such mobile phone pictures required permission and the payment of a fee (upheld in a Rome court).

There is little doubt that the issue of access and definition of image right will become an increasingly key battlefield between media and clubs over the next decade, as delivery systems and technology extend their market share and become more robust.

Club channels and the development of a broadband football market

Some analysts argue that eventually if the money on offer from traditional broadcasters becomes too small, then clubs across Europe will be tempted to go it alone, or set up their own channels. It is even mooted that clubs will be delivering exclusive subscription matches via the web across broadband networks and ostensibly cutting out traditional broadcast networks and migrating the sport from television to the web.[2] However we remain highly sceptical of this outlook not least because as noted above, this is not how fans socially watch the sport, while the building of robust and reliable broadband networks remains some way off, despite the advances that are being made (albeit unevenly) in this section of the new economy.

Significant changes in the UK broadband market are taking place which may have implications for clubs and their ability to use the web to exploit their IP. 2002 has seen BT, the troubled telecom company in the UK, reposition broadband at the core of its business. As the dominant player in the market, the company's Chief Executive Ben Verwaayen set a target of one million broadband customers by summer 2003, rising to two million in 2004 and five million by 2006. Central to the ability of BT raising its required £1.5 billion of retail revenue by 2005, is that a third of this will come from broadband uplift (the *Guardian*, 25 March 2002). There is little doubt that broadband usage in the UK is beginning to pick up pace, with BT reaching its one million target during the summer of 2003.

It is worth noting that the figures (OFTEL, July 2003) indicate that almost half the homes in Britain (47 per cent) are connected to the Internet. Interestingly this suggests that a ceiling has been reached as this figure shows little significant year on year change. What is changing is the number of these home users who are migrating to some form of broadband package. In July 2003, it was estimated that 19 per cent of these Internet homes are using a broadband connection (either ADSL or cable modem). This figure has risen from only 5 per cent in May 2002. It has been argued that the speed of growth (estimated to be 30,000 a week in 2003) outstrips the demand for both mobile phones and Internet dial-up services on their introduction (Hewitt and Pinder, 2002). However this still constitutes about 10 per cent of the homes in the UK and suggests that while broadband is growing it has someway to go before it becomes a mass infrastructure for delivering content.

This research also shows that some analysts remain unconvinced that the roll out of broadband across the UK, at least in the short term, will provide the platform required to sustain the video streaming of matches across the web. Graham Lovelace of Lovelace Media Limited argues:

> that BT's aspirations are overly optimistic. Broadband has been sold to an unsuspecting UK consumer market on the technological advantage. No media since the development of radio, cinema, whatever it is, has ever been sold on technology. But if you think most usage of the Internet is to pick up e-mails and monitor one or two websites, what really does broadband Internet give you? So we think that is overly optimistic and is being sold on the wrong advantage, plus the actual data capacity rates that BT through ADSL can ever offer is the maximum of 512 kilobytes per second. Now that's if no one else on your street is using it at the same time, that's a maximum saving.
>
> The critical thing for the [football] clubs is that to deliver full broadcast video requires between two and four megabytes per second and you don't just want to deliver one channel, you want to deliver several channels, simultaneous coverage, plus pictures within pictures so you need enormous amounts of capacity to actually deliver what those who are seen to deliver the applications actually want from this.
>
> Interview with author, 10 April 2002

In other words, what is being described as broadband for much of the UK market is in fact a two-dimensional slightly faster service. For example, the cable operator NTL offers a range of services under their broadband provision. One is at 160 kps, another at 600 kps and their top speed package at 1 mb. Thus broadband actually can mean a number of differing services. While the cable operators such as NTL struggle to restructure their debt laden companies, the future of a fast broadband mass market remains a distant proposition particularly in the UK. Paul Wright, formally Marketing Director of Sports.com and now founder of Aura Sports, a digital media agency, shares the scepticism about broadband being a viable platform for video streaming.

> Well I think the reality of broadband is it's basically just faster Internet access rather than what it's jazzed up to be in terms of video streaming [...] I think the video element has always been over-hyped because I don't think the rights position is clear yet to make it happen, regardless of whether there is broadband infrastructure or not. The other thing I think we have to ask ourselves is are people seriously going to watch a

small box on an Internet, something live relative to being able to watch it on TV?

Interview with author, 10 April 2002

Thus it appears Manchester United's policy of viewing both digital television and the web as distinctive but connected platforms to deliver differing content seems a prudent strategy. We would argue that live matches, and even extended highlights packages will require a digital TV platform, with goals and short highlights packages being of interest to web based platforms. However this is not the agreed wisdom in the new media economy.

Exploiting the web

The start of the 2003/4 season saw English Nationwide semi-professional Conference League set up its own broadband channel (The Footballers' Football Channel) which it believed was robust enough to charge subscriptions to net users of almost £50 a season or £1.99 a week to get access to highlights packages involving clubs such as Margate and Farnborough. We are highly sceptical of the long-term viability of such a project which seems more in keeping with the misplaced Internet optimism of the late 1990s.

The attractiveness of streaming match highlights via the web has been a cause for concern of Football League clubs still reeling from the collapse of ITV Digital. In trying to meet the challenges of the new media environment, the Football League took the unprecedented move of collectively selling its Internet rights in an attempt to commercially exploit the value of all its member clubs. John Nagle, the Head of Communications at the Football League, explained the strategy behind the collective agreement:

> Our clubs are slightly different to the Premier League. It's really to do with how the League has always been. The clubs are much stronger together than they are apart. And by packaging their rights together in a collective way they are more valuable than they were individually.

Interview with author, 7 May 2003

In June 2000 the League struck a five-year deal with NTL subsidiary Premium TV. The deal was unusual in that NTL paid £65 million for an initial five-year licence to manage 73 club websites and moreover, the right to set up a joint company with the League, FLPTV, that would share any future commercial revenue from the venture. Nagle explained further:

> What we were saying was that if you want to start a company with us you have to give us a certain amount of money to buy into the one-hundred-and-something-year history and the brand we have established and our clubs have established. Then we can start talking about making money.

Interview with author, 7 May 2003

The deal was struck in a way that League clubs could maintain some direct control on their new media rights but also bring in outside expertise to run the actual sites. The valuation of the rights reflected the market at that time, new television deals having been struck and football seemingly on the up. However, as the market changed with the collapse of ITV Digital and the movement of NTL into bankruptcy the deal was renegotiated. NTL had paid £30 million of the rights fee and the remaining rights fee was scrapped. Instead, the profit sharing agreement was activated with an 80/20 split in favour of the Football League. Although FLPTV had more than 1.4 million registered users by mid 2003 the sites were not necessarily making much money. Press speculation that the venture would collapse mounted on the news of a major financial restructuring of the company and 20 redundancies in May 2003. As Nagle admitted, 'The elusive trick is turning what is an enormously popular venture in terms of hits into hard cash.'

To this end FLPTV have struck centralised deals with Bet365 and Sporting Index to promote football betting throughout the League network. Clubs brand these services to suit their needs and take a direct share of the profits. All 73 League clubs also have premium subscription services where fans can access match highlights, radio and data services and localised advertising accompanies the League's centralised marketing deals. Incentivising clubs to make the most of their websites has proved problematic. Issues of how revenues are shared across the three Leagues and how traffic to each site equates to commercial value have led to some sharp practices. Stories of clubs employing staff to make repeated visits to club sites in order to boost figures is one example. Overall Premium TV boasts 2 million subscribers to its total of 80 club sites, including Premier League clubs Newcastle United and Aston Villa and Scottish Premier League side Rangers. Although October 2003 saw Aston Villa pay Premium TV £2.3 million to unwind a complex shareholding arrangement with the club. Nagle reiterated that the advent of new media and its commercial value for clubs through betting, e-commerce and the exploitation of football data has transformed the balance between the game and the traditional media:

> You have got this relationship between football and the media that has grown up together. It's worked well for both sides. The media helped football clubs to grow. Football helps sell newspapers. It has been a 50/50 relationship. With the advent of new media and the entrepreneurial maverick football chairmen with their own websites they are now media providers as well. They can provide the news and the stories and the relationship has started to change.
>
> Interview with author, 7 May 2003

As we have seen, most Premier League clubs have developed their own websites, some in partnership with Premium TV. Initially these were often used simply to give information and sell club merchandise. It is also true that getting information about the club out to supporters quickly remains one of the key ways in which fans use new media to enhance their knowledge about club activity. However it was initially envisaged that new income would be generated from streaming audio–visual material which fans would pay an additional premium to view.

For elite clubs, with a large national and international fan base, such as Liverpool FC this has resulted in them being able to charge £34.99 for its e-season ticket. Working with their media partner Granada (who secured a 9.9 per cent stake in the club for £22 million in 1998), this gives access to eight channels through its LiverpoolFC.TV portal. Content includes access to match day radio commentary, exclusive interviews, e-mails from the manager, a wide range of archive footage including access to the innovative series of short documentaries entitled *100 Days that Shook the Kop*, all delivered via LiverpoolFC.TV.

Liverpool FC run this venture as a joint business with media group Granada (as do Arsenal). As of September 2002, about 10,000 had signed up for this package with Liverpool (*Revolution*, 4 September 2002). In Scotland, by late 2003 a similar subscription base existed for Rangers, through its Rangers World packages, which form part of its Internet operation with partner Premium TV, thus indicating that a market does exist for such services. Interestingly, Rangers estimate that about 60 per cent of subscribers are UK based, while the remainder are dotted around the globe. As Sponsorship and New Media director Damian Willoughby from the club suggests with regard to the Rangers experience of new media:

> We were hugely optimistic about what the Internet could deliver. Both in terms of brand building and more importantly in terms of revenues. But like a lot of companies involved in new media, we've been disappointed in terms of what its actually delivered in terms of merchandising, advertising and sponsorship. We are now in a more realistic era of looking at what it can deliver [...] and clearly there remains huge potential for development for the club.
>
> Interview with authors, 5 September 2003

Rangers' Old Firm rivals, Celtic, have also introduced subscription layers to their website through the Celtic Replay subscription package which gives access to additional material for £4.99 a month. Unlike Rangers they have not sold these rights to a media partner. The advantage being they have a greater autonomy over online development and retain all revenues generated through this source, rather than split income with a joint venture partner. The downside however being that by refusing to sell to NTL at the height of the dotcom bubble in the late 1990s, they missed out on the £31 million deal which in hindsight grossly overvalued football online rights.

One central element of these new media strategies has been the importance of radio or audio coverage for the clubs. As this does not require a broadband platform for delivery, it is worth noting that online radio rights for clubs have become increasingly important. This is particularly the case for clubs such as Celtic and Rangers who have a large fanbase in North America. Away from the high profile wrangles over live television rights, the issue of determining the value of online audio rights has been important in the battle for control between clubs, leagues and governing bodies. The clubs have seen splitting the value of the radio and online audio rights (with clubs retaining the latter) as a key marker in a longer battle to retain and extract more value from a range of rights associated with the club.

A survey by *Broadband World* (August 2003) showed how all the English Premier League clubs, with the notable exception of Charlton Athletic, charged between £20 and £40 a season for 'premium' content on the web such as goals packages and highlights of matches. Over 80 per cent of the club websites in the English leagues are run by the NTL Europe subsidiary Premier TV. Their 'World' format provides a generic template for all those English sites which they run, which as noted above also includes Rangers in the SPL. While clubs with a large local and global fan base (such as Manchester United, Celtic and Liverpool) may be able to extract some financial value from their web presence a range of problems exist which make it unlikely that club websites will provide a substantial revenue stream for more than a handful of clubs.

Significantly, Mike Flynn, the CEO of Fast Web Media (www.fastweb media.com), one of the largest sports website publishers in the UK, argues that while access to rights to live streamed matches remains an issue, he is not convinced that the web is currently the best medium for live football. He suggests:

> I think we are some way off showing full games over the net. I don't think the desire is there to watch games in full on your PC or laptop, when you can watch them in a bar or in your lounge. Highlights and interviews are ideally suited, especially to fans that are only interested in their own team. However, that is not to say that we will not get to the situation where games are being broadcast as a whole. That will definitely happen, but not for a couple of years.
>
> White, 2003

We would argue that while revenues from traditional broadcast sources for football will fall in real terms over the next five years, they will remain significant. Like so many media developments before, the Internet will not kill football on television, but will offer additional value for some elite clubs to generate possibly substantial revenues over the next 5–10 years.

Football clubs and SMS

While the growth in the UK mobile phone market has stalled, it still means that three-quarters of the adult population has a mobile. This is important as the development of the SMS market for football clubs has been identified as a significant revenue stream for clubs launching their own services. For example, in the UK alone in 2002, 16.8 billion text messages were sent, this was an average of about 43 million a day. In comparison, in 1997, 10 million were sent in the entire year (MDA, 2003). The evolution of a text alert market for sports has also been significant. At Arsenal they initially introduced a free SMS service in 2001, before bringing in a subscription-based model with its media partner Granada Media. As the club's then Broadband manager Peter Smith noted:

> It didn't get quite so many people, as you can imagine but there were still significant numbers of people who were interested, I think probably 2,500–3,000 people took it up so that's where we started (to evolve our subscription based website sections).
>
> Interview with author, 8 April 2002

At other clubs fans are paying up to 20p per alert for updates on goals and news from their favourite football clubs. Most major clubs, in partnership with media and telecom partners (an example of how the Manchester United and Vodafone partnership acts more like a franchise than a traditional sponsorship arrangement) have launched some sort of SMS service.

However the real revenue growth had been predicted to come from the launch of the next generation of mobile phones (3G) which offer pictures and video content. The new UEFA Champions League deal of 2003 saw for the first time the governing body sell 3G rights for this competition. This allowed mobile users to see clips of goals five minutes after they happen (Gibson, 2002b).

A recent report into new media and sport has suggested:

> Premium sports content will be a strategic weapon of considerable significance for telecom companies seeking to drive sales of their 3G mobile devices [...] sports rights holders will experience an initial boom in the sale of their 3G right as telecom companies struggle for market share.
>
> Clarke, 2002: 2.3 Executive Summary

Once again however the development of this particular market looks likely to take longer to evolve than initially predicted. In the UK, Hutchison 3G, which paid £4.4 billion for its licence, launched in 2003 under its brand name of 3. However things have not run smoothly with regard to 3G with problems around the technology involved, pricing structures for packages and crucially the issue of content. As media commentator and editor of New Media at the *Guardian* Owen Gibson has argued:

> Hutchison paid £40 million to the English Premier League to show video coverage of goals through 3G phones. [...] a lot of people didn't think

about what people wanted, it was sold on technology, technology saying well this can be done so we should do it and the clubs I think got over excited because they saw the chance to take control of their destiny.

Interview with authors, 9 April 2002

Despite signing a three-year deal, they have only managed to launch in the final year of that contract, which means that they have no realistic hope of recouping their investment in this particular contract. In addition, in September 2003, 3 were offering three months free access to Premiership Goals to new customers signing up for the new VideoTalk 3G service. In October 2003 3 renewed its rights deal with the Premier League, this time in a joint contract with Vodafone worth £30 million over three years (2004–2007) for all 380 Premier League matches. The deflation in value from the previous contract emphasised a reassessment of how attractive mobile VOD actually is to fans. At the start of the 2003/4 season 3 had only attracted 155,000 subscribers to its Premier League service (Durman, 2003). This made the decision to share the 2004 rights with Vodafone even more puzzling. The exclusivity of the offer heavily promoted by 3 had been dropped and with it any competitive advantage the new mobile service provider might have had over its rivals. Vodafone's global prominence and supplementary deals for the wireless rights to the Champions League are likely to further consolidate the mobile telecommunications market.

3G remains a new technology, which if the SMS market is any indicator may develop in directions which have currently not been envisaged by those telecom companies which have secured the licences. However the market will continue to evolve and mobile telephony is clearly now embedded in football fan culture and society more generally. T-Mobile, who launched their 3G service in 2004, had secured media partnership deals with a number of clubs, notably the Old Firm but we would argue that 3G will remain a peripheral source of income for most football clubs. Bigger clubs with strong brand identities are the likely winners from this particular innovation in football media.

Conclusion: new media, what's this for?

What we have argued is that while some elite football clubs have been keen to develop their new media (digital, Internet and mobile telephony) services, differing business models have emerged. All the clubs seek to generate additional revenues from these developments, and while the broader aim of connecting with supporters has not been totally abandoned, many clubs driven by their position as either a plc or a commercial business view the converting of fans to customers as central to any revenue generation strategy.

Clubs such as Manchester United, Arsenal, Chelsea, Liverpool, Rangers and Celtic in the UK are all building infrastructures as they seek to exploit their IP through advertising, sponsorship and increasingly subscription driven models. Most view this as a long-term evolution as the rights market evolves and various barriers remain in the creation of both a genuine mass-market broadband Internet platform and a mass audience digital television network.

They recognise that the hype and unrealistic expectations which accompanied much of the Internet development in the late 1990s has not actually helped viable business models to evolve. However, by 2004 it is clear that those clubs who have remained committed to new media development and have re-scaled the impact it will have on their business are well positioned to move forward over the next decade. During which time the migration of online rights to clubs will increase, while robust platforms across broadband and mobile telephony will ensure that football fans are interacting with their clubs in some new and potentially lucrative way (for the clubs) over the next five years.

The English Premier League deal in 2004 resulted in more rights being retained by the clubs to exploit via the web and their own television channels. This will consolidate partnerships with various media companies as we have noted above. However while collective rights selling remains central, longer term there is likely to be a battle as the big clubs seek to secure a larger return on their new media investments. The issue of overseas rights will remain crucial for clubs such as Manchester United and Liverpool. As Paddy Harverson has argued:

> I don't think, we're suggesting that the core domestic Premier League rights be sold individually because I think that would fundamentally seriously damage the structure of domestic competition. But we think a good example is the international rights whereby we get 1/20 of the income from international rights sales and yet we know we are by far a long way the most popular club and the most watched club overseas so we get the same amount of money Southampton get. No disrespect to them, [but] how many viewers round the world tune in to watch Southampton, they tune in to watch us.
>
> Interview with author, 25 April 2002

Television revenues will remain crucial to many clubs, however those elite clubs such as Manchester United are able to spread their dependence on this source of income through their other increasingly global commercial activities.

One financial issue will be how long clubs will back loss making new media ventures. Even global football brands such as Real Madrid and AC Milan are struggling to make a profit from their TV channels (Koranteng, 2001: 37). One can envisage a handful of globally branded football teams making a return on their investment, but for the majority of football clubs, domestic terrestrial and satellite deals will remain crucial. The Internet, even with broadband developments will not usurp television. We remain unconvinced that the web is the right platform to show live games to supporters. Others will disagree, and FC Barcelona for example hope to webcast some of their games when the current deal with Via Digital runs out in 2003 (Koranteng, 2001: 36).

It seems likely that the web will however provide a source of information and news (mostly free) both to and between supporters and an increasingly large subscription based output (including goals and exclusive interview content) which fans can pay for if they wish.

Clubs such as Arsenal remain upbeat about the business opportunities that new media developments offer them. Peter Smith, their then Sponsorship and Broadband Manager outlined the next stage in the club's development:

> A lot of it will depend on TV rights and what the new contracts say. We're lucky enough to be in a position where if the deal is centralised we will exploit it because we are big enough. We're also big enough to go out and sell our own rights after the current deal. We want to be exploiting our rights more in five years' time, we want to be penetrating into people's houses more, we want to be hitting our supporters more often with our team and our product and our brand, we want to be taking our brand much further.
>
> Interview with author, 8 April 2002

In reality the revenue generating powers of Internet, 3G and digital platforms remain uncertain. For the majority of football clubs throughout Europe we suspect they will remain peripheral to other areas of the clubs' business for a long time to come. There is no indication that these new technological developments will do anything other than speed up the widening gulf that already exists between a European footballing elite and the rest. Elite clubs (in terms of fan base, success and global appeal) such as Manchester United, Liverpool, Barcelona, Real Madrid and Juventus will, to varying degrees increasingly exploit their fan base to generate revenues through these platforms. Some clubs, such as Manchester United are well advanced in both strategic and infrastructural terms.

Yet by focusing on these new platforms as primarily a source through which to make money, they also risk in the longer term alienating sections of their fan base who already feel they are paying too much to watch football. As clubs become more determined to exploit all aspects of their IP, they must strike a balance between the club as a commercial entity and recognising the social and cultural dimension involved in supporting football clubs. This also raises wider journalistic issues of access, as clubs seek to control the flow of information coming from players and management. As clubs seek to develop 'exclusive' content for services that fans will pay for, this battle between clubs, players (often with contractual obligations outside of the club) and traditional media outlets – dependent on football news to attract readers, listeners and viewers – is set to become more complex.

It also remains important that football remains available, in some shape or form on free-to-air television giving access to a mass audience. A point to note is that while the demographics of football supporters have shifted over the last decade as the game has become more middle class, the sport in certain markets, such as Scotland for example, remains a predominantly working class activity. In such circumstances clubs such as Rangers, who estimate that their average supporter earns about £14,000 are acutely aware that many of these supporters simply do not have Internet access, never mind the means to secure a relatively expensive broadband connection. In the new media environment, class remains an important issue, and access to this economy remains determined quite often by patterns of economic and cultural capital.

Thus free-to-air remains important for football's profile. Only this way will the longer-term health of the game be sustained, helping to create the next generation of football fans. Football becoming a niche entertainment product, interesting a hard core of fans willing to pay extensively to view the sport, is not necessarily the best long-term future insurance policy for the game. Yet despite this, as we examine in the following chapter, this is a scenario that some clubs appear happy to embrace.

Chapter 6

A league of their own?
The Old Firm and SPL TV

Scotland's armchair fans have the future of the game in their remote control.
Hugh Keevins, the *Daily Record*, 3 April 2002

The SPL TV debacle highlights football's decline. And once clubs falter, they rarely recover; once revenues disappear, they rarely return.
Ian Bell, Ten on a losing streak, *Business AM*, 9 April 2002

Anyone who thinks this is a bluff [SPL TV] will receive something of a shock when the channel hits the screens in the summer.
Scottish Premier League spokesman, the *Sunday Herald*, 20 January 2002

Introduction

It was a television executive's dream football match. A bank holiday game to decide the championship between two of football's oldest rivals. All the ingredients that television requires from live sport were present, with a few extras thrown in for good measure. A stadium seething with 60,000 fans cranked to fever pitch; a referee with blood streaming from an open wound caused by being struck by a coin thrown from the crowd, and a fan deciding that the quickest way to exit the stadium was to fall from the top of one of the highest football stands in Britain. Violence, aggression, drama, passion and an Old Firm football match in the middle of it all, just the sort of qualities BSkyB wanted from Scottish football and had paid over £11 million a season to secure.

In the Scottish Premier League (SPL) Hospitality Box high above Celtic Park, Vic Wakeling, Managing Director of Sky Sports, watched beside his host for the day Roger Mitchell, Chief Executive of the recently formed SPL. Mitchell set about trying to dampen the media coverage associated with a frantic sporting event which threatened to spiral out of control. Yet the closeness and corporate bonhomie between the media and football executives seemed to symbolise the synergy that existed between the industries. Each seemingly happy with their close relationship, which appeared to benefit both industries. Despite the difficulties that day both men were supremely confident that a long and fruitful relationship lay ahead between the cream of the Scottish game and the largest pay-TV broadcaster in the world.

Yet here was a match that had been staged in the early evening of a Bank Holiday Monday for the sole benefit of television and thus allowing a large majority of the fans to spend much of the day drinking before the title-deciding game. This would prove to be a major factor in contributing to the ferocious atmosphere inside the ground that day. A game that would feature on all the news channels that evening and make headlines across the Scottish and UK newspaper market the next day.

Yet within the lifetime of this BSkyB/SPL deal, Wakeling and Mitchell wouldn't be on speaking terms, with Sky refusing to speak with the Chief Executive. The relationship would have irrevocably broken down and the game in Scotland plunged into crisis. At its core would be the issue which has run throughout this book; the battle for control of the football industry.

This chapter focuses on the impact of the particular relationships between football and the media outlined above for the industry in smaller European countries. In particular it presents a case study of the situation in Scotland and attempts there to introduce new business models in the delivery of televised football into a pay-TV market. In the light of the previous chapter, we examine the wider implications of leagues attempting to by-pass traditional broadcasters and set up their own pay-TV channels.

Throughout the 1990s we have seen how income derived from a re-regulating broadcasting market has resulted in television becoming the financial underwriter of the sport. As a result of the growing importance of the television market to the financial well being of the sport, the wider economic structure of television markets have played a growing role in the uneven development of the sport across Europe in a manner previously unseen in the sport. As football has increasingly marketed itself as primarily a television 'product', so those clubs operating in the elite leagues of large and competitive television markets have benefited the most from this process. Those leagues, and as we have seen in the case of Italy and Spain in Chapter 3 in particular some elite clubs, have been able to extract more revenue than ever before from broadcasters keen to either retain a domestic share of a market (such as beleaguered PSBs) or to establish themselves in new markets, such as pay-TV.

Thus while broadcasting income has become central to the financial well being of elite clubs (and as we saw in Chapter 2 football clubs more generally) particular structural problems are being faced by those clubs operating in small television marketplaces. Even clubs with a large fan base, such as Celtic and Rangers in Scotland, who between them have almost 100,000 season ticket holders find that the value they can extract from the collective selling of league rights is determined by the external factor of the size of their domestic television market. The case in Scotland (population just over 5 million) is heightened by its proximity to England (population about 55 million) which has one of the largest and most competitive television markets in Europe. Thus the economics of the television market meant that a club in the lower echelons of the Premier League in England could expect in 2001 to secure up to six times the revenue from domestic television income that Celtic, the champions of the SPL, could expect.

As we will discuss below, from within the Scottish situation, the financial inequality within the European game has led some clubs to seek to participate in leagues other than those with which they have been historically associated. In pursuing this aspiration, the clubs unleash a host of issues relating to the economic, legal, regulatory and cultural status of the football industry within national and state boundaries. In many ways this desire for these most rooted of cultural institutions to slip their moorings and sail into larger oceans, highlights some of the tensions that exist between the local, national and global economies.

From the Scottish League to the SPL

On 5 May 1998 Scottish football ditched over a hundred years of tradition. Ten Scottish clubs broke away from the Scottish Football League, arguing that they could dramatically increase their revenue generating power as a separate elite league. By July of that year Roger Mitchell left his post as Chief Operating Officer at EMI/Virgin in Italy and was appointed Chief Executive of the Scottish Premier League (SPL), buoyed by a new television deal with BSkyB which locked itself into the Scottish game paying £45 million over four seasons to the SPL. A year later the league was expanded to 12 clubs following a settlement with the Scottish Football League which used some of the money from the new SPL television deal to compensate the clubs left behind.

At the very core of the setting up of the Scottish Premier League (SPL) in 1998 was the belief that more income could be generated for Scottish football from a range of media platforms. Heavily influenced by the seemingly endless buoyant football television rights market across Europe, his experience of the Italian television market and the extravagant financial predictions associated with new revenue streams from both digital television and the Internet, the SPL under Chief Executive Roger Mitchell placed his media strategy at the centre of the SPL's revenue generation programme.

However endemic structural problems remained in a relatively small league, in a small television market, dominated by a more powerful and glamorous neighbour. The new improved SPL was still dominated by the Old Firm, Celtic and Rangers, whose stranglehold on the Scottish game had intensified during the late 1980s and through the 1990s, with Rangers in particular almost untouchable on the domestic front. The clubs also controlled the key decisions the SPL took by voting together on key issues, and thus able to strangle a voting system that required an 11–1 majority to pass motions. In so doing the Old Firm were replicating on a smaller scale the control exercised by a number of powerful clubs in England since the setting up of the FA Premier League in 1992.

Of more immediate concern for Mitchell was the question of how to extract more value out of a league that appeared at times uncompetitive and operated in a small television market. Mitchell was keen to develop the overseas potential of the Scottish game. The strategy appeared to be to generate a healthy revenue stream by selling domestic broadcast rights across both terrestrial and pay-TV platforms, and augment this by using the new media opportunities offered by the Internet to promote and sell the game overseas. However one problem with the global Internet market was that the Old Firm, and Celtic in particular, were also waking up to the potential diaspora audience that might exist in North America and Australia for matches and information about the Old Firm. The retaining of audio rights has been an important aspect for clubs hoping to drive traffic to their websites from overseas. The other major problem was that, put simply, compared to the marketing of the English Premier League, with its television stronghold from Scandinavia, to Asia, to South Africa, the Scottish game didn't appear on the global radar screen of television.

The case of SPL TV

The SPL under Roger Mitchell had always believed that the various broadcasters were getting Scottish football too cheaply. They looked south of the border at the vast sums which had been poured into the sport by television during the 1990s and felt that the game in Scotland had been selling itself short. Under Mitchell's guidance the SPL since 1998 had actually increased fourfold the external revenue coming into the game. Central to this had been the £45 million four-year deal with BSkyB which was due to end in 2002. Under this arrangement, BSkyB broadcast 30 live matches a season, the bulk involving Celtic and Rangers and generating between £2 million and £2.5 million for each of the Old Firm. The remaining clubs received in the region of £600,000 per season from this deal.

Initial informal discussions with Sky about the next television deal began in March 2001 and the noises coming from the broadcaster were that they were happy with the Scottish game and keen to do business again. At this stage it was even being mooted that any new deal could be worth up to £40 million a year to the SPL. However during the summer of that year a row developed between the Old Firm and the rest of the SPL clubs about the allocation of any future television revenue. The Glasgow clubs wanted 80 per cent of any new deal, arguing that this was justified by the subscribers attracted to games involving the Old Firm.

Two issues are worth noting here. First, this split would have been way in excess of the percentage received by the elite clubs in the English Premier League. Here the television money is split among the clubs with roughly 50 per cent allocated to all clubs for being in the league, 25 per cent related to final league position and the final percentage is determined by the number of appearances on the screen. As a result the gap between the top and bottom clubs, while substantial, is not massive. Second, such a position that two clubs should each take 40 per cent of the television revenue earned by a league does not take into consideration the issue of 'mutuality' which is implicit in any competitive league structure. In other words, the Old Firm need teams to play against to have a viable television 'product', and the other clubs argue that this should be recognised in any division of television income.

This very public row involving the SPL and the continued stories linking the Old Firm to a move to a league other than the SPL (discussed in more detail below) did little to strengthen the league's position with regard to a new television deal.

However as we discussed in Chapter 2, other factors in the wider media environment began to undermine the value of any new deal. BSkyB, having completed a major deal with the English Premier League, began to go cool on any significant increase to its outlay on the Scottish game. As relations between Sky and Mitchell collapsed, the SPL found itself in a rapidly changing market, with few potential suitors seeking its wares.

As noted in Chapters 2 and 3, the collapse of the ITV Digital deal with the Nationwide clubs and the crumbling in the value of football rights across Europe (Chapter 3) completely altered the broadcasting ecology. Allied with the doubts about digital take up among both broadcasters and the government and the advertising recession which showed no sign of abating, the SPL could not have picked a more economically hostile moment to bring a new concept to market. In one sense it appeared their hands were forced to some extent, as conflicting reports suggested that BSkyB were either simply going to offer the same type of £11.25 million a season deal, or offer one with a slight increase. Neither came close to the proposed selling of the main broadcast package over three years for £110 million, which was being accredited to sources 'close to the negotiations' as late as October 2001 (*Business A.M.*, 12 October 2001).

Indeed the noises coming out of the SPL during this month seemed to indicate that a new three-year deal was almost done, with the Old Firm clubs finally agreeing to take 40 per cent between them of the television revenue, but with additional PPV income also in the pipeline. However when Stewart Thompson, Marketing Director of the SPL, confirmed in November 2001 that the league was seriously considering setting up a stand alone pay-TV channel noting that, 'It would be owned by the SPL and would be available through all satellite and cable platforms' (*Business A.M.*, 2 November 2001) the situation changed.

On Mitchell's advice, backed by the rest of the SPL, including of course the Old Firm, BskyB's proposed offer was rejected before it was formally made. By December 2001 the negotiations with BSkyB had broken down (as had relations between Wakeling and Mitchell) and full attention was given to the development of an SPL TV business despite the relatively short timescale involved. Journalist Michael Grant feels that at this stage:

> Sky got irritated with Roger Mitchell's attitude and what they saw as his poor judgement of the value of what they (the SPL) were selling.
>
> Interview with authors, 20 January 2003

While Mitchell had always been convinced that such an innovative and revolutionary concept as a league-owned television channel was economically viable, others had viewed the development of SPL TV as primarily as a negotiating tool with BSkyB. However at this crucial juncture all the SPL clubs backed their Chief Executive's bold strategy, a fact not lost on the ten non-Old Firm clubs, when the Glasgow teams would suddenly scupper the project at the last minute.

The idea was deceptively simple in theory, but extremely complex to develop in practice. SPL TV would be a dedicated football channel controlled by the members of the league. This would involve the league employing production companies to bring the channel to the screen. Ironically, given the adverse publicity they suffered as being one of the key stakeholders in the failed ITV Digital, Granada were eventually identified as the preferred production company for the new channel. In this they were helped by the footballing archive they could bring to the magazine aspects of the channel, which would augment the live matches, most likely to be two games a week.

In addition, a call centre would need to be hired, possibly from Sky, to co-ordinate subscriptions, while staff would need to be recruited, to, among other things, sell advertising, attract sponsorship etc. Then on air presenters would need to be contractually tied down. Much of this work would of course be out sourced, but would still involve heavy front end investment on the part of the SPL in the start up period of the channel. Crucially of course a distribution deal with a digital platform carrier would need to be agreed, and of course paid for. Given BSkyB's monopoly of the pay-TV market, in all likelihood any such arrangement would have involved Sky Digital and possibly NTL the cable operator. Of course crucial in any subscription service would be the setting of the fee level. Would fans be willing to pay £7.99 a month, perhaps on top of their existing BSkyB outlay to watch the SPL?

Despite the complexity in successfully launching a station from scratch in such a relatively short space of time, positive noises continued to come out of the SPL early in the new year with regard to the likely success of the project (*Soccer Investor*, 22 January 2002). The consultants who were working on the project were Reel Enterprises, a respected group of consultants led by David Rogan. Rogan, formerly of Reuters, also had close links with the FA Premier League and would be heavily involved with their Chief Executive Richard Scudamore as they prepared their pitch for the sale of Premier League rights from 2004 onwards. Reel Enterprises had done a range of media consultancies related to the issue of rights and were viewed as leaders in their field. The SPL budget for the consultants' involvement was estimated to be in the region of £200,000 (*Sunday Herald*, 7 April 2002). It is clear that at this stage those closest to the project were firmly convinced that the station could successfully launch in the late summer of 2002.

When the SPL TV project was finally vetoed, the Chairman of the SPL Lex Gold claimed that in fact there had never been a bid of any sort from BSkyB for the pay broadcast rights. The financial impact on the monopoly player in the

UK pay-TV market of its massive outlay in securing English Premier League rights for the season starting in 2002, was also being felt and suddenly an additional outlay for the rights to the Scottish game didn't appear a priority. This appears to have been the view of Douglas Odam, the Rangers financial director who at this juncture remained extremely positive about the future prospects of SPL TV. He noted that:

> Sky didn't want to increase their offer at all, so at this stage the SPL clubs sat down and debated whether that was the correct way to go. We recognised that the market the Scottish game is commanding has grown and yet we are not being offered any more money for it. That is because Sky has overspent for their English rights.
>
> The *Herald*, 5 February 2002

It was probably the case that BSkyB were prepared to offer about £40 million for a new deal, but as the plans for SPL TV gathered pace, relations between the head of Sky Sports and the SPL's Chief Executive broke down completely. BSkyB simply refused to speak to him.

The battle raged among various analysts with regard to whether the figures stacked up to make the proposed new channel, the first of its type in the world, a feasible, and more importantly profitable entity. In late 2001, BSkyB had 5.7 million subscribers in the UK, of which it was estimated that 600,000 were in Scotland. What is unclear is how many of these subscribers are attracted primarily by the lure of football coverage, and whether watching the SPL was central to their subscription. More difficult to predict was how many would be willing to pay up to an additional £100 a season to watch Scottish football. The SPL indicated that it thought it could attract anything from 120,000 subscribers (*Soccer Investor*, 22 January 2002) to 200,000 viewers (*Sunday Herald*, 7 April 2002). Crucially it would require 90,000 subscribers to break even. A figure that ultimately the Old Firm would feel was too difficult to secure.

Among other aspects being reported, was a proposal that the highlights package should not be sold to terrestrial television, thus making SPL TV a must see for fans wanting to watch their team in action. In addition, Michael Grant suggested that Roger Mitchell had also considered not allowing SPL TV to join the News Access Agreement, thus denying terrestrial television any access to goals, incidents or even SPL press conferences (*Sunday Herald*, 7 April 2002). The fact that these types of course of action were even on the table, all mechanisms which would push up the exclusivity value of SPL TV, also indicated the extent to which the role of the supporters was all but absent from any thinking with regard to strategy. Under this scheme, fans would have to pay to see any action, the notion of any free-to-air access (through a highlights package) held to be central in any television rights package would be ignored in the drive to extract greater value from the SPL, a cost to be borne entirely by the supporters.

It also raised an issue that we examined in the previous chapter with regard to dedicated club channels; that of journalistic access to non-rights holders of footballing events. It has been suggested that at one stage it was being mooted that only selective access would be given to journalists at news conferences. One can only imagine the level of media hostility such action would have provoked from the excluded sections of the Scottish media.

Attempts to maximise the value which can be extracted from exclusivity in such a case also raises the potential clash with sponsors who may be seeking a wider exposure. It seems clear that a successful SPL TV channel, delivering 200,000 dedicated Scottish football fans, would be of considerable interest to a certain cache of football sponsors such as Umbro and Tennants. Not least in the case of some companies as the projected male demographics of such an audience would clearly include a large proportion of early adapters of key products. However larger, more mass market based sponsors such as the SPL's headline sponsor, the Bank of Scotland, were said to be less than pleased that they may disappear from terrestrial screens and find their brand migrating to a small niche audience.

The project was also subject to a review by KPMG, which according to Kenny Kemp resulted in subscription figures being lowered by 30 per cent; a lowering of growth rates for the channel and a re-adjusting downwards of the pricing structure (Kemp, 2002). The income figure they predicted was £15 million a year to start with, building over the coming seasons. Indeed it was suggested that in fact the concerns raised by the KPMG review helped convince the Old Firm that the risks involved in the project remained too great (the *Scotsman*, 9 April 2002). Following the collapse of the project much of the subsequent press coverage focused on the concerns expressed by Celtic and its Chief Executive, Ian McLeod. However there is little doubt that the outgoing chairman of Rangers, entrepreneur David Murray, played a key role in blocking the development of the channel.

At a meeting of the SPL in April 2002, less than four months before the start of a new Scottish football season, the proposed revolutionary television channel was finally killed off in a move that plunged the Scottish game into crisis, and immediately resulted in one SPL club, Motherwell, going into administration.

8 April 2002: the end of SPL TV

The voting structure of the SPL required that 11 votes were needed to pass any decision. To this end, the two Old Firm clubs voted as one thus ensuring they could block any proposal with which they were unhappy. At a meeting of the SPL at Hampden Park in Glasgow on 8 April 2002, the Old Firm, to the great surprise of the other clubs, voted to block the implementation of SPL TV. The project was dead. Just over a week later the other 10 clubs in the league signalled their intention to quit the SPL giving two seasons' notice (they officially tendered their resignation on 1 August).

The reasons given by the Old Firm for their failure to support SPL TV, a project that all the other clubs appeared to back, was outlined by the then Celtic Chief Executive, Ian McLeod. He noted that:

> Fundamentally our decision not to support the current proposal is based on the incompleteness of information available, the high level of business risk attached to the project that is not adequately addressed and the lack of firm substantiation of the plan assumptions.
>
> The *Scotsman*, 9 April 2002

Significantly, the joint statement from the Old Firm also highlighted their concern about the key issue of media rights. They argued that the proposed SPL TV project did not have sufficient safeguards built into it to protect the media rights of the clubs if the project were to fail. This was viewed as important because the SPL would in fact transfer the league's media rights to SPL TV. One also suspects that the Old Firm were less enamoured than the other clubs about having their valuable media rights assets (certainly the most valuable in terms of any of the SPL teams) locked into a high risk project. In particular when they also expressed concerns about the 'lack of clarity in the SPL proposal for the governance and control of the channel's operation' (the *Scotsman*, 9 April 2003).

At a meeting with members of the Celtic Trust in May 2002 he reiterated the issues which resulted in both Old Firm teams rejecting the proposed SPL TV channel (www.celtictrust.com). At this meeting it was clear that the collapse of ITV Digital had heavily influenced their decision. Contrary to the SPL chairman's claims, McLeod insisted that the SPL did in fact reject a BSkyB offer, then taking the view that a better offer could be achieved, however the Celtic Chief Executive acknowledges that the subsequent collapse in television football rights across Europe badly impacted on this decision.

There is little doubt that the Old Firm initially viewed the SPL TV project as part of a wider negotiation ploy to extract more revenue and a better deal from BSkyB. However with the collapse of ITV Digital and the implosion of football rights across Europe, BSkyB simply did not need Scottish football, and certainly not at the price they were looking for.

In addition McLeod questioned the market research carried out in support of the project claiming that it exaggerated the potential audience. In particular he was unconvinced that the subscriber numbers outlined for year one were attainable, with lift off for the station being viewed as crucial to its long-term success. While the research had been carried out by the respected media rights consultants Reel Enterprises, the football industry in general had been awash with overly optimistic consultants' reports with regard to media revenue streams for a number of years. Banks (2002: 114) notes how consultants Fletcher Research had only a few years previously been predicting that PPV (which up until now had failed to take off significantly) would be worth £450 million a year to the Premier League in England.

McLeod also suggested that even if SPL TV was on course to fulfil the business plan, it would not have made money until year 3 and that any financial forecasts had not taken into account the collapse of the ITV Digital deal (Celtic Trust, 2002). There also appeared to be a lack of clarity with regard to the product that would appear on the screen. This included suggestions that in comparison with BSkyB's coverage fewer cameras might be used to help lower costs. Given the risks involved, both Old Firm clubs were also concerned about the issue of liability should SPL TV crash in a manner not dissimilar to ITV Digital, and that while the project was interesting, it was too high risk in an uncertain marketplace.

Ultimately central to the failure of the SPL TV project was the shuddering financial impact the collapse of ITV Digital in March 2002 would have not only on English football, but football across Europe. The failure of that company to attract subscribers in sufficient numbers to the Nationwide League football it championed, signalled the extent to which television had misjudged a rapidly shifting market and that consumers and supporters were simply not going to continue indefinitely paying for more and more football driven subscription services (see Chapter 2).

Stuart Cosgrove, Head of Nations and Regions at Channel 4, and previously involved with sport at the channel knows the problems involved in developing a new station. He has seen first hand the struggle the company has had launching its digital channels Film on Four and E4. Even with the cross promotion of an established brand such as Channel 4, the earliest either of these channels was likely to break even would be five years. He claims he was 'on the positive side of sceptical' about the potential success of a new Scottish football television channel. He wanted it to work, as a successful SPL TV would be both culturally innovative and possibly economically important in helping boost the independent production sector within the commercial television market. Given the difficulty Channel 4 had in making money from its two new stations, Cosgrove remained unsure if the projected subscriber numbers for SPL TV could be realised.

However there was, he felt, another key factor in the failure of the SPL TV concept. That was the inherent business outlook of the football industry with regard to the revenue generated by selling broadcast rights. For most clubs the selling of these rights means money upfront at the start of a deal, with additional payments throughout the period of an agreement. This money was viewed as vital in paying wages and helping to attract or retain key players on long-term contracts. As Cosgrove argues:

> There is a cultural flaw inside football. Up until [SPL TV] football clubs have been used to receiving money in advance for TV rights. They get a cheque from a funder. This [SPL TV] meant you will have to invest in the business, grow the business, not take value from the business until such a time as it grows profitable. That was its biggest flaw. I think SPL TV could

have succeeded commercially, built only on the basis of a five to seven year business plan, in which they [clubs] weren't taking value in the early years.

Interview with authors, 8 January 2003

Thus SPL TV meant clubs investing upfront and deferring a large part of their income to a later date. Given the notoriously short termism which characterises the economics of the football industry this was always going to be a difficult revenue model to sell. In their joint statement issued after they blocked the proposed channel, this was indeed one of the areas highlighted by the Old Firm. As they argued:

> The pay TV channel could absorb other income sources as initial funding. SPL media rights payments successfully negotiated for payment to clubs next year from areas other than pay TV, could be required to fund start-up costs, placing inappropriate risk on otherwise certain income streams to the clubs.
>
> The *Scotsman*, 9 April 2002

Thus the clubs viewed guaranteed income from the sale of other media rights as being absorbed by the fledgling channel.

The setting up of a dedicated football channel controlled by a league is of course not a new business model and has been suggested before. The English Premier League has floated the idea of starting its own channel as far back as 1992, with Arsenal's David Dein being approached by the Swiss Bank Corporation about a project called Project Premier (Fynn and Guest, 1994: 67). While nothing came of this particular project some viewed such ideas – the setting up of a league controlled channel – as a potential negotiating ploy by members of the league. However, as Simon Banks has suggested:

> In order for the clubs to draw immediate income from a Premier League TV Channel [...] it would need significant outside investment, as offered by the Swiss Bank Corporation in 1992.
>
> Banks, 2002: 123

However, the combination of the worst advertising recession seen across the media industry for 30 years, and the downturn in the value of sports rights across Europe, certainly made it more difficult to attract financial institutions willing to take the long-term risk to invest in such a project.

We also suspect, although the Old Firm would deny this, that in April 2002, they were pursuing an alternative agenda. At this specific juncture the clubs were convinced that structural change within the UK and/or the European football market would result in the Old Firm plying their trade in a league other than the SPL in a relatively short time. As a result of this, they simply did not want to be locked into a four-year broadcasting deal which would have tied up the majority of their media rights during this period.

Does anyone want to play with us?

Throughout the gestation period of the proposed new television channel, there had been ongoing speculation relating to the possible move of the Old Firm out of the Scottish game to play in some other league. This might be in either an already existing league such as the English Premier or Nationwide League, or the formation of some new pan European structure involving clubs from other European countries who were also playing their football in a relatively small television market.

The wider issue of the role that television rights and income have played in the structural evolution of the game in Europe has been discussed in more detail in Chapter 3. However in a Scottish context, there had been rumours about structural change involving more than domestic tinkering with the Scottish game since the late 1990s. By this stage the Old Firm had become convinced that they were not extracting the value for their media rights that their fan base and appeal deserved. They also felt that their dominance of their domestic league was having a detrimental impact on the clubs' ability to compete successfully in Europe where the record of both clubs had been dreadful for some considerable length of time. The relative lack of television income, compared with the revenues being secured by clubs in the Premier League in England, meant that the Old Firm felt they had difficulty in attracting the top players to come to the clubs which would allow them to compete at the highest level in European competition. This situation was also being compounded by the poor level of competition in the domestic league where a club other than the Glasgow teams had not won the championship in Scotland since Alex Ferguson's Aberdeen had briefly broken the Old Firm's dominance of the domestic game in the 1980s.

Of course relative to the other teams in the Scottish league the Old Firm were financial giants. They attracted massive home gates, by the late 1990s for example they had almost 100,000 season ticket holders between them and generated substantial revenue through their corporate and commercial revenue generating operations. For example, by 2001, the combined turnover of the Old Firm was £89 million (Rangers £47 million and Celtic £42 million), the combined turnover of the rest of the SPL clubs was £40.9 million (Pattullo, 2002: 42–46). However despite this position of strength within the domestic game, the twin engines of both local and global media developments had begun to result in them casting envious glances south of the border and further afield.

As we discussed in the previous chapter the evolution of the Internet began to raise the possibility of developing global markets among the various diaspora of fans which existed around the world. These fan bases having evolved and been sustained due to the politically and culturally inflected rivalry that existed between the clubs and which had often helped give the Old Firm a certain uniqueness (Boyle, 2004). During a period when clubs, often being run as plcs, began to increasingly view themselves as brands, the Old Firm rivalry helped give both clubs a distinctive identity within the footballing world. When this global outlook was allied with the explosion in the domestic value placed on football by media corporations in the increasingly competitive UK television market that we discussed in earlier chapters, then the Old Firm, giants in a small television market, felt that economically, they were playing in the wrong league.

In 1999 there had been newspaper speculation about the possible departure of the Old Firm to join an Atlantic League. Here the Glasgow clubs would join select teams from Belgium, Holland, Portugal and Sweden in a mid-week league which would involve games against teams such as Ajax, PSV Eindhoven, Porto and Sporting Lisbon. The economic logic was that in drawing from these small domestic media markets you could create a potential market of 50 million. As a result, television derived revenue would increase substantially. As with previous threats to its authority, discussed in Chapter 3, UEFA dismissed the plan while at the same time recognising the problems of large clubs in small domestic markets and the growing financial gulf between a group of television rich European elite clubs and the rest. Partly as a result of these concerns there has been a restructuring of the UEFA Cup competition from 2003 that will now adopts aspects of the UEFA Champions League group stages format, thus guaranteeing more matches, and more television revenue, for clubs.

Since the late 1990s there has also been much discussion of the two Glasgow clubs leaving Scotland to play in either the English Premier League, or more recently in 2002, in either the Nationwide Division One, or a restructured post ITV Digital collapse Phoenix League. The latter thus giving the much maligned English First Division a potential fresh appeal to television with a spiced up league which would allow the Old Firm to play in England. Problems involving the governing national bodies of the sport in Scotland and England, as well as UEFA and FIFA exist with regard to letting teams play outside of their geopolitical leagues. However while there may be opposition, precedents do exist, with football clubs in Wales and Northern Ireland playing in leagues in England and the Republic of Ireland respectively. What appears to have blocked any move so far is not the disdain of UEFA or FIFA, whose power to block any moves could even be challenged in the European Court as a possible restriction of trade for the clubs, rather the shifting attitudes of governing bodies in England, and those of the club chairmen in that country, who remain unsure of the potential benefit the Old Firm would bring to their game.

Significantly there is a counter argument to that put forward by the Old Firm. It has been suggested (Banks, 2002: 138–140) that the failure of the Glasgow teams to make any significant impact in European competition is not related to their domestic location in a small television market. As Simon Banks has pointed out, clubs from small television markets such as Slavia Prague from the Czech Republic, Norway's Rosenborg and Austria's Sturm Graz have all successfully reached the second group phase of the UEFA Champions League, something that neither of the Old Firm had managed to achieve, by 2003.

All of these clubs generate less domestic television income than the Old Firm, and Banks argues that:

> The Old Firm's complaint that low domestic television revenue is a reason why they are unable to compete in Europe is baseless.
>
> Banks, 2002: 139

He concludes that if the Old Firm complain about the lack of domestic competition as another factor in their European failure, then the only sensible solution is to shift the massive inequalities in wealth within the Scottish game.

> The league could become more competitive if mechanisms for a more equitable method of revenue distribution were adopted.
>
> Banks, 2002: 140

Banks suggests that this is a move that will be resisted by the Old Firm, who seek instead a solution elsewhere.

Of course all of this speculation about the Old Firm re-locating has done little to enhance the unity of purpose of the clubs who constitute the SPL. Journalist Michael Grant who covered this story for the *Sunday Herald* notes that there was extensive behind the scenes briefing from the clubs, Celtic in particular, over a period of years talking up a potential move to England. However, he also notes that:

> There were countless stories about the Old Firm moving to England. The constant feature in all of them was that neither UEFA nor FIFA changed their opinion. Both remained implacably opposed to the move because of the huge ramifications it would have for the game. [...] However it did create a climate of unease about the stability of Scottish football, which suited the Old Firm when it came to broadcasting deals because they wanted the other ten (SPL clubs) to feel vulnerable and dependent on them.
>
> Interview with authors, 20 January 2003

In retrospect it is clear that such a strategy actually forced clubs to look to a future without the Old Firm, and may as a result have helped strengthen their resolve not to be driven by the Glasgow clubs' agenda.

Of course any media lobbying and manipulation were not the sole prerogative of the Old Firm. For example, persistent rumours that Celtic and Rangers had been secretly negotiating with BSkyB while the SPL TV project collapsed were completely untrue. However they helped serve the purpose of the other ten clubs in casting the Glasgow teams as the villains of the piece and allowed them to argue that if the Old Firm did not want to play in Scottish football, then Scottish football did not want them. One of the most significant changes

ushered in by these protracted and recurring rumours of the impending departure of the Old Firm, all feverishly reported with varying degrees of accuracy by
the Scottish media, has been to shift the climate of opinion in Scotland. This
has moved in a relatively short period of time from one in which the thought of
the Old Firm leaving the Scottish game was both unbelievable and potentially
devastating to those clubs left behind, to a mood which now views such a move
as both not inconceivable and actually something that in the long term might in
fact benefit the game in that country.

Football across frontiers: Europe

The Old Firm watched with interest in the early months of 2003 as the English
Premier League responded to official concerns from the European Commission
that the selling of exclusive live rights to only one television channel (in this
case BSkyB) was a form of price fixing as well as being anti-competitive. As we
discussed in Chapter 2 what was really at stake here was the concept of collective rights selling of football, something which had been integral to the British
game since the early days of the sport's uneasy relationship with broadcasting.

However the stakes were raised in August 2003, when Celtic's main shareholder, the Irish millionaire Dermot Desmond, intimated that he would be
taking legal action against the 2004 BSkyB/Premier League deal on the
grounds that those involved were operating a cartel. He argued that:

> It's pretty apparent that Sky, the Premier League, and maybe the BBC have
> got together and formed a little cartel to decide how they are going to
> break up the rights to give out the gold, silver and bronze. That's not
> transparent, it's not in the interests of football and something has to be
> done about it.
>
> Interview on BBC Radio Five Live, 4 August 2003

Basing his case on European Union Competition Law, Desmond set the wheels
in motion for a challenge to the deal initially through the UK Office of Fair
Trading. At the core of this case was a) the right of clubs to sell their own television rights and b) the right of clubs such as Celtic to play in other leagues,
such as the English Premier League. In 2004, this action is ongoing, and those
who dismiss it lightly will do well to remember the impact of Bosman on the
game (another case which was originally treated as unimportant).

In 2002, the SPL signed a two-year deal with BBC Scotland, with, for the
first time, a number of Old Firm games being screened across the UK on the
BBC. The deal was worth £18 million until season end 2004 and saw a weekly
live match being screened on the Sunday. A couple of points are worth noting
here. No radio coverage existed as the Old Firm remained keen to retain their
ability to deliver audio coverage of matches via their websites. Indeed it would
be radio and online rights which would delay an ultimate settlement between all

the clubs, which would finally occur early in 2003. The compromise finally agreed saw the Old Firm retain some of their rights to broadcast matches via their websites (on a subscription basis) but paying some element of compensation to the clubs featuring in these matches. On the television front, archive rights have finally reverted to the clubs, again this is something of more potential value to the Old Firm clubs, as we argued in the previous chapter, as both clubs bundle this material as part of an online subscription package.

However for some club chairmen, the new deal was nothing short of a disaster. Motherwell's Chairman, John Boyle, argued the outcome had been calamitous for the Scottish game. He told us that he felt that live free-to-air football on the BBC was seriously impacting on audiences, to such an extent that even the visit of the Old Firm was no longer filling grounds. The loss of revenue from falling attendances was also not being adequately covered by television income. As a result, a combination of easily available football on television and the high admission prices at matches was potentially strangling the football economy in Scotland.

By early 2003, a peace of sorts had broken out among the 12 clubs. It was clear that the Old Firm were going nowhere in the short term, while the SPL, with the Glasgow clubs onboard, clearly offered a better opportunity to extract broadcasting revenue in the short term at least. However the endemic structural problems of the Scottish game had been clearly highlighted during this time, with corresponding erosion of trust between all involved. With the departure in November 2002 of the SPL Chief Executive Roger Mitchell, not only did the league emerge from this turbulent period without its key media strategist, but with no long-term media strategy in place.

How long the stability of the SPL would remain, given the inherent tensions between the Old Firm and the other ten clubs, would however remain to be seen. Shortly after this settlement, stories emerged that a Spanish business consortium were attempting to set up a European league called, rather confusingly, the Golden Cup. If this twin league came about, it was certainly envisaged that the Old Firm would be asked to join, while still playing in their domestic league (the *Sunday Herald*, 2 February 2003). Meanwhile Dermot Desmond's legal action in 2003–2004 demonstrates that one impact for smaller leagues/ television markets in the new media age is an ongoing sense of instability, as the larger clubs seek to relocate, not on cultural or social grounds, but strictly financial criteria.

Conclusion

While this chapter has focused on the failure of the proposed SPL TV channel in Scotland, it does raise a number of wider related issues that characterise the evolving relationship between the football and media industries. What is becoming clear is that the issue of media rights, and implicitly the associated concern about who controls 'media content' is helping to put structural change back on the footballing agenda. Of course in one sense, as earlier chapters have discussed, this aspect of the relationship between broadcasting, in particular, and football has always been part of the fabric of the uneasy partnership. What is different about the contemporary scenario however is that the developing media infrastructures when allied with the changing economic and cultural manner in which aspects of media are consumed, means that issues of rights and ownership are becoming more complex.

For example one possibility which the proposed SPL TV channel also raised was the possible longer-term synergy between the traditional notion of broadcasting companies operating within nation-state boundaries (and the rights being sold correspondingly) and the potential global network that exists through something like the Internet.

Stuart Cosgrove of Channel 4 suggests that longer term what may have been lost was the opportunity to use the SPL brand, driven by the Old Firm as the most powerful clubs in the league, to address both the domestic Scottish market through the channel and to innovatively tap into the wider fan base that exists for these two clubs in particular.

> The chance to connect those two converging media eras. The global nation-state based broadcaster and the global based Internet transmission systems that are still in their infancy. That's where the loss is [of SPL TV] if there is any.
>
> Interview with authors, 8 January 2003

This growing tension between the locality of a club, and its global brand image is also important because it works to financially enhance the elite of the game, rather than the greater good of the wider sport.

What the SPL TV project also exposed was the extent that the media, as a revenue stream for football, has become so overwhelming as to potentially de-stabilise aspects of traditional footballing infrastructures. As John Boyle, Chairman of Motherwell has indicated:

> From being a life saviour (SPL TV), the failure of the project has been a disaster that will fundamentally restructure the economics of football for every single club in Scotland.
>
> Interview with authors, 31 January 2003

Significantly, part of this process has resulted in the return of an age old concern among football clubs, the fear of adverse effect of live coverage on attendances at games. In addition, Boyle argues that the pricing structure for games, means that it can cost over £50 to take two children to a match, which they may be able to watch free-to-air on BBC television.

Another aspect to this crisis has been the ongoing debate about the various merits of clubs, as opposed to a league selling the rights of matches for the broader good of the competitive base of that league, or the sole benefit of the individual club involved. While the Scottish case is heightened in intensity by the fact that the elite clubs of the game in that country operate, to all intents and purposes, in two parallel economies, with the super clubs of the Old Firm enjoying a turnover, excluding broadcasting income, of almost ten times that of the majority of other clubs in the SPL, never mind Scottish football as a whole. The SPL service to illustrate the damage that structural inequalities in the economics of football can have for the long-term health of competition. The challenge facing the governing bodies of the sport is to find mechanisms which allow them both to encourage greater competition across and within league structures, while keeping on board those powerful elite clubs who are able to extract a commercial media value from their global appeal. Failure to do so may in the longer term see aspects of the chronically uncompetitive Scottish SPL being replicated in other leagues across Europe, with of course an impact on the collective value of any rights being sold.

Yet despite all the discussion of structural change prompted by the factors outlined in this chapter, something else emerges which we feel is significant and indicative of a counter tendency. For despite changes at the pan European level of the game, through the re-structuring of the Champions League (as discussed in Chapter 3), at a domestic level, it appears that national leagues remain remarkably resistant to change. The traditional roots of domestic football, shaped by nation-states are embedded deep in the cultural psyche of football fans throughout Europe. This may be, we would argue, perhaps to a greater extent than either media strategists realise or some footballing businessmen would like to believe. Certainly the systemic structural change involving the domestic Scottish league envisaged by some in the game still appears some way off.

If, as we have argued throughout this book, that one of the common themes which informs the relationship between the footballing industry and the media is a concern about control, then the failed SPL TV deal is also an important indicator of the current balance of power in this relationship. There is little doubt that a successful SPL TV would have presented a considerable threat to the dominant pay-TV platform player in the UK, BSkyB. Not so much in the short-term loss of Scottish football from its portfolio of sport, although some indications of a drop off in subscriptions in Scotland to Sky indicate that it has had some impact – even to merit a suggestion that they will bid again for the SPL rights in 2004 – rather in the challenge that it would offer to the business model of sports pay-TV which Sky has developed with great success in both the UK and increasingly throughout Europe (see Chapter 3).

While SPL TV would have to be carried on the Sky Digital platform (thus generating up to £2 million in revenue for the carrier), but it would still have set a dangerous precedent, and seriously undermined Sky's position, given that by 2002, the company had successfully seen off all newcomers in the UK pay-TV market. The danger being that had SPL TV been successful it would have encouraged other clubs to think more innovatively about restructuring aspects of their domestic environment. This crucially at a time when the next round of rights negotiations with the crown jewels in Sky's portfolio, the English Premier League, was beginning to move onto the agenda. The English Premier League would undoubtedly be interested in a successful SPL TV business model, giving it leverage as it sat down to discuss the value of its league with the monopoly pay-TV organisation, Sky.

However, longer term, one could also envisage a successful SPL TV model threatening the collective English Premier League concept. The elite clubs may seek to restructure in a differing configuration which may maximise the under exploited value of the elite clubs within the higher echelons of the Premier League. If it had been successful, SPL TV would have been a difficult genie to put back in the bottle, and the experience of a small domestic league on the margins of European football would have initiated another wave of structural change throughout the footballing and media industries of the Continent.

In many ways it took an administrator with someone like Mitchell's background in the world of media rights and television markets to champion such a high risk and innovative strategy. It would have been hard to imagine a 'traditional' risk averse football business manager thinking in such a manner. Even at the end of his tenure, Mitchell, whose experience of the television market he gained from his time in Italy, was still convinced that the concept of SPL TV would have worked:

> I'm more convinced than ever it would have worked. We did all the research, did all the costings and would have needed around 100,000 subscribers. I still think the idea was perfect for the type of country Scotland is: small, yes, but with a remarkably high loyalty factor towards what we were trying to sell, which was football. In the business, we call it 'narrow channel exploitation'. In terms of subscribers, there were enough passionate people out there for us to have secured our must-have audience.
>
> The *Herald*, 23 November 2002

Ultimately this particular market concept remained untried. However the interest shown from other leagues around the world in the SPL TV project suggests that in a different economic climate, within a more relaxed regulatory rights market, the dedicated pay-TV football channel, controlled by the clubs, may yet become a business model with which fans will become familiar in the future.

Central in the last two chapters have been various aspects of the opportunities and challenges offered to both the footballing and media industries by the evolving Internet as a global network of communication. The next chapter opens this debate further to assess its importance, not simply with the club game and domestic environment, but on the global game and world-wide media events. In particular it also focuses on the impact an increasingly global, digitised, interactive mediated game is having on its relationship with supporters.

Chapter 7

The new World Wide Web of football

Interactivity and the fan

Sometimes it seems to me that all today's progress in electronics is made only and exclusively to further a more complete, a more satisfying representation of football.

Parks, 2003: 69–70

If you've wondered about the point of digital television, this season's screening of the Champions League is one answer. Never mind one or two matches live on the same night, the whole lot will be shown this season.

The Times, Champions League Handbook, 15 September 2003

Introduction

Throughout this book we have argued that football has held centre stage in the evolution of new media services in the UK and beyond. The reasons, to reiterate, are that football has a captive, ready-made audience of eager fans who also in significant numbers happen to mutually belong to a demographic of 'early adopters' of new information and communication technologies. The fact that men in their mid-twenties to mid-thirties are the highest consumers of football and new media technologies has not been lost on the sports media industries eager to market new services to generate new revenues.

One only has to look at the way new media products and services, from digital television to 3G mobile phones, have targeted this group to understand what is at stake. The companies that have used football in their promotional strategies read like a who's who of the global media and telecommunications industries. NTL, Telewest, BSkyB, Granada Media, BT, Vodafone, Orange, O2, T-Mobile, Nokia and Siemens have all invested large sums of money in promotional campaigns including advertising and sponsorship to woo the British football fan.

An example of this process came in the months preceding the 2002 FIFA World Cup in Japan and South Korea. South-East Asia, a hotbed of technological innovation appeared an ideal setting for the collision of football and new media and Internet companies and mobile networks used the global mega event to great effect to roll out new products and services. Although previous World Cups had seen innovations in new media, especially dedicated websites produced or licensed by FIFA, the 2002 World Cup saw an explosion in football related new media services.

Underlying the growth of new media services was the maturity of particular new media markets in the UK and other industrialised nations. Where the 1998 FIFA World Cup could be equated with the 'take-off' phase of domestic Internet use, the 2002 event took place in a progressively more mature Internet environment. By June 2002 the Government's National Statistics Office estimated that 11.1 million households in the UK could access the Internet. It was reckoned that 57 per cent of adults had accessed the Internet at some time in their lives, which equated to 26.3 million people. These changing demographics of new media use were general indicators of wider changes in media consumption and experiences which FIFA and their commercial partners sought to exploit.

This chapter seeks to analyse the ways in which new media services, specifically interactive services, have attempted to create new experiences for football fans. At the heart of this process is the increased commodification of football fandom with new media services establishing new relationships between the interests of global capitalism and football as a form of popular culture. Crucially, the relationship between football and new media is viewed as being increasingly intertwined in a complex web of relationships between football authorities, players and agents, sponsors and advertisers, the media, telecommunications companies and fans.

There are new patterns of organisation and production in the football industry many of them driven in part by the needs of global media. Many of these changes are being guided by the belief that new media provide new opportunities of experiencing football, providing fans as consumers with a wider choice of football related information and entertainment. In many ways this is a reflection of the broader ubiquity of the neo-liberal ideology that runs through the new media industry itself. As Lister *et al.* (2003: 20) have argued more generally:

> People are seen as being able to make individualised lifestyle choices from a never-ending array of possibilities offered by the market. This ideological context then feeds into the way we think about the idea of interactivity in digital media. It is seen as a method for maximising choice in relation to media texts.

If we apply this analysis to the relationship between football and new media we can envisage a world where more and more services are created to entice football fans to engage with new technologies. Increasingly, the corporate world of football is encroaching on all aspects of the football culture. Whether it be information about fixtures or results, accessing audio–visual images, engaging in discussion and debate or playing football related games, the football industry caters for the desires of the end-user, the fan as consumer. The notion of information technologies providing greater 'choice' has been woven into the marketing strategies of the media sport industry. This is not only a choice in programming but also a choice in where a programme takes you and how a viewer might interact with it. The emerging importance of interactivity is reflected in the following analysis of global sports markets by Westerbeek and Smith (2003: 146):

> It is simply not enough for spectators to passively sit and watch a sporting contest on their television screens. People want to be drawn into the event, even if it is from the comfort of their own homes.

The belief that media companies and new media services must provide added value through interactive services and gaming to entice new consumers is writ large in the contemporary culture of the media sports industries. Innovation in the delivery of sports content through interactive services, virtual advertising, video-on-demand and i-gaming are seen as crucial to the survival of the industry in the face of stiff competition from other entertainment industries, particularly the games industry.

What is ironic about the processes of industrialisation and commodification of football and new media is that they occur at a time when end users are viewed as having more control over media. In the new media age, the consumer of digital media is arguably more competent in manipulating and intervening in the communication process than past generations. The evolution of the Internet and associated technologies has built-in the ability of the individual to engage on a one-to-one or one-to-many or many-to-many basis, short-circuiting the top-down, hierarchical model of industrial media production. As seen in the music and film industries the rise in prominence of file sharing across peer-to-peer networks has undermined the ability of corporate media to control the distribution and uses of media content. However, as we shall go on to discuss, these options appear to be increasingly curtailed by technological, economic and regulatory processes. The clampdown of copyright holders discussed in Chapter 4 is one manifestation of these processes and continues to have a wider effect on the evolution of new media services connected to football. The fears of football rights holders that media piracy could undermine their ability to leverage income from new media technologies remains a pressing issue as it has in other entertainment industries. Before going on to look at the way new media services are being delivered to football fans we shall first consider what the idea of interactivity actually means when set against the above.

Interactive football: a new industry

Interactivity has become something of a mantra for contemporary media and telecommunications executives. After significant investment, digital media infrastructures including digital television, the Internet and mobile telecommunications have opened up huge potential for interactive services and experiences for viewers, surfers and SMS 'texters'. At the heart of interactive technologies is the desire to provide content that transcends the linear reception of analogue television into a more dynamic, active participation of the user. Whether via the Internet or iTV interactive services enable fans to find both depth and breadth of coverage at the same stroke. From aggregated websites that combine a plethora of information and entertainment features under one umbrella to specialist niche sites that provide comprehensive information based on specific interests, interactive new media are transforming the way football is communicated.

As we have stressed throughout the book with respect to new media, innovation in interactive media is primarily realised by the imagined uses of such technology. As Lister *et al.* (2003: 67) point out, 'such visions are driven by cultural values on which a technological imaginary is based and not technological necessities'. This reflects a more sceptical view on the potency of new technology to transform society. As May (2002: 29) has argued in his reinterpretation of Lewis Mumford's history of technological change, 'humans shape the social context which produces technological advance'.

With regard to football and interactivity this has meant that new media innovators have had to capture the imagination of football fans to engage with the various services on offer. This has meant that any new media service has had to appeal to the sensibilities of football fans and the types of information that have broader value and meaning in the general football culture. Simply delivering news and information on football or providing online chat rooms for fans to engage with each other may not automatically guarantee an audience for such content.

One reason for the lack of any clear formula for website design, even within a niche field such as football, is the very dispersed and individualised nature of new media production. Because the barriers to entry in the production of new media have been lowered by increased accessibility to technology and networks and less prohibitive costs of production and distribution there have been a plethora of sites devoted to the game. Website production is relatively easy. All it takes is some basic knowledge of using an html editor, access to a host server and know-how to transfer the files across from a personal computer to a server.

Following the mass appropriation of ICTs in the home and the rise of desktop publishing in the 1980s and 1990s personally produced websites have proved another extension of the DIY culture of contemporary media production. In terms of football websites, many are fan-driven and produced out of enthusiasm for the game and a particular club. Much like the explosion of football fanzines in the late 1980s (Haynes, 1995) fan websites, or e-zines, are created from a labour of love motivated by passion and heavily tied to the construction of cultural identities. As with the fanzine phenomenon most are not-for-profit and produced outside of work hours. The dispersal of new media production has therefore opened up a whole new communicative space for football fans.

The latest incarnation of new media spaces used by football fans are weblogs. Blogs are often simple efficient means of publishing views and opinion online in an open and accessible format. Blogs break down barriers to publishing and enable the reader to respond directly to published work via a message board system. Football blogs are typically created by individuals in their spare time and provide commentary and rhetoric on a plethora of topics based on recent events with links to various news sources. Because of their openness blogs are often full of irreverent and acerbic comment. In the context of football, they may also be confrontational and invariably anti-establishment. Although blogs are rarely if ever produced for commercial gain, some fan sites have turned early entry into the online world into a profit.

Some of the early fan based websites took a familiar trajectory in the evolution of fanzines into magazines operating in the fully-fledged publishing industry. As with other sectors of the dotcom boom in the late 1990s, those sites that transformed a good idea into a highly successful website attracted corporate finance and venture capitalists eager to make a fast buck. Examples of supporters turning a bedroom pastime into a multi-million pound business are few and far between. But early forays into the Internet did transform the lives of some. Tom Hadfield set up the website Soccernet at the age of 12 with the help of his journalist father. Hadfield had started using the Internet in 1994 and came across the idea of launching a football website when he began exchanging e-mails with an increasing number of ex-patriot English fans eager to hear news about their team. Soccernet became one of the most frequently visited websites in the UK and in 1997 the company was sold to the *Daily Mail* and General Trust. In 1999 at the height of the dotcom boom a 60 per cent share in the site was sold to Disney for £15 million which now runs the site under its ESPN sports brand. Hadfield and his father went on to create another start-up, an education site Schoolsnet, and the teenager was rewarded for his entrepreneurial talent by being named a 'global leader of tomorrow' by the world Economic Forum in 2000.

However, Soccernet is one of a few exceptional examples of a recreational pastime becoming a global business. For the most part, commercial sites have been developed from within the existing sports media industry. The evolution of the industry for interactive sports content on the web has been characterised by a series of false dawns and misjudged investments. As we noted in Chapter 5 the new media sports boom of the late 1990s was something of a false dawn. Large write-downs in the value of new media companies and the liquidation of many of the leading brands, including Sports.com, Sportal and Quokka Sports in the new media sports sector, followed an initial phase of rapid expansion. The main premise for the introduction of e-commerce in sport was the fact that sport had paved the way for other eras of new media technology bringing a ready-made audience to the new medium. The history of media sport is a testament to the mutual benefit the two industries enjoyed primarily through the twentieth century (Boyle and Haynes, 2000). For many in the sports industry the Internet promised a similar opportunity. The main business model of sports Internet start-ups included subscription services to specialised information/ content, pay-per-use sites with video-on-demand or pay-per-view content, sports retailing with football merchandise or online betting, arguably the most lucrative area of sports e-commerce.

Sportal and BT: tales of our times?

The story of the rapid rise and fall of trailblazing new media sports companies is revealed in microcosm by the company Sportal. At its height, Sportal was viewed as the third largest Internet start-up in the UK behind auction site QXL.com and travel company Lastminute.com (BBC, 2001a). The company was running the websites of some of Europe's leading football clubs including Bayern Munich and AC Milan as well as sponsoring Euro 2000. Established in 1998 by Rob Hersov with backing from former employers' financial consultants Morgan Stanley and News Corporation, Sportal quickly gained a reputation for being a leading online brand.

The company would receive further investment from Microsoft and Italian media mogul Silvio Berlosconi and established subsidiary websites across Europe. The site aimed to provide access to premium audio–visual content as well as rolling sports news and was driven by a slick design and cutting edge technology. In May 2000 the company was on the verge of a takeover by French global media corporation Vivendi Universal for the massive sum of £270 million. The deal collapsed amid speculation that the dotcom boom was about to end and the global advertising industry was moving into recession.

Although the site boasted 300,000 subscribers and generated $1 million of advertising revenue per month (BBC, 2001b) by early 2001 the company was hurtling towards bankruptcy. Finally in November 2001 the online bookmaker UKBetting.com bought the sports portal for a paltry £1. Sportal had once been a leading light in the new media marketplace with bold and brash investment in sports rights and massive advertising campaigns. The demise of the site was indicative of over-confidence in the new media market with inflated projections of advertising revenue and attractiveness to sports fans.

In April 2001 industry research had predicted the decimation of the online sports market due to over-crowding (Forrester Research, 2001). Expectations that betting would bolster the market were viewed as overly optimistic and the scale of the online sports industry would be significantly offset by interactive television. As the advertising slump bit hard into the revenues of the new media industry the online sports market was characterised by further consolidation of leading brands. As well as acquiring Sportal, UKBetting merged its betting interests with Sportinglife.com and developed its football interests in buying another leading light of football websites, Teamtalk.

The US based Sports.com, which among others had received backing from sports marketing company IMG supplied online sports content to the likes of the *Financial Times*, Manchester United and AOL, became the biggest casualty of the dotcom crash. On the eve of the 2002 World Cup the site was put into administration and the assets of the company were sold off to the survivors of the online crash. As with Sportal the domain name was licensed to a rapidly expanding online gambling company Sportingbet using the customer base of Sports.com to drive an increase in its registered users.

As the dust has settled on the pioneering years of the World Wide Web what is clear is that established brands of the mainstream UK media and telecommunications industries – most notably the BBC, BSkyB and BT – have effectively exploited public trust in their ability to innovate new media technologies. This faith has subsequently been carried into an array of new media services. As we shall go on to discuss in more detail below, the BBC has proved highly successful in appropriating existing content and delivering interactive media through its websites and digital television channels. While the BBC has not commercialised its new media output, with the exception of beeb.com a subsidiary of BBC Worldwide, it has nevertheless made a significant contribution to a dramatic shift in media habits. The BBC's website is one of the leading destinations for online news in the UK and has also extended the global appeal of the corporation in direct competition to global portals such as Microsoft's MSN and Yahoo.

Similarly, as we noted in Chapter 5, in spring 2002 BT made strategic moves to significantly increase the number of UK households with broadband connections to the Internet. The goal was to create 5 million broadband Internet users by 2006 from a base of 350,000 in 2002. BT had previously been heavily criticised by industry watchdogs OFTEL for its sluggish roll out of broadband and its prohibitive pricing to third party broadband suppliers. In cutting the price of broadband services to below £30 per month and instigating a £10 million television advertising campaign, one of the largest ever witnessed in the UK, the 'no frills' service was designed to initiate significant take-up of high-speed connections.

Key to the strategy was the development of broadband content and applications to entice Internet users to migrate away from dial-up connections. In November 2002 BT announced a new partnership with a resurrected Sportal brand now being licensed by UKBetting. The on-demand service provided streaming action and highlights from various sports including football from the UK, Italy, Brazil and Argentina. The broadband channel also developed a premium pay-per-view service with full delayed 'as live' coverage of Italian Serie A games.

BT also entered into alliances with broadcasters and leading Internet brands as a means of challenging the technologically superior offering of UK cable operators NTL and Telewest who could deliver telecommunications and digital television in the same package. A promotional alliance with BSkyB enabled BT to offer discounted connections to BSkyB subscribers with the reciprocal benefits for BT Openworld customers who wanted to subscribe to the digital satellite broadcaster. In autumn 2003 BT launched another strategic partnership with global Internet portal Yahoo. Yahoo had previously steered clear of service provision and BT's Openworld service had struggled to attract enough new customers to its own interactive content seen as a poor relation to other portals such as AOL, MSN and Lycos. The strategic partnership represented a converging set of interests by telecommunications and new media content providers as a new generation of new media households begins to emerge. The partnerships also marked a degree of consolidation in the new media environment potentially stifling competition for the mass market of Internet provision.

The political economy of new interactive sports media has mirrored the broader consolidation of the global media and telecommunications industries. Start-up companies that have introduced innovative delivery systems, such as Quokka Sports 'immersive' technologies or Sportal's on demand services, have been subsumed into the interests of existing media production and distribution networks. In this sense, new media represents less of a challenge to established media organisations, more a new way to conquer emerging markets. Sport, with football at its helm, is frequently touted by industry executives as a key content to woo consumers to purchase new technologies that provide that little bit extra than what they are accustomed to. As we have already alluded, online betting has gradually become the killer utility for any sports website and it is to the issue of the rise in football gambling that we now turn.

Football and online betting

Betting on the Internet has transformed the configuration of those who fancy a flutter on football. Although gambling has long been an important facet of football culture in the UK, not least through the football pools, online betting has dramatically influenced the structure of football related industries. To the uninitiated, going into a high street bookmaker has always been shrouded in mystery. Admission to being a gambler still carries negative connotations. However, the anonymous world of online gambling has opened up a new lucrative sector in the industry and seduced a new wave of customers. Bereft of any restrictive social or physical barriers and notable for its ease of use, online gambling has become a serious threat to the established betting industry in the UK. The figures on the scale of online betting are sketchy and can vary quite widely. A survey by Merril Lynch in 2003 estimated that the global online gambling market was worth $6.3 billion (O'Connor, 2003).

The development of betting sites located in offshore tax havens prompted the UK Treasury to rethink its method of levying the betting industry with major concessions to the industry to reduce the levels of duty in high street bookmakers. In the spring budget of 2003 the Government introduced a 15 per cent tax on gross profits rather than a tax levied on the transactions over the counter. The move was designed to stem the flow of money heading offshore by making the UK companies, in particular the established giants of the industry, more competitive. The Government's Gambling Review in 2001 made recommendations for the Government to support the development of online gambling but within renewed regulatory guidelines that sought to license websites with gambling facilities and establish measures to prevent juvenile gambling. In July 2003 the Government produced the Gambling Bill (DCMS, 2003) with the proposal to create a new regulatory body for gambling in the UK, the Gambling Commission, and establish some economic guidelines for online gambling most notably the ban on UK advertising for overseas betting companies.

Throughout the late 1990s and into the new century the industry saw a stream of new websites and entrants to the betting market. Gibraltar based Victor Chandler, who began their international online operation in May 1999, quickly managed to build its reputation as an alternative to the 'big three' of Ladbrokes, Coral and William Hill. New media betting exchanges undermined the dominance of the traditional market by providing competitive odds and linking up with key sports brands. The UK betting industry has also faced competition from other European and global betting operators. During Euro 2000 Italy's Snaisports made large inroads into the football betting market. The global aspect of betting has also made an impact beyond the UK. In July 2003 Hong Kong legalised football betting for the first time opening up a huge market for UK online agencies (the *Evening Standard*, 28 July 2003). Previously black market betting cartels had dominated football gambling which was largely based on the popularity of the English Premier League (Thomas, 2003). By establishing a legitimate betting market with licences for offshore companies the Hong Kong Government hoped to levy a betting tax to help offset their spiralling deficit.

Information about sports betting has always been a key content driver for new media. When the sporting press began to blossom in the early nineteenth century, *Bells Life*, one of the most eponymous titles of the Victorian sport era, became a key stakeholder for the aristocratic 'fancy' for prize fighting. Similarly, the development of the telegraph enabled the transfer of betting information on horse-racing to the sporting press, which in turn allowed newspapers to aggregate the odds being calculated from the 'Tattersall Rings' – the exclusive betting enclosures. The football pools was for many years the dominant form of football betting and was well supported by the rise of broadcasting which made ritual listening of the Saturday afternoon full time scores. However, with the rise of fixed odds betting on football and competition from the National Lottery the pools has gone into rapid decline.

In the modern era of media sport, interactive television promises to be the most powerful marriage of informative data, instant electronic betting and live action. The future prospect of gambling through an iTV portal will continue to be important in any bidding process for television rights to major sport, particularly football which has seen the biggest growth in the betting industry. In 2001 the English Premier League supplemented its deal with BSkyB by a further £22.5 million payment for interactive services including betting. Rights holders now account for the prospective revenues from online betting in their valuations of rights and levels of exclusivity. Other innovations such as 'Footy Flutter' introduced by IndexGaming allows fans to place bets via a premium rate telephone number, where the call charge is the stake, have added to the surge in football betting since the change in the tax levy.

Any new media portal that makes a claim to sporting credentials must have at its disposal a window to online betting to keep the fans coming back for more. While high definition pictures remain a distant pipe dream for sports webcasters, sports sites need to offer an incentive beyond breaking news stories and associated exclusives. Betting, along with merchandising, is the most lucrative e-commerce opportunity for sports websites. It may be e-commerce, but it is still one of the oldest sporting trades in the world.

The level and accessibility of football betting does raise concerns. It could be argued that the use of credit cards and 'e-cash' makes gamblers more irresponsible with their money as debt becomes invisible. On the social front, online betting is largely anonymous and solitary again hiding the dangers of addictive behaviour around gambling. New pressure groups such as GameCare offer support to gamblers and have pressurised the Government to enforce specific codes of social responsibility on online and interactive gambling companies. Unlike the high street bookmaker online betting services can build a database on their customers with details of when they bet, what on and how much. Such marketing armoury is open to abuse and so far there are few limitations on the commercial exploitation of such information.

Football and interactive television

The conventional wisdom about watching television is that people like to 'tune in' and 'switch off'. The classic profile of the 'couch potato' is someone – usually male – comfortably sitting at home absorbing the images of multichannel TV while stuffing themselves with junk food and beer. While many of us may recognise a diluted form of these traits in some of our closest family and friends, audience research in media studies since the 1980s has revealed that such stereotypes differ greatly with how people actually experience television. The concept of the 'active viewer' actually creating meaning from television messages built on wider social, cultural and psychological processes has led to a far more complex picture of how we consume the medium.

The basic premise of contemporary audience research is that viewers understand television programmes by deploying complex interpretative strategies. Moreover, how television fits into the household and everyday life becomes as important as the analysis of what appears on screen. These environmental factors reveal a lot about how people appropriate media technologies into their home and how they are then incorporated as part of the fabric of the household (Silverstone, 1994).

Certainly the television industry has attempted to adapt to the options offered with digitisation by incorporating interactive elements into their programmes. As O'Regan and Goldsmith (2003: 92) point out:

> Interactive television is not only emerging in new formats and distribution platforms such as the Internet, but is also an added element thoroughly at home with existing old analogue media such as prime-time television.

Interactive television blurs some of the boundaries between the so-called 'lean back' experience of watching television and the 'lean forward' experience of personal computing. However, as we shall go on to see even this simplified analysis of how new media technologies are consumed is not straightforward and has caused some major head scratching within the industry as to how best to use the technology to build an audience.

The concept of interacting with the television set while watching a football match therefore takes on quite profound significance. For if we are already actively engaging with our televisions at the level of making sense of the medium (which for football fans may include screaming at the television) how do viewers interpret the multi-layered complex networking of information available through interactive television?

One short answer has been that they haven't. Studies conducted in both the United States and the UK reveal that viewers are incredibly reluctant to 'interact' with their televisions beyond interpreting what is already on screen. In a 2003 industry survey of the likelihood of US households adopting interactive television found that 72 per cent of respondents showed no interest in 'interacting' with their television sets (Johnson, 2003). More seriously for the fledgling industry was the finding that in homes already geared up for interactive services very few actually participated in interactive elements based around programmes or advertising.

Crucially, what many thought would lead to the absolute convergence of the Internet and television just has not happened. Rather, interactive has had to fight its own battle in order to gain recognition from the audience who are reluctant to learn the knowledge or competencies to take part. A similar study in the UK by the Future Media Programme at the London Business School (Brodin *et al.*, 2002) revealed that viewers saw interactive television as an enhancement of the linear programming rather than a fully-fledged alternative to the World Wide Web. Indeed, the television industry itself has turned to the concept of 'enhanced' television rather than the term interactive that suggests an all-singing all-dancing Internet experience.

The initial hype that accompanied digital television has perhaps damaged the initial take up of these services. As the Internet did not live up to the much-predicted path of taking over our lives, so interactive television has proved short on inspiration and ideas as broadcasters struggle to find a format to engage the viewer. Part of the problem has been the lack of convergence between new media technologies. Interactive television has many of the properties of the Internet most importantly the 'return' path back to the producer of the content. However, it has evolved in a very different manner.

Where the World Wide Web is an open space with no ownership of the network, with its protocols or language (HTML), interactive television is a far more controlled environment. The various platforms for digital television in the UK use different protocols for delivering interactive services that are heavily patrolled. Where Freeview uses MHEG based technology and NTL and Telewest use HTML and Javascript, BSkyB use a proprietary system developed by Open TV thus programme makers and advertisers wanting to develop inter-active services for the digital satellite channel must adopt the authoring and digital format required of that system. This makes the production of interactive programming potentially expensive and restrictive. Unlike the Web which has standard formats and protocols that anyone can use, interactive television has numerous barriers to entry that ensure the controller of the digital platform, BSkyB, has a near unassailable power in how the technology develops. This restricted technology of interactive television has an important bearing on its ultimate uses which are likely to be significantly different to using the web. As the survey by Brodin, Barwise and Canhoto (2002: 4) suggests:

> Many people in homes with iDTV have never even tried any of the interac-tive services, while others have been discouraged by poor reliability, slow access, and weak content. The main successes to-date have been iDTV games and gambling, although operators have found it hard to make these profitable.

The different technologies and the way in which they are delivered by digital satellite, digital cable and digital terrestrial platforms has also led to confusion among consumers and acted as a deterrent to advertisers. This has been a problem for BSkyB who launched the Open service in 1998 and went on to invest £2 billion in transferring all its customers to digital STBs (Tryhorn, 2003). Interactive elements such as player cams and multi-camera angles were early features of Sky Sports Active, the satellite broadcaster's interactive sports channel. Sky Sports have explored the possibilities of what the technology can deliver but such services are often nothing short of gimmicks and provide a dis-traction from the main event. For example, a new interactive feature introduced by Sky Sports was a game called 'Beat the Pundits'. Here interactivity is allied to a fan's involvement in the game with all the associated views and opinions that accompany such activity. Viewers are asked to make predictions throughout the coverage of a live game in parallel with the studio experts. As with other forms of interactive gaming – innovated with reality television programme formats such as *Big Brother* – by encouraging viewers to join-in-from-home and playing against the panel the game seeks to enliven the whole experience of watching a match. While we might agree that listening to football pundits often provokes a strong reaction we might question the longevity of such an exercise after a couple of plays. Herein lies the problem of interactive elements associated with the actual programming of football; most fans simply want to watch the game.

A key strength of digital television is the ability to record data on individual viewers as they use the system allied to 'one-click' purchasing. This has great benefits for advertisers and direct marketing via what has now become known as t-commerce. Since the launch of Sky Sports Active the satellite broadcasters' strategy has been to recoup as much money as possible via its interactive services and advertising. After spending enormous sums of money on new technology and building a customer base of 7 million by the end of 2003 the company has sought to commercialise as many aspects of the interactive experience it can.

The broadcasters most lucrative commercial venture has been interactive betting. BSkyB has attempted to generate revenues from interactive betting via Sky Bet that enables fans to gamble on a range of events during the game from first goalscorer, to scoreline and result. Unlike conventional sports betting where all bets are closed prior to the event, Sky Bet operates a rolling betting scheme constantly updating the odds as the match progresses. The service is also accompanied by a separate commentary to update the viewer on the various odds being offered. As Charles Malir the marketing director of Orbis, a sports betting software supplier was quoted as saying in the *Financial Times*:

> Imagine sitting down to watch the FA Cup Final with your mates, and being able to bet from your TV remote control on whether David Beckham will score the penalty – appeal for this kind of fun betting will be huge.
>
> Ward, 2001

Although the revenue from interactive services such as Sky Bet remains a small proportion of BSkyB's overall revenue (£72 million of £2,331 million turnover by March 2003) it is expected to rise, as interactive television becomes more commonplace. A survey of interactive television sports by *Screen Digest* (2003) forecast revenues to grow to $2.79 billion by the end of 2008. Although such figures are invariably wildly optimistic the suggestion that interactive television will rapidly expand over this period is persuasive. As the former Chief Executive of BSkyB Tony Ball suggests interactive television is a 'generational' time bomb, as '65 per cent of multichannel homes have teenagers and they're going to be the homemakers of tomorrow' (Cantos, 2003). The key measurement in this respect is the annual revenue per user (ARPU), which by March 2003 stood at £364 and is set to rise to £400 by 2005 (BSkyB, 2003).

Such figures drive home the changing environment of pay-TV in the UK. Viewers are far more likely to spend additional money on home entertainment on top of the initial outlay on installation and subscription costs. In the case of

BSkyB football has driven many of these changes and is the reason why the broadcaster continues to invest incredible sums in rights fees.

Enhanced television brings the perception of choice to the viewer. The ability to choose from an extended menu, whether it is interactive games, betting, in-depth information about players and teams, all adds up to a complex viewing experience. This point was noted by the BBC's Head of Football Niall Sloane who remarked that he was 'always a little bit dubious' about giving the viewer the ability to change the perspective of watching a game via interactive channels. Rather, it is the ability of broadcasters to increase the capacity to show more sport by opening up interactive channels that shows most promise. Reflecting on his personal experience Sloane commented:

> I saw the initial models of 'here you can watch the match from a low angle' or 'here's fifteen minutes of the game you can concentrate on the left-back'. I look at myself and say 'you're too old to get this'. But I look at my children and they weren't bothered in terms of watching different angles. I think the best interactivity comes when you are offered different games. Like in a World Cup or maybe look at the Wimbledon model when you've got four matches to flick around between. I think that's proper interactivity and that I get.
>
> Interview with the authors, 22 April 2003

For pay-TV channels it is the ability to offer multiple games via different payment structures that is ultimately changing the coverage of football rather than the ability to change and interact with programmes. In 2003 BSkyB developed its football rights in two significant deals. First, the capture of Champions League rights (see Chapter 5) gave Sky Sports the opportunity to deliver up to eight games in the group stage of the tournament. The ability to divide the digital signal into further channels is a step change in the volume of football available on British television.

Second, the capture of the Premier League's delayed 'as live' package completes the circle in the satellite broadcasters coverage of the league. In a deal worth an estimated £60 million Sky Sports could not only broadcast an entire Premier League game 'as live' the evening after the match but also make highlights available of every other game not transmitted under the live agreement. Match highlights could therefore be delivered as part of a video-on-demand (VOD) interactive service whereby fans could make micro-payments to view the games of individual clubs.

As we discussed in Chapter 5 VOD has already begun on club websites but would not match the quality of sound and image delivered via digital television. We would therefore argue that the distinction between television and the Internet remains marked. As Brodin, Barwise and Canhoto (2002: 4) suggest, 'iDTV is television with interactivity, not the Internet with moving pictures'. As the technologies of new media develop broadcasters will become more attuned to the needs of viewers. This is particularly important for public service broadcasters who need to balance wider political objectives with the changing landscape of television production and distribution.

The BBC, new media and football

Throughout its history the BBC has pioneered new broadcast technologies under a predominantly expansionist strategy in an attempt to provide the British public, the licence fee payers, with a broad range of services. Sport has taken an inexorable place in the BBC's output and has become synonymous with its history and status in British culture. As we have argued elsewhere (Boyle and Haynes, 2000) sport has been central to the development of broadcasting and has frequently provided an umbrella for the introduction of new technologies innovated by the BBC. The BBC helped pioneer the first pan-European television broadcasts from the World Cup in 1954 and introduced the use of colour television in 1967 during the coverage of Wimbledon. More recently, the introduction of interactive television services of the same tournament in 2001 represent a further landmark in the BBC's innovation of new media technologies in the coverage of sport.

However, the BBC's move into the delivery of digital content via the BBC website and interactive television has raised issues about its role in the new media marketplace. Not least are the allegations by the commercial media sector, both broadcasters and Internet publishers (including the online press) that the BBC has overstepped its role in the new media sector to the extent that the scale of the operation has undermined the growth and diversity of the industry. The place of Internet and interactive services in a public service broadcaster does present some interesting issues. In particular, should public money raised through the licence fee be used in a way that potentially distorts the new media market at the expense of potential competitors? Moreover, how the BBC reacts to these allegations in its continuing political manoeuvring to keep its Royal Charter and financial support through the licence fee presents an interesting conjuncture to investigate its new media activity.

From the launch of BBC Online in 1997 the BBC has defended its right to move into what John Birt, the Director General of the Corporation throughout an era of dramatic change in the 1990s, has called the broadcaster's 'third medium' (Naylor et al., 2000: 142). The Corporation clearly views its move into the delivery of online content as central to its public service commitments and received official Government approval to fund these activities from the licence fee in 1998. In a strategic reorganisation of the BBC's interactive services in 2001 the Corporation's online, interactive television and digital text services were brought under a single brand BBCi.

The expansion into a tri-media public service broadcaster has placed the BBC in the political spotlight. In August 2003 the Government opened public consultation in a detailed review of the BBC's online services. The review aimed to focus on the BBC's performance against the terms of its original consent accepted in 1998 and the impact the site had on the UK Internet market. In preparation for the review the BBC produced its own report on the place of BBCi in its public service remit. In a clear statement of intent the report outlines the key philosophy of its online service:

> Above all, the BBC's online service is the clearest expression of the idea of the BBC as a free public space in broadcasting, where the UK's disparate voices and cultures can encounter each other on equal terms and with mutual respect.
>
> BBC, 2003: 5

The role sport and football play in this context is interesting as it represents one of the key growth areas of new media and the BBC's services. Sport has gained more prominence in the BBC's strategy to bolster its public service credentials. As Niall Sloane explained:

> I think there is a more positive attitude with the BBC, both at the Director General level and throughout the BBC. In the past sport didn't have a seat at the top table in the way the executive of the BBC works. Now it does.
>
> Interview with the authors, 22 April 2003

The impact of the departure of Greg Dyke as Director General early in 2004 on this situation remains to be seen.

Although the value of sport to the BBC management may have had its ups and downs, to the audience, sport and the BBC remain strong bedfellows. In a market impact assessment of the BBC's website, by City consultants KPMG, sport represented the second most popular genre on the BBC site behind news (KPMG, 2003). Sports pages represented 16.9 per cent of page impressions a significantly high proportion of visits. More interestingly, analysis of the sports website users suggested that the BBC site showed a very high frequency of visits by a relatively low number of unique users. This suggests that unlike news websites, sports websites attract a niche market (young to middle-aged men) with very active use and participation. Finally, the report estimated that the BBC sports website had a 20 per cent share of the sports market in the UK (KPMG, 2003: 123) giving it a major presence in the new media sports industry.

The KPMG analysis of the market impact of the BBC sports website makes it clear that BBCi operates outside the principal activities of most sports websites which is to make money. Where most sports related websites are geared towards driving revenue through e-commerce, betting and advertising, the BBC does not offer any of these facilities. Neither has the BBC entered into the delivery of 'push services' where charges are made for personalised constantly updated services and as a public service broadcaster it has no intention of providing VOD services or pay-per-view via its websites. Nevertheless, the critics of the BBC will continue to persist in their complaints that the BBC website continues to have a gravitational pull on Internet users taking them away from advertising sponsored sites or other premium rate services. The Government's review of the BBC's online services will be critical in how this dispute is settled. Industry lobbies such as the British Internet Providers' Association have called on new regulation of the BBC with budgetary ceilings and demands that the BBC websites make links to news services of its commercial rivals.

In light of mounting complaints the BBC took measures to offset such criticism. In March 2003 the Corporation announced the reallocation of resources from its websites into interactive television as a strategic shift in its new media policy. There was a halt to the development of new websites with 100 job losses and a diversion of spending into the development of interactive features across its programming. By moving its resources back into the core business of making programmes the BBC made moves to head off any future criticism of its new media spending.

In the defence of the BBC's online activities one can point to the efforts it has made to build what it has called 'communities of interest'. By offering discussion forums and a route back to programme producers via e-mail and text messaging the BBC has opened up the extent to which licence payers can feed into the communication network. This collaborative approach to building online communities is reiterated in the BBC's sports coverage and the ways in which the BBC website supports the television coverage. Viewers can e-mail their points of view to the website, some of which are picked up by the programme producers and used in the panel discussions during half-time analysis of games. Moreover, discussion boards develop asynchronous communication among viewers based on their interests and passions.

The BBC's view of 'cyberspace' sits very comfortably with the ideas of some of the webs early pioneers and advocates of the 'virtual community' (Rheingold, 1993). In this view of new media participation interest groups on bulletin boards constitutes a new space of empowerment. It is a rhetoric that also neatly matches the ethos of football communities in general. Football communities can be characterised as being unswervingly loyal, increasingly geographically dispersed, but brought together by common concerns and interests. Moreover, many of the participants of the online message boards are unknown to the others and may even be anonymous. Such discussion forums and chat rooms have come under suspicion for these very characteristics with fears that participants may not be what they seem, with Microsoft publicly pulling the plug on its MSN chat rooms in September 2003. However, in the context of football, message boards can often be liberating and provide a communicative space for the free-flow of ideas and opinions. Although, of course, they can also raise a new set of legal difficulties for sites which hoist them. Rivals.net had to close a number of their message boards in October 2003, when fans started posting the names of a number of footballers allegedly involved in the rape of a 17-year-old girl. These names had not been officially put into the public domain and the case was subject to an ongoing police investigation. The website feared legal action from lawyers wishing to protect the reputation of their players.

What is more insidious is the way in which the social and cultural characteristics of online communities are increasingly harnessed for commercial ends. Sites increasingly demand users to register before entering sites whether or not they have to pay for access. This information can then be stored and used for direct marketing purposes filling the online universe with more and more 'spam'. The BBC at least provides a safe harbour from the creeping commercialisation of new media sport. The Corporation has had to steer clear of being seen as overtly commercial in its coverage of sport. Prospects of a BBC sports channel have, according to Sloane, been 'oft talked about and frequently rejected'. As Sloane outlines this is primarily due to 'the political ramifications of the BBC using licence fee money to set up a sports channel' which would be far reaching. The need for a dedicated sports channel has been negated somewhat by the BBC's online activity and increasing output for broadband users. Similarly, the possibilities for opening up BBC1 and 2 for interactive access to multiple coverage of games as the demand arises also lessens the need for a separate channel. In the final section of the chapter we review the way in which the 2002 World Cup represented a new phase in the development of new media services and conflicts it posed for rights holders.

FIFA World Cup 2002: online 24/7

More than any other sporting occasion, including the Olympic Games, the FIFA World Cup produces intense and ubiquitous media coverage. In Chapter 4 we referred to Whannel's (2002) notion of a media vortex that pulls in all news stories around the exploits of renowned stars and celebrities to the exception of anything else that might be happening in the world. Similarly, the World Cup produces a vortextual effect on all media outlets immediately prior and during the event. Included in this global media mix, jostling for position with the national broadcasters who had paid a total of £60 billion for the rights to the World Cup, was the Internet. According to FIFA figures the official website for France 98 had received a total of 1.1 billion hits during the 33 days of the tournament. This figure was set to rise sharply during the 2002 World Cup in Japan and South Korea.

The World Cup in 2002 was interesting in terms of the development of sport on the web for several reasons that we sketch out briefly below. First, it heralded a new era of partnership between the governing body of the sport and a leading global brand in the emerging new media industry. In September 2001 Yahoo signed a rights agreement to become the producer of Fifaworldcup.com, the official website of the tournament, as well as joining FIFA's exclusive club of 15 official sponsorship partners for the 2002 and 2006 World Cups. For FIFA the alliance obviously brought much needed expertise into the running of the official site that had proved so popular during the 1998 finals.

For Yahoo it represented a strategic change in its approach to content delivery from being an aggregator and portal (where content producers paid for the privilege of receiving exposure from one of the web's leading brands) to a situation where it bought into the exclusive delivery of content in order to draw exposure to its brand via a co-sponsored website. The move represented a broader shift in the alliances of major web brands, such as Google's supply of search engines for leading portals, and a realisation from sports administrators that web development is best left to those with experience and global clout. At the time of the deal in 2001 Yahoo claimed a worldwide user base of 200 million many of whom would be channelled towards FIFA's official site for the duration of the 2002 finals. In the event the official website recorded 2 billion unique visits with an average 130 million page views per day at the height of the tournament (FIFA, 2003).

A second significant development in 2002 was the decision to allow fans to access streaming video of each and every game via the web. There is a general belief in the sports industry that as the level of Internet users reaches saturation point and a significant percentage of online users are connected to broadband networks that rights holders will cede some of the live audio–visual rights to Internet content suppliers. The key to these changes is dependent on the damage done to television rights packages, especially live broadcasts that have a premium price tag.

Fears that online distribution of live football would undermine the value of such rights are obviously well founded. In the case of the World Cup, for example, successive rounds of negotiations for live rights has led to protracted arguments about the value of rights not least because the potential for piracy via global communications networks is ever-present. As the music and film industries have discovered to their cost, digital distribution of content can seriously affect the value of rights and their market. Rights holders have therefore been cautious in their approach to opening up footage to the Internet.

However, the 2002 World Cup represented something of a watershed in this respect with the delivery of four-minute highlights of every game two to three hours after the final whistle. Pressure to enable access to live matches via the web had been dashed early on by both FIFA and the German television rights agent Kirch. This followed the IOC precedent of policing web content of the 2000 Olympic Games in an attempt to allay broadcasters' fears that their rights were not infringed. Internet retransmission rights had originally been included in the broadcast rights deal signed by Kirch in 1996 when the value of web rights was negligible. The German media giant would later go into administration but had spun off a separate company KirchSports later re-branded Infront to broker the World Cup rights effectively saving FIFA's blushes.

Yahoo's service was called 'FIFA VIP Club' and provided a secure portal for fans to subscribe at a flat rate fee of $19.95 (£14). Yahoo also made an archive of previous World Cup 'classic games' available free of charge including full television footage of the 1966 final (minus the Wolstenholme commentary). A crucial aspect of the release of highlights on the web was that the footage was exclusive to Fifaworldcup.com. Although national broadcasters around the world had paid multi-million dollar fees for the World Cup television licences they were prohibited from screening any of this footage on their associate websites. This meant that the BBC, who had contentiously paid £170 million in a joint bid with ITV for the 2002 and 2006 tournaments, could not show any footage of the finals on their website even within their online news bulletins. Throughout the 2002 finals audio–visual news output was heavily policed by a specialist rights management agency NetResult. Monitoring and forcibly withdrawing unlicensed footage and abuse of licensed logos further cemented the need for fans to receive information via an official website that carries advertising and tie-ins to FIFA's sponsored partners giving the World Cup site maximum exposure.

The third important dimension of online coverage from Japan and South Korea was the social impact it had on how people accessed information about the tournament. Given the time difference between South-East Asia and Europe many of the games were played at unsociable hours way out of peak time viewing. A huge debate raged across the UK with the prospect of important World Cup matches taking place during standard working hours and fans wondering if their employers would allow time off to watch the crucial games involving England and Ireland. With more than 50 per cent of adults in the UK accessing the Internet by the summer of 2002, with a large proportion of these combining access at home and at the workplace, the web came into its own during the finals. Text commentaries were delivered online and supplied by numerous football sites. Similarly, mobile phone operators moved into the football market with prolific zeal offering discounted subscription services with text message updates of goals, goalscorers and match reports.

The FIFA president Sepp Blatter reiterated the importance of the web for delivering information on demand shortly after the deal with Yahoo had been struck:

> This is particularly significant for fans in different time zones to Korea and Japan, for example Europe is up to 9 hours behind. By launching this video highlights package FIFA has listened to the voices of football fans across the globe and has responded by providing the ultimate way to stay in touch with the action.
>
> FIFA, 2002

However, FIFA has been reluctant to release how successful the subscription site had been during the finals. Television and radio clearly maintained the important advantages of immediacy and it is debatable how attractive the streaming of highlights would be when games were repeated during peak time viewing each evening.

Moreover, the BBC offered digital satellite viewers the opportunity to view the day's action via an interactive menu across its BBC channels; a more attractive proposition than watching highlights on the web. Nevertheless, the ability of fans to time-shift their viewing patterns was an indicator of how such technologies might develop around global media events such as the World Cup. While the 2006 finals in Germany will not create similar problems for fans, the demand from fans to access archival material and alternative viewing via interactive television or the web is set to increase.

Conclusion

What we have attempted to outline in this chapter is the changing landscape of new media services as they relate to the consumption of football. The communicative space of football has become increasingly global in the new media age. If football fanzines represented an era of change in the reportage of football, the Internet and interactive television signify a profound shift in the production and distribution of football as an entertainment industry. New media have done this by opening avenues for fans to engage with the game in new ways and to experience new forms of communication.

At the same time we have seen increasing activity by established media into new media services increasingly intent on commercialising as much of this new media space as possible. Many of the new media companies trying to take advantage of football's appeal have fallen by the wayside unable to find a way of capturing a big enough market to convince advertisers they are worthy of investment. The market has therefore been characterised by consolidation through merger and acquisition and a host of alliances between global web brands and sport.

One benefactor of new media technologies has been the BBC, that has neatly integrated much of its sports broadcasting with the web and innovative elements of interactive television. Its success in building one of the largest and most frequently visited sports websites has thrown it open to the accusation that it has abused its position as a public service broadcaster. However, it might be argued that its coverage of football on the web and interactive television has held true to the driving cultural ethos of the web that has long idealised the power of networks to bring disparate communities together under shared interests.

Conclusion: the only game?
The media and the football industry in the twenty-first century

The game is about those who play and those who pay.
Celtic manager, Martin O'Neill, BBC Radio Five Live, 24 April 2003

The words culture and citizenship are rarely closely connected within contemporary debates.
Nick Stevenson, 1999: 59

The whole thing with sport's television rights now is it is on a fulcrum. We are seeing the past disappearing before our eyes and before we know it there will be a whole new order simply brought about by finance.
David Hill, Former Head of Sky Sports and current Chairman of Fox Sports, September 2003

Football, commerce and citizenship in the new media age

Football has always been a commercial industry. In Scotland, the 'Old Firm' was a term first used to highlight the financial benefits that accrued to both Celtic and Rangers as far back as the nineteenth century as they jointly exploited their unique rivalry and turnstile appeal. What we have argued in this book is that the movement of the game into the new media age appears to have simply intensified and refined what has been a longer historical process. Having said that, this ongoing process of commercialisation has witnessed a step change in the new media age. This process, as we have discussed in previous chapters has been set against a wider crisis in public television, the consolidation of European pay-TV platforms, and the bedding into the social fabric of new mobile communication technologies.

It seems likely that public and pay-TV platforms will operate together within an increasingly commercial television environment. One of the problems faced by Public Service Broadcasters (PSBs) is that they are struggling to differentiate themselves in a multichannel media landscape. Their strength remains the potential breadth of their audience, despite the steady growing access to pay television in most European markets. However we would argue that despite the general downturn in football rights since its highpoint in 2000, which has allowed a return of sorts to the coverage of the sport on free-to-air channels, anomalies with regard to access still exist in this process.

When Scotland played Lithuania in a vital Euro 2004 qualifier at Hampden Park in Glasgow in October 2003, the game was carried exclusively live on the pay-TV channel Sky Sports. This important national game was not available live on free-to-air television. Such games are media and cultural events which pull in viewers whose primary interest is not necessarily in the football, but is rather driven by wider cultural and national factors (Blain *et al.*, 1993). Yet the rights holders, the Scottish Football Association (SFA), who lament the poor profile of the national game in Scotland, were happy to sell the rights to such an important match for short-term financial benefit, ignoring the wider negative impact that removing the Scottish national team from national television may have on its profile and development. In the new media age short-term thinking among rights holders is still very much in evidence.

In differing contexts and from various perspectives writers such as Hoggart (1996), Scannell (1989, 1996) and Garnham (2000) have all argued about the civic/cultural role that media systems, broadcasting in particular, have had in embedding cultural practices in society. In many ways football, and its historic interface with the media provide a good example of a cultural form which through its symbiotic relationship with a public service framed system of broadcasting framed by public service ideology has become part of the wider fabric of cultural life in many societies.

Globalisation and new media football

What we have argued throughout this book is that the new media age, or digital age if you prefer, marks another staging post on the longer road of commercialisation which the media and football industries have been embarked on since their first meeting. We remain unconvinced that untold riches lie ahead for those parts of the football industry that want to exploit the new wave of technological innovation for their own ends. It seems to us that while consumers (and we mourn the apparent passing of the term citizens in this debate) engage with aspects of the communications industry in increasingly complex ways, certain fundamentals remain constant. Much of the rhetoric about global marketplaces and brands with regard to clubs and players, will remain exactly that; rhetoric. Yes, patterns of global fandom are shifting and changing as the Internet and digital technologies allows faster and more varied forms of worldwide dissemination of information and entertainment, but for many they also remain rooted in the more local and national environments as well.

These patterns of cultural activity remain complex and require an ongoing empirical awareness allied with theoretical framing. For example much of the early summer of 2003 saw the British, Spanish, and to a lesser extent the American media speculating about the future of footballer David Beckham, as it became clear that the Manchester United player would be moving from the English Champions. His eventual departure to Real Madrid, and the ensuing public relations battle between him, his Manchester United manager and the club gained plenty of media attention. For some commentators, such as Tom Bower (2003b), the saga epitomized all that was rotten in English football. For Bower it was a corrupt sport, driven by greed, media hype and vested interests with a coterie of agents and middlemen all getting rich on the back of the national game.

What aspects of this polemical analysis also highlighted were the increasingly complex relationship between stars, football and popular media culture as the globalisation of the game continues.

It might be argued, that as the process of globalisation appears to intensify with ever more instant and globally oriented communicative systems in the new media age, that European football and popular culture in general is becoming more 'Americanised'. Yet as Mike Steinberger, writing from the USA in the *Financial Times* pointed out, the Beckham transfer saga, with Manchester United supposedly selling one of their top stars and marketing assets to a rival, demonstrated that in certain aspects European sport remains very different culturally and economically from the US. He argued:

> There are really only two instances in which a pro team [In America] will voluntarily part with a superstar; when it can trade for someone better, or when it can no longer afford to keep them. [...] It has long been an article of faith that European football is becoming Americanised – that the game is being lost to the mercenary values and obsession with marketability that drive American sports leagues. No doubt, Real's interest in Beckham is partly motivated by business considerations. But viewed from the other side of the Atlantic, the circumstances of Beckham's imminent departure from Manchester could not look less familiar.
>
> Steinberger, 2003: 19

In other words, the fact that the US media were at all interested in David Beckham – who was touring the USA at this time with his wife Victoria – tells us something about globalisation and the role media play in helping to create and sustain 'stars'. Yet as Steinberger notes above specific cultural and economic forces still help to shape the particular context within which popular culture and the football industry both in the UK and the rest of Europe operate.

In this respect, while the pace of change may quicken in the new media age, as information gets circulated via differing communication networks, at its cultural core, specific national aspects of the sport continue to look remarkably similar to that which existed in the pre-digital era. Indeed the plethora of scandals that engulfed the English game in the autumn of 2003 was actually amplified patterns of behaviour that pre-date the latest injection of media money and interest. There has always been bad behaviour among a section of young

English males. What is different in the new media age is the levels of wealth involved, the more intense media scrutiny from a larger and more complex commercially focused industry and a complicit popular press who are happy to both help create and condemn aspects of celebrity culture. As Burke *et al.* (2003) suggest:

> with the media and clubs combining to increase the profile – and thus the profitability – of clubs, pay levels for the top players are unlikely to drop soon, despite increasing resentment among many fans. The media attention is undoubtedly unprecedented, with players' agents, PRs, tabloid and broadsheet reporters, paparazzi, tipsters ranging from club bouncers to ground staff, all combining to keep the stories, and the cash, coming.

Thus even in a globalising age, specific cultural traits remain important. Put simply, the values and norms of a society continue to shape the footballing culture that it produces.

As Stevenson (1999: 67) has argued:

> The 'globalisation thesis' is in danger of underestimating the relative permanence of national cultures and their ability to respond to changes. Whether it is through national holidays, watching television, reading newspapers, listening to the radio, speaking a language or applying for a passport, the nation remains a primary form of 'cultural' address.

To this list we would add following football and supporting a particular team.

Early autumn 2003 saw the business and sports pages of the UK press covering the surprise departure of the Manchester United Chief Executive, Peter Kenyon, to their Premiership rivals Chelsea. Under their new owner, billionaire Roman Abramovich, the acquisition of Kenyon suggested that Chelsea were hoping to compete with the elite clubs of Europe, not only on the field of play, but also in the wider global marketing stakes. Yet for all Kenyon's marketing expertise, is it possible to simply create a global football brand at a club which has won little of significance in recent times and does not have a profile outside of the English Premier League?

We would argue that while the new media age, through increasingly global communicative systems, offers the potential for profile in diverse worldwide markets (and indeed in some limited cases, such as that of Beckham the brand, this value has been realised), in general terms simply because such systems exist does not mean that an unproblematic form of global influence will simply follow. Chelsea will first need to be successful and to re-invent (or indeed create) a distinctive culture surrounding the club in order for it to have any purchase or value in overseas markets. Unlike a cluster of clubs such as Real Madrid, Juventus, Manchester United, Liverpool and Celtic, they have no immediate significant global diaspora of fans to connect with.

For many supporters, football remains a cultural form distinguished from others by its mixture of a sense of place, identity, history and emotion. It will continue to offer this rich cultural mix (when it stops doing so, the game will really die) as media systems mutate and evolve, driven evermore by the demands of a complex and contradictory marketplace. The ongoing commercialisation of the sport simply reflects the more market driven culture within which the sport operates and comes with the attendant dangers which see the economic drive dominate the cultural agenda and not vice versa. A failure of political nerve to recognise the wider social and cultural significance and value of media systems (rather than their purely economic importance) will simply accelerate this already quickening process of market driven regulation.

Even those who dislike the sport, and all that it appears to have become as media money has flowed into the elite end of the game, will recognise the longer-term damage that the migration from a public media culture to a private cultural domain will bring for the sport. By association this also impacts on the wider symbolic role that football plays in the process of cultural and national identity formation.

The creation of a civic space and the broad democratising process talked about by Scannell (1989) which public service media has historically helped to foster – with all its imperfections – appears to have been in retreat for much of the last two decades. However, the early years of the new century has seen a more robust stance being taken by broadcasters such as the BBC as it seeks to carve out a position for PSB in a digital age. As we have noted elsewhere in the book, its encroachment into the digital market as a publicly funded provider has been controversial, with claims that it is actually distorting the market and inhibiting the commercial growth of competition in certain sectors such as the online provision of news.

However under its former Director General Greg Dyke, there is little doubt that sport, and football in particular, had been given greater prominence in the Corporation's strategic thinking. The impact on this of his departure from the BBC in 2004 remains to be seen. In addition, it seems to us that a more aggressive approach from publicly funded media is not necessarily something which we should be concerned about, given the dominance that market driven media exert over the communications landscape.

For many years organisations such as the BBC were viewed as part of the broadcasting establishment, with an attendant arrogant and paternalistic view of its world place. The growth in competition, described in the opening chapters of the book, have resulted in the once 'new kids on the block', such as BSkyB, themselves now becoming part of the broadcasting establishment. In many ways the Sky brand is now synonymous with football in the UK, and we would argue they have helped to set the agenda for how the sport is covered by television in that country. There always remains the longer-term possibility that a new generation of supporters will enjoy the Sky experience to such an extent that it will become infinitely more appealing (and cheaper) to watch in pubs, clubs or at home than trying to get a ticket to attend an actual top flight game. The arguments about the balance between live sporting attendances and live media coverage of football, such a fixation in the years between the 1950s–1980s, may not have disappeared in the digital age, and indeed may be about to make a return over the next decade.

A re-statement of the cultural value of popular culture, not simply its economic worth, is a challenge for a sport that has always worn its civic responsibilities lightly down through the years. As we embark on a new century, with the new possibilities that media development offer in terms of extending and creating new communicative spaces for us all to engage with, it appears that this challenge remains beyond any vision that custodians of the sport appear uninterested in engaging with.

Beyond the pitch: economics and politics

Of course crucial in mapping and shaping future developments will be the wider economic and political context in which the evolving communications industry operates. In the UK, for example despite a slowish uptake, digital television has been boosted with the launch in 2003 of the BBC led free-to-air digital terrestrial system, Freeview. The sports content of this package is also beginning to grow with Setanta Sport, the Irish sports company, adding to its pay-per-view sports channel and web based presence (with Setantasport.com, the most popular sports website in Ireland already) with proposals for a free-to-air sports channel. With Freeview being in 2.5 million homes by December 2003, satellite and cable digital systems already in up to 10 million homes, the UK digital market is beginning to bed down. However real concerns remain about the viability of the proposed switch from analogue to digital, which the UK Government hopes to carry out by 2010. With some media executives, such as the former BSkyB and Channel 5 executive David Elstein, convinced that this is an unrealistic deadline (it was originally 2006) and that the UK television market will not be ready for an analogue switch off for many years well beyond 2010 (interview with authors, 18 October 2002).

Clearly the creation of a mass digital television market place (with both a robust free-to-air and pay sector) will dramatically impact on the way in which football, and sport in general, is mediated, bought, sold and packaged. This will no doubt lead to an increasing extension of the cross platform entertainment model used by reality programmes such as Channel 4's *Big Brother* and the BBC's *Fame Academy* into the realm of sports coverage in the new media age. Yet how significant this form of interactivity and cross media platform synergy will be in fundamentally altering the mediated experience of football is hard to call. We remain convinced that as much will remain the same as change around the culture of the game.

As suggested above, it is expected that major sporting events in the future will continue to utilise digital technology primarily for revenue generation, so for example, FIFA World Cups may make individual games available on distinct digital channels, rather than selling the whole tournament, or Olympic Games will create dedicated sports channels focusing solely on particular events. Our concern is that current research indicates that the driver for future evolution will be extracting additional commercial value from coverage, rather than primarily enhancing and respecting the broader cultural and social values generated by collective sporting experiences which have broadly characterised media sports development in the last century.

The wider regulatory environment within which the broader telecommunications systems operate will also take time to settle, with super UK regulator OFCOM, not fully operational until 2004. It is also clear that the European Commission's (EC) interest in the relationship between media and sport will intensify over the next decade, particularly as they seek to create a climate in which the new media economy can flourish. There are already wider implications for public service television sport of the EC's 2003–2004 attempts to restructure deals struck by the European Broadcasting Union (EBU) which buys events such as the Olympics and the FIFA World Cup for free-to-air public service broadcasters throughout Europe. The EC are challenging the EBU right to buy sports rights collectively claiming it is anti-competitive and part of a cartel that excludes other broadcasters. However, should the EC follow through on this, then the door opens for commercial broadcasters to simply cherry pick top events, again undermining public service television. Such an outcome, according to broadcasting consultant Richard Russell 'would cause irreparable damage to the interdependent worlds of sport and television' (Russell, 2003).

It is always difficult to predicate how such patterns of regulation will develop in practice. What we have looked at in this book is the evolving battle lines between elite football clubs, as 'upstream' media content providers and media organisations as 'down stream' distribution systems, as both parties have attempted to reposition themselves as both providers and deliverers of football content.

That already complex nexus between sport and media is set to become even more byzantine as the battle lines get redrawn between public and private digital media cultures and the role of regulation, both national and international in media development and marketplaces. A process that is set to increase over the next decade as regulators (some interested in the cultural role of media, others in its commercial evolution) strive to keep pace with a digital mediascape which threatens to perpetually run ahead of regulatory frameworks.

This uneven digital television revolution in the UK also highlights another important aspect of any analysis of the social impact of these technologies. First, convergence, as predicted by analysts to mean people using their computers as televisions and vice versa, an important model for many in the sports market, has not happened. Put simply, the television and the computer will remain discrete, but related parts of the domestic fabric of homes for a number of years to come. Television executives no doubt remain wary of the encroachment of Internet use into the time spent viewing television. There are signs that advertisers are thinking more carefully about where they spend their money and in what medium. Advertisers are increasingly sophisticated in their use of the Internet and it will continue to compete with the more expensive medium of television. However, in our review of the new media sports environment it is clear that television remains a far superior experience for sports fans. As we've argued earlier, a lot of the Internet led business models for sports content, and football in particular, have simply failed to understand how football fans interact with, and watch the sport. Television will remain both a key financier of football and the most important media showcase for the sport for many years. This is not to say that patterns of interaction between differing media technologies will not occur, or indeed converge in some areas, rather that it will be a much more uneven, and unpredictable process than many originally envisaged.

Second, the way these digital technologies become embedded in our everyday social lives is not always in a manner that is easily predicable. As we argued in previous chapters, the rise of a text based process (texting on mobile phones) in a supposedly overwhelmingly visual age, is one such example. Another is the resilience and rise of radio as an important media form in the digital age. While digital radio is only slowly gaining a market in the UK (2 per cent of all radio listeners by August 2003), the success of Freeview, mentioned above, has seen a dramatic growth in radio listening via television. Since the launch of Freeview this has risen by 27 per cent while online radio listening also is growing with 17 per cent of the 16–24-year-olds group listening regularly via the web (*Revolution*, July/August 2003).

This was not something that the industry widely expected, with a range of digital radio channels being given excellent exposure via digital television. This process demonstrates how particular patterns of social engagement with these communicative technologies remains inherently difficult to accurately predict, with new revenue streams often emerging from unlikely sources, as was the case with SMS. For example, much is being made of the potential of wireless Internet connections (Wi-Fi), offering public locations where people could simply open their laptop and connect. The potential structural impact for existing payment structures and competition of such developments or the growth of voice-over Internet protocol (VOIP) which would eliminate both local fixed lines and Wi-Fi are potentially enormous. Yet how realistic a mass market scenario Wi-Fi actually is remains open to debate. Are you likely to simply take out your expensive laptop in a coffee shop located in a crowded city centre and be able to concentrate for fear of someone coming along and simply grabbing it? This process of trial and error is likely to continue as we find our way around the digital landscape and adapt it to suit our own lifestyles and patterns of popular cultural consumption.

The new media age has seen two related media systems developing new relationships of co-existence: the global Internet and the more nation-centred television service. Furthermore, digitalisation has facilitated a growing tension between the national governing bodies of the game and clubs. As administrators strive to keep the game patrolled within national boundaries, with strict rules for international engagement through competitions such as the Champions League, clubs with transnational appeal such as Celtic and Ajax are driven by the lure of greater media revenue available by playing in transnational leagues. In differing ways both processes represent the globalising challenges offered to both sport and media in the new media age.

As we have argued throughout the book the digital age is increasingly one driven by commercial values and the wider economic climate in which the market remains the central driver of the digital economy. In late 2003, the ongoing global economic downturn is still adversely impacting on media/ advertising budgets in the UK. Media spend, which is the lifeblood of commercial television in this year is down 2.6 per cent, in a sector already suffering from a number of years of declining revenue in real terms. All this impacts on the general climate within which the football industry operates and of course has become more and more important as television rights income has become central to the football economy.

What is certain is that elite clubs will continue to chip away at retaining their core media rights as they increasingly seek to exploit these using new media technology. Sometimes this will be done in partnership with existing media (e.g. digital television), at others it will lead to direct competition (e.g. over issues of access and print/online media). Whether longer term this process is good for the overall football industry is probably doubtful. The elite and richer clubs will continue to see the gap between them and the others in the game grow, as market forces determine the direction of the game. Without some form of regulation and intervention this process will simply accelerate.

Throughout its history the game has shown a remarkable ability to re-invent itself as each new communication technology has come along. The challenge in the new media age is for the stakeholders in the game to strike a balance between commerce and culture, the local and the global and short-term gain and the long-term well being of an important cultural form.

The battle to control the game in the media age is not new. In the digital century we are simply entering the next phase of that ongoing struggle. It is a struggle that tells us much about the wider relationship between popular culture and the media, and its intensity shows no sign of abating.

Notes

Introduction

1 In Lievrouw and Livingstone's (eds) extensive work *The Handbook of New Media* (2002), sport does not merit a single mention despite the extent to which it has been one of the major cultural forms targeted by new media entrepreneurs as a key 'content' provider for new media forms.

5 Battle for control: football clubs and new media strategy

1 A Jupiter MMXI survey reported in *Revolution* (17 July 2002) indicated that in 2001, 70 per cent of the paid for online content market went on porn, while games, finance and business news made up most of the rest. Sport didn't feature to any great extent.
2 Both Andrew Lee, a sports and media analyst from Dresdner Klienwort Wassertein and Glen Kirton, head of football at Fasttrack were quoted on this in the June 2002 issue *Football Business International*.

Bibliography

Baker, M. (2001) 'Against all odds', *New Media*, the *Guardian*, 4 June.

Banks, S. (2002) *Going Down: Football in Crisis*, Edinburgh and London: Mainstream.

Barrett, S. (2002) 'Fergie's Digital Army', *Revolution*, 4 September.

Barrie, C. (1999) 'OFFdigital', the *Guardian*, 19 July.

Barwise, P. (2002) 'The value of the digital prophets', *FT Creative Business, Financial Times*, 23 April.

BBC Television (2002) *Football: Against the Wall*, BBC1 documentary, 7 May.

BBC (2000) 'Start-ups threaten corporate giants', available at http://news.bbc.co.uk/1/hi/business/905883.stm, 1 September.

BBC (2001a) 'Sportal seeks buyer', available at http://www.news.bbc.co.uk/1/hi/business/1321075.stm.

BBC (2001b) 'Internet bookie buys Sportal', available at http://www.news.bbc.co.uk/1/hi/business/1632108.stm, 1 November.

BBC (2002) 'Digital TV switchover "still on track"', available at http://www.news.bbc.co.uk/1/hi/uk_politics/1952770.stm, 26 April.

BBC (2003) 'Public service in an online world. London: BBC', available at http://www1.thdo.bbc.co.uk/info/policies/online_review.shtml.

Bell, E. (2002) 'It's a funny old game', the *Guardian*, 1 July.

Birch, D. (2002) 'Transactions will kick-start 3G', the *Guardian*, 23 May.

Blain, N. (2003) 'Beyond "media culture"; sport as dispersed symbolic activity', in Blain, N. and Bernstein, A. (eds) *Sport, Media, Culture: Global and Local Dimensions*, London: Frank Cass.

Blain, N. and Bernstein, A. (2002) 'Sport and the media: the emergence of a Major Research Field', *Culture, Sport, Society*, 5 (3), Autumn: 1–30.

Blain, N., Boyle, R. and O'Donnell, H. (1993) *Sport and National Identity in the European Media*, Leicester: Leicester University Press.

Bose, M. (2002) 'Botham protects his image', the *Daily Telegraph*, 13 September.

Bower, T. (2003a) *Broken Dreams: Vanity, Greed and the Souring of British Football*, London: Simon and Schuster.

Bower, T. (2003b) 'United no longer', the *Guardian*, G2, 12 June, pp. 2–4.

Bowers, S. and Teather, D. (2000) 'ONdigital comes clean over pay-TV launch', the *Guardian*, 16 November.

Boyle, R. (2004) 'Football and social responsibility in the new Scotland: the case of Celtic F.C.', in Wagg, S. (ed.) *Soccer and Social Exclusion*, Frank Cass: London.

Boyle, R. and Haynes, R. (2000) *Power Play: Sport, the Media and Popular Culture*, Harlow: Longman.

Boyle, R. and Haynes, R. (2002) 'New media sport', in Blain, N. and Bernstein, A. (eds) *Sport, Media, Culture: Global and Local Dimensions*, London: Frank Cass.

Boyle, R. and Haynes, R. (2003) 'Media matters: issues in media management in the football industry', in Trenberth, L. (ed.) *The Business of Managing Sport*, Palmerston North: Dunmore Press.

Boyle, R. and Haynes, R. (2004) 'The football industry and public relations', in L'Etang, J. (ed.) *Critical Perspectives in Public Relations*, New Jersey: Lawrence Erlbaum.

Boyle, R., Dinan, W. and Morrow, S. (2002) 'Doing the business? The newspaper reporting of the business of football', *Journalism*, 3 (2): 149–169.

Brodin, K., Barwise, P. and Canhoto, A.I. (2002) *UK Consumer Responses to iDTVReport*, London: London Business School, available at http://www.idtvconsumers.com

Brown, A. (ed.) (1998) *Fanatics! Power, Identity and Fandom in Football*, London: Routledge.

Brown, M. (2003) 'Prebble fears TV's future is in Sky', the *Guardian*, 6 June.

BSkyB (2003) British Sky Broadcasting Group plc results for the nine months ended 31 March 2003.

Burke, J., Campbell, D. and Asthana, A. (2003) 'Too much to soon?', the *Observer*, 12 October.

Campbell, D. (2002a) 'Spent forces', the *Observer Sports Monthly*, May, No. 25.

Campbell, D. (2002b) 'In a league of his own', *Sport Business International*, June.

Cantos (2003) 'BSkyB – interim results', interview with Tony Ball, Chief Executive of BskyB, available at http://www.cantos.com

Carrick, C. (2002) 'Crozier fear for ITV', *Daily Telegraph*, 7 April.

Cashmore, E. (2003) *Beckham*, Cambridge: Polity.

Cassidy, J. (2002) *dot.con: The Greatest Story Ever Sold*, London: Allen Lane.

Cassy, J. (2001) 'Armchair fans vote with remote', the *Guardian*, 9 October.

Castells, M. (2000) *The Rise of the Network Society*, second edition, Oxford: Basil Blackwell.

Cellan-Jones, R. (2001) *dot.bomb: The Rise and Fall of dot.com Britain*, London: Aurum Press.

Celtic Trust (2002) Celtic Trust Briefing, September, Glasgow.

Clarke, R. (2002) *The Future of Sports Broadcasting Rights: A SportBusiness Report, Executive Summary*, SportBusiness: London.

CNN (2003) 'Nike endorsements hit $1.4b', available at http://www.money.cnn.com/2003/08/18/news/companies/nike_endorsements/index.htm, 18 August.

Collins, R. (1998) 'Supper with the devil – a case study in private/public collaboration in broadcasting: the genesis of Eurosport', *Media, Culture and Society*, 20 (4): 653–663.

Conn, D. (1998) *The Football Business: Fair Game in the 90s*, London and Edinburgh: Mainstream.

Conn, D., Green, C., McIlroy, R. and Mousley, K. (2003) *Football Confidential 2: Scams, Scandals and Screw Ups*, London: BBC Worldwide.

Cornish, W. (1999) *Intellectual Property*, fourth edition, London: Sweet & Maxwell.

Couchman, N. (2002a) 'Public image limited', the *Guardian*, 1 May.

Couchman, N. (2002b) 'The computer game case', The MediaGuardian, available at http://media.guardian.co.uk/medialaw/story/0,11614,707778,00.html, 1 May.

Cox, B. (2003) 'Paying the piper but not calling the tune, lecture on TV in the digital age (11/2/03)', The MediaGuardian, available at http://www.media.guardian.co.uk accessed 12 February.

Crabtree, J., Nathan, M. and Roberts, S. (2003) *Mobile UK: Mobile Phones and Everyday Life*, London: iSociety, The Work Foundation.

Day, J. (2002a) 'Image rights battle threatens press freedom', the *Guardian*, 1 May.

Day, J. (2002b) 'ITV brand counts the cost', the *Guardian*, 2 April.

DCMS (2003) *Modernising Britain's Gambling Laws: Draft Gambling Bill*, London: HMSO (CM5878).

Deloitte & Touche (2003) *Deloitte & Touche Annual Review of Football Finance 2001/2*, London.

Dempsey, P. and Reilly, K. (1998) *Big Money Beautiful Game*, London: Nicholas Brealey.

Dobson, S. and Goddard, J. (2001) *The Economics of Football*, Cambridge: Cambridge University Press.

Doward, J. (2002) 'So who killed ITV Digital?', the *Observer*, Sunday, April 28.

Doyle, G. (2002) *Introduction to Media Economics*, London: Sage.

Durman, P. (2003) 'They said they would lead the way in 3G with 1m users by Christmas. What do they know?', the *Sunday Times*, 12 October.

FIFA (2002) 'fifaworldcup.com to offer video highlights of all 64 FIFA World Cup™ matches', available at http://fifaworldcup.yahoo.com/02/en/020429/2/f42.html.

FIFA (2003) 'OC website goes multilingual', available at http://fifaworldcup.yahoo.com/02/en/030225/4/9w.html.

Fitzpatrick, N. (2001) 'Raising the stakes for stats', *SportBusiness International*, December.

The Football League (2002) 'Statement by the Football League Board on the contract with ITV Digital', available at http://www.footballleague.premiumtv.co.uk/today/view/page_detail/0,,1079484928,00.html, 21 March.

Forrester Research (2001) 'The online sports survival guide', press release of report, available at http://www.forrester.com/ER/Press/Release/0,1769,563,00.html.

Fynn, A. and Guest, L. (1994) *Out of Time*, London: Simon and Schuster.

Fynn, A. and Guest, L. (1999) *For Love or Money: Manchester United and England – The Business of Winning*, London: Andre Deutsch.

Gardiner, S.J. and Gray, J.T. (2003) 'Protecting the "crown jewels" of sport', *SportBusiness International*, July, Issue 82, p. 52.

Garnham, N. (2000) *Emancipation, the Media and Modernity*, Oxford: Oxford University Press.

Garraham, M. (2002) 'David Beckham', *Creative Business* supplement, *Financial Times*, 22 January.

Gerlis, S. (2002) 'The route to web riches', *SportBusiness International*, May.

Gibson, O. (2002a) 'Football's big balls-up', *New Media*, the *Guardian*, 22 April.

Gibson, O. (2002b) 'Broadcasters battle for Champions League rights', available at http://media.guardian.co.uk., 15 July.

Gibson, O. (2002c) 'ITV Digital sale raises just £27m', The Guardian Unlimited, available at http://media.guardian.co.uk/itvdigital/story/0,11829,814789,00.html, 18 October.

Gibson, O. (2003a) 'What are the legal issues?', The Guardian Unlimited, available at http://media.guardian.co.uk/broadcast/story/0,7493,902737,00.html, 25 February.

Gibson, O. (2003b) 'ITV football man switches teams', the *Guardian*, 4 April.

Giulianotti, R. (1999) *Football: A Sociology of the Global Game*, London: Routledge.

Glanville, B. (1991) *Champions of Europe: The History, the Romance and Intrigue of the European Cup*, London: Guinness Publishing

Granada Media (1999) Granada Media plc Annual Report 1998.

Greenfield, S. and Osborn, O. (2001) *Regulating Football: Commodification, Consumption and the Law*, London: Pluto Press.

Guardian, the (2002) 'BT is the only game in town. But will it play fair?', Finance Notebook, 25 April.

Hamil, S., Michie, J. and Oughton, C. (eds) (1999) *The Business of Football: A Game of Two Halves?*, Edinburgh and London: Mainstream.

Hamil, S., Michie, J., Oughton, C. and Warby, S. (eds) (2000) *Football in the Digital Age: Whose Game is It Anyway?*, Edinburgh and London: Mainstream.

Hart, S. (2002) 'United picturing big profits as secret trials are exposed', *Daily Telegraph*, 22 September.

Harvey, J., Law, A. and Cantelon, M. (2001) 'North American professional team sport franchises ownership patterns and global entertainment conglomerates', *Sociology of Sport Journal*, 18: 435–457.

Hawkey, I. (2002) 'The £30m mannequin', *Sunday Times*, 8 September.

Haynes, R. (1995) *The Football Imagination: The Rise of Football Fanzine Culture*, Aldershot: Arena.

Haynes, R. (1998) 'A pageant of sound and vision: football's relationship with television, 1936–60', *The International Journal of the History of Sport*, 15 (1): 211–226.

Hesbrugge, R. and Wipperfurth, F. (2001) 'A Bottomless Pit?', *Sportel01*, October.

Hewitt, P. and Pinder, A. (2002) *Monthly Report to the Prime Minister: Office of the e-envoy*, 7 May, Office of the e-envoy: UK Government.

Hodgson, J. (2003) 'EC to probe Premier "price fix"', the *Observer*, 7 September.

Hoggart, R. (1996) *The Way We Live*, London: Pimilico.

Horrie, C. (2002) *Premiership: Lifting the Lid on a National Obsession*, London: Pocket Books.

Horsman, M. (1997) *Sky High: The Inside Story of BskyB*, London: Orion Business.

Johnson, I. (2003) 'Are viewers adopting interactive TV?', *Admap*, January, Issue 435.

Jolley, R. (2001) 'Sport needs to raise its game', *Revolution*, 25 July.

Jones, T. (2003) *The Dark Heart of Italy: Travels Through Time and Space Across Italy*, London: Faber and Faber.

Jowell, T. (2002) 'Statement on ITV Digital by the Rt Hon Tessa Jowell MP Secretary of State for Culture, Media and Sport', House of Commons, 62/02, available at http://www.digitaltelevision.gov.uk/press_notices/dcms82_02.html, 26 April.

Kelso, P. (2002) 'Arsenal trader wins court fight', the *Guardian*, 13 December.

Kemp, K. (2002) 'Why vested interests killed off a commercially viable SPL TV', *Sunday Herald*, 14 April.

Koranteng, J. (2000) *European Football Channels*, London: SportBusiness International.

Koranteng, J. (2001) 'European Football Channels', London: A SportBusiness Report.

KPMG (2003) 'Market Impact Assessment of BBC's Online Service', available at http://www.culture.gov.uk/global/consultations/2003+current+consultations/cons _bbci_review.htm.

Lane, S. (1999) 'The problems of personality merchandising in English law: the king, the princess and the penguins', in Barendt, E., Firth, A., Bate, S., Gibbons, T., Palca, J.

and Ensor, J. (eds) *The Oxford Yearbook of Copyright and Media Law 1999*, Oxford: Oxford University Press.

Langley, Hon. J. (2002) *Carlton Communications plc Granada Media plc v The Football League*, Approved Judgment, Neutral Citation No. [2002] EWHC 1650 (Comm).

Law, A., Harvey, J. and Kemp, S. (2002) 'The global sport mass media oligopoly', *International Review of the Sociology of Sport*, 3 (4): 279–302.

Lessig, L. (2001) *The Future of Ideas: The Fate of the Commons in a Connected World*, New York: Random House.

Lievrouw, L.A. and Livingstone, S. (2002) 'The social shaping and consequences of ICTs', in Lievrouw, L. and Livingstone, S. (eds) *The Handbook of New Media*, London: Sage.

Lister, M., Dovey, J., Giddings, S., Grant, I. and Kelly, K. (2003) *New Media: A Critical Introduction*, London: Routledge.

Lovejoy, J. (2002) *Sven Goran Eriksson*, London: CollinsWillow.

De Lussanet, M., Nordan, M.M. and Mendez, M.A. (2002) *3G's Belated Break-Even*, Techstrategy Report, Forrester, September.

Maguire, J. (1999) *Global Sport: Identities, Societies and Civilisations*, Cambridge: Polity Press.

May, C. (2002) *The Information Society: A Sceptical View*, Cambridge: Polity.

MDA (2003) Mobile Data Association: Resource Centre, available at http://www.mda-mobiledata.org/resource/hottopics/sms.asp, 23 January.

McGill, C. (2001) *Football Inc. How Soccer Fans are Losing the Game*, London: Vision Paperbacks.

Miller, T., Lawrence, G., McKay, J. and Rowe, D. (2001) *Globalization and Sport*, London: Sage.

Molskey, N. (1999) *European Public Broadcasting in the Digital Age*, London: FT Media and Telecoms.

Monti, M. (2001) 'Competition and sport the rules of the game', paper given at the Conference on Governance in Sport – European Olympic Committee – FIA – Féderation Internationale de l'Automobile – Herbert Smith Swissotel Brussels, available at http://europa.eu.int/rapid/start/cgi/guesten.ksh?p_action.gettxt=gt&doc=SPEECH /01/84l0lRAPID&lg=EN, 26 February.

Morrow, S. (1999) *The New Business of Football: Accountability and Finance in Football*, London: Macmillan.

Morrow, S. (2003) *The People's Game? Football, Finance and Society*, Basingstoke: Palgrave Macmillan.

Murdock, G. (2000) 'Digital futures: the age of convergence', in Weiten, J., Murdock, G. and Dahlgren, P. (eds) *Television Across Europe*, London: Sage.

Naylor, R., Driver, S. and Cornford, J. (2000) 'The BBC goes online: public service broadcasting in the new media age', in Gauntlett, D. (ed.) *Web.Studies: Rewiring Media Studies for the Digital Age*, London: Arnold.

O'Connor, N. (2003) 'The online betting market', available at http://www.betting market.com/onlinebetting.htm.

OFTEL (2003) *Key Trends in Fixed and Mobile Telephony, and Internet*, London: OFTEL.

O'Regan, T. and Goldsmith, B. (2003) 'Emerging global ecologies of production', in Harries, D. (ed.) *The New Media Handbook*, London: BFI.

Papathanassopoulos, S. (2002) *European Television in the Digital Age*, Oxford: Polity.

Parks, J. (2003) *A Season with Verona*, London: Vintage.

Pattullo, E. (2002) *Football Clubs and Finance, Market Report, 2002*, London: Key Note Market Intelligence.

Pericles Trifonas, P. (2001) *Umberto Eco and Football*, London: Icon Books.

Redhead, S. (1993) *Football with Attitude*, Manchester: Wordsmith.

Redhead, S. (1997) *Football and the Millennial Blues*, London: Routledge.

Research and Markets (2003) 'Digital and Interactive TV Markets: Service Development and Uptake to 2007', available at http://www.researchandmarkets.com/reports/28362/.

Rheingold, H. (1993) *The Virtual Community*, London: Secker and Warburg.

Rowe, D. (1996) 'The global love match: sport and television', *Media, Culture and Society*, 18 (2): 565–582.

Rowe, D. (1999) *Sport, Culture and the Media: The Unruly Trinity*, Buckingham: Open University Press.

Russell, R. (2003) 'Commercial cherry-pickers pose threat', *SportBusiness International*, September, Issue 84, p. 27.

Samualson, P. (1996) 'The copyright grab', *Wired*, available at http://www.wired.com/wired/archive/4.01/white.paper_pr.html, January.

Scannell, P. (1989) 'Public service broadcasting and modern public life', *Media, Culture and Society*, 11: 135–166.

Scannell, P. (1996) *Television and Radio in Modern Life*, Oxford: Blackwell.

Screen Digest (2003) *The Global Business of Sports Television*, London: Screen Digest.

Shah, S. (2002) 'Football League demands ITV Digital investigation', the *Independent*, 12 April.

Silverstone, R. (1994) *Television and Everyday Life*, London: Routledge.

Singh, T. and Carter, T. (2003) 'Tottenham 1, Arsenal 0, Barcelona 0', *SportBusiness International*, March.

Soccer365.com (2003) 'Premier League Reject TV Solution', 29 May.

Steinberger, M. (2003) 'Baffled by Beckham's fallen star', the *Financial Times*, 17 June, p. 19.

Stevenson, N. (1999) *The Transformation of the Media*, London: Longman.

Sugden, J. and Tomlinson, A. (1998) *FIFA and the Contest for World Football*, Oxford: Polity Press.

Szymanski, Stefan (2002) 'Collective selling of broadcast rights', *Soccer Analyst*, 3 (1).

Taylor, Lord Justice (1990) *The Hillsborough Stadium Disaster: Final Report*, London: HMSO (CM962).

Teather, D. (2001) 'Zenith attacks ITV', the *Guardian*, 25 September.

Thomas, D. (2003) *Foul Play: The Inside Story of the Biggest Corruption Trial in British Sporting History*, London: Bantam Press.

Timms, D. (2003) 'A hard nut to crack', *New Media*, the *Guardian*, 27 January.

Toft, T. (2003) *TV Rights of Sports Events*, European Commission, Competition DG, Brussels, 15 January.

Toomey, J. (2002) 'The Future of Music', *Texas Intellectual Property Law Review*, 10: 101.

Tryhorn, C. (2003) 'BSkyB hits 7m subscribers three months early', the *Guardian*, October 1.

Tunstall, J. and Machin, D. (1999) *The Anglo-American Media Connection*, Oxford: Oxford University Press.

Walsh, A. and Brown, A. (1999) *Not for Sale!: United for United: Manchester United, Murdoch and the Defeat of BSkyB*, Edinburgh: Mainstream.

Walsh, C. (2003) 'Beckham: now or never', the *Observer*, 27 April.

Ward, A. (2001) 'Television Gambling', *Creative Business* Supplement, the *Financial Times*, 13 March.

Waterman, D. (2001) 'The economics of Internet TV: new niches vs mass audiences', *The Journal of Policy, Regulation and Strategy of Telecommunications, Information and Media*, 3 (3): 215–229.

Westerbeek, H. and Smith, A. (2003) *Sport Business in the Global Marketplace*, London: Palgrave Macmillan.

Whannel, G. (1992) *Fields in Vision: Television Sport and Cultural Transformation*, London: Routledge.

Whannel, G. (2002) *Media Sports Stars: Masculinities and Moralities*, London: Routledge.

White, D. (2003) 'Back of the net', *Broadband World*, Issue 1, August.

Williams, J. (1999) *Is It All Over? Can Football Survive the Premier League?*, Reading: South Street Press.

Williams, J. (2002a) 'Football's leaving home', in Perryman, M. (ed.) *Going Oriental: Football After World Cup 2002*, Edinburgh and London: Mainstream.

Williams, J. (2002b) 'The new football elites', *Leicester Mercury*, 6 April.

Williams, J. (2002c) 'Good business for clubs – but is it good for fans?', *Leicester Mercury*, 16 November.

Williams, R. (1974) *Television, Technology and Cultural Form*, London: Fontana.

WIPO Arbitration Panel on Domain Names (2000) Pierre van Hooijdonk v. S.B. Tait, Case No. D2000-1068, available at http://arbiter.wipo.int/domains/decisions/html/2000/d2000-1068.html.

WIPO Arbitration Panel on Domain Names (2002) Francesco Totti v. Jello Master, Case No. D2002-0134, available at http://arbiter.wipo.int/domains/decisions/html/2002/d2002-0134.html.

Index

Aberdeen FC 129
Abramovich, Roman 100, 162
adidas 85, 88
American websites 106
appearance money 83–5
Arsenal FC 16, 19, 36, 76–9, 82, 89,
103–4, 111, 113, 116
Aston Villa FC 110
attendances at football matches 16, 40,
133–4, 163–4

Ball, Tony 46–7, 150
Bank of Scotland 125
Banks, Simon 29, 62–3, 126–31
Barwick, Brian 31
Barwise, Patrick 98, 151
BBC (British Broadcasting Corporation)
13, 17–23, 30–2, 49, 57, 69, 106,
132–4, 144, 152–8, 163–4
Beckham, David 24, 71–5, 86–9, 161–2
Beckham, Victoria 86, 161
Bell, Ian 118
Bell, Tim 88
Bells Life 146
Bergkamp, Dennis 82
Berlusconi, Silvio 59, 61, 143
Bernstein, A. 1
Berry, George 91–2
Berti, Genevieve 63
Best, George 71
betting 55, 110, 143–7, 150
Big Brother 149, 164
The Big Match 18
Birt, John 21, 152
Blain, N. 1, 24, 54
Blair, Tony 42
Blatter, Sepp 157
Bosman, Jean-Marc (and Bosman case)
72, 80, 85, 91, 101, 132

Botham, Ian 77
Bower, Tom 161
Bowyer, Lee 81
Boyle, John 133–4
BP (company) 89
Bradford City FC 36
Bradford stadium fire 19, 43
British Broadcasting Corporation *see* BBC
British Internet Providers Association
154
British Satellite Broadcasting 19
British Telecom (BT) 35, 107–8, 138,
144–5
broadband technology 107–9, 115–17,
144, 156
Broadband World 112
Broadcasting Act (1990) 20
Brodin, K. 151
Brylcreem 88
BSkyB 9–13, 20–2, 27–37, 42–50, 54, 56,
60, 66–9, 96, 99–104, 118–26, 131–2,
135, 138, 144–51, 163
Buchler, David 39–40
Burke, J. 162
Burns, David 40–1, 43

Cable and Satellite Act (1984) 20
Cambridge United FC 36
Campbell, Denis 99
Canal Plus Technologies 37, 53–4, 58
Canhoto, A.I. 151
Cantona, Eric 87–8
Carlton Communication 29–43
Cashmore, Ellis 87
Castells, M. 53
Celtic FC 16, 105, 111–12, 119–35, 159,
162, 167
Celtic Park 118
Champions League 4, 31–2, 35–6, 45–6,

56, 61–7, 80–3, 101, 104, 113, 130,
   135, 138, 151, 167
Chance, David 36
Channel 4 18, 127
Channel 5 32, 49
Charlton Athletic FC 112
Chelsea FC 100–1, 162
civil society 57
Clarke, R. 113
Coca-Cola 83, 88
colour television 152
commodification of football 12, 17, 28,
   73, 76, 97, 139–40
company status for football clubs 10,
   129–30
competition policy 29–30, 44–9, 65–7,
   101, 132
computer games 91–2
conference league 109
Conn, David 9
contracts with players 72–5, 80–8, 92,
   97
Cornish, W. 76
Cosgrove, Stuart 127–8, 134
cost per hour of television sport 23
Couchman, N. 82
Crabtree, J. 98
Cragnotti, Sergio 1
Crozier, Adam 39, 89
cultural change 25
culture of football 8, 24, 162–4
Cup Final matches 18
cybersquatting 90

Dacourt, Olivier 81
Daily Telegraph 92–3
Day, Julia 75
Dein, David 40, 128
Deloitte & Touche 39, 96
Department of Trade and Industry 46
Derby County FC 18, 80
deregulation of broadcasting 23–4
Desmond, Dermot 132–3
Diageo 77
Diana, Princess of Wales 76
digital television 3, 5, 13, 25, 27–37,
   42–57, 62, 69, 96–8, 109, 138, 148,
   150, 164–7
Dobson, S. 9, 18, 21
domain names 75, 89–90
Doward, J. 30
Dupont, Jean-Louis 91
D'Urso, Andy 93

Dutch football 65
Dyke, Greg 19–21, 163

Elstein, David 164
endorsements 76–7, 85–6
English national team 1, 88
European Broadcasting Union 55, 165
European Commission 29–30, 44–9,
   51–2, 61, 65–9, 81, 85, 101, 132, 165
European Council (Nice, 2000) 48, 66,
   74
European Court of Justice 78–9, 91, 130
European Economic Interest Grouping see
   G14 group
European SuperLeague 64
European Union Directive on the
   Information Society 74
Eurosport 54
Everton FC 19, 97, 105

Fame Academy 164
fans see supporters
fanzines 90, 141–2, 158
Ferdinand, Rio 1, 81
Ferguson, Alex 87, 129, 161
FIFA 64, 91, 130–1, 139, 155–7; see also
   World Cup
FIFPro 91–2
Figo, Luis 72–3, 83
Fitzpatrick, N. 93
Fletcher Research 126
FLPTV 109–10
Flynn, Mike 112
Football Association (FA) 13, 16, 32, 39,
   48, 69, 83–4, 88–9; see also Premier
   League; Scottish Football Association
Football Fans Union 40
Football Foundation 48
Football League 16–19, 29–49, 84,
   109–10
football pools 146
The Footballers' Football Channel 109
Fowler, Robbie 73, 81
free-to-air television 12, 15, 22–5, 28, 49,
   53–7, 67–9, 116–17, 124, 133, 160,
   165
Freeview 30, 42, 53, 149, 164, 166
Fynn, Alex 15, 58, 64

G14 group 63–4, 66, 81
Gambling Bill (2003) 146
GameCare 147
Gardiner, S.J. 69

Garnham, N. 160
Garraham, Matthew 86
German television 56, 69, 100
Gerrard, Bill 81
Gibson, Owen 113–14
Giulianotti, R. 25
Glasgow Rangers *see* Rangers FC
globalisation 11–14, 24, 57, 75, 161–2, 167
Goddard, J. 9, 18, 21
Gold, Lex 123
Golden Cup 133
Goldsmith, B. 148
Google 156
government policy for sport 19, 42–3
GPC International 39
Grabiner, Stephen 30
Grade, Michael 17
Granada Media 29–43, 103–4, 111–13, 123, 138
Grant, Michael 122, 124, 131
Gray, J.T. 69
Greenfield, S. 10–11, 22–3
Guardian 106
Guest, L. 15
Guinness brand 77

Hadfield, Tom 142
Hagi, Gheorge 91–2
Harris, Keith 38, 41
Hart, Simon 92
Harverson, Patrick 101–6, 115
Hawkey, Ian 85
Heart of Midlothian FC 16
Henderson, Michael 71
Hersov, Bob 143
Heysel Stadium disaster 19, 43
Hibernian FC 16
highlights programmes 17, 22, 28, 31–2, 48–9, 104, 109, 124, 151, 157
Hill, David 7, 159
Hoggart, R. 160
Holborn PR 39
Hooijdonk, Pierre van 90
hooliganism 19, 24
Horrie, C. 16–17
Horsman, Matthew 32
Hutton, Will 9

image rights 71–8, 82–9, 92–7, 106–7
Independent, the 7, 20
Independent Television Commission (ITC) 30, 43

IndexGaming 147
intellectual property (IP) 5, 10, 73–5, 78, 89, 97, 103, 107, 114–16
interactive services 139–41, 145, 149–51
interactive television 98, 148–9, 152–5, 158
International Olympics Committee (IOC) 156
Internet resources 4–5, 13, 25, 29, 37, 45, 53, 66 70, 89, 94 117, 121, 129, 134–6, 139–49, 156–8, 165–6
Irvine, Eddie 77
Italian television 57–61, 99–100, 106–7
ITV Digital 27–49, 96, 99, 122–3, 126–7
ITV network 16–21, 69, 157

Johnson, Simon 47
Jones, Tobias 58–9
Jordan, Michael 89
Jowell, Tessa 42–4

Kahn, Oliver 91–2
Keane, Robbie 81
Keane, Roy 93
Keen, Alan 43
Keevins, Hugh 118
Kelso, Paul 27
Kemp, Kenny 125
Kenyon, Peter 46, 102, 162
Kewell, Harry 81
KirchMedia 56, 100, 156
Koranteng, J. 54
KPMG 125, 153

Laddie J. 77–9
Lane, S. 76
Langley J. 41
Law, A. 11
Lee, Mike 36
Leeds United FC 81
legislation on broadcasting 20
Leicester City FC 80, 102
Lessig, Lawrence 75, 95
Lievrouw, L.A. 2–3
Lister, M. 139, 141
live football on television 18, 22, 25, 28, 31–5, 44, 68, 104, 109, 112, 134, 163–4
Liverpool FC 19, 103, 105, 111, 115, 162
Livingstone, S. 2–3
London Weekend Television (LWT) 17
Lovelace, Graham 108

Lycos 103
Lynam, Des 31

Machin, D. 58
McLeod, Ian 125–7
McManus, J.P. 100
Magnier, John 100
Malir, Charles 150
Manchester City FC 81
Manchester United FC 1, 12, 16, 19, 36, 46, 73, 76, 80–1, 86, 88, 92–3, 100–9, 113–16, 162
Mandic, Bernie 81
Marcotti, Gabriel 58–9
Marie Claire 87
market failure 99–101
Marks and Spencer 88
Marr, Andrew 34
Match of the Day 17, 21, 49, 93, 98
Maxwell, Robert 18
May, C. 141
Melvin, Andy 20
merchandising 73–5, 79–83, 87, 110
message boards 154
Microsoft 143, 154
Middlesbrough FC 93
Miller, T. 12, 25
Mitchell, Roger 118–24, 133, 136
mobile telephony 66, 70, 98–100, 105–7, 112–15, 159
Monopolies and Mergers Commission 46
Monti, Mario 44, 48, 65, 67
Moore, Glenn 7
Morgan Stanley 143
Morrison, Steve 33, 40–1
Morrow, Stephen 8, 68
Mother (advertising agency) 35
Motherwell FC 125
Mumford, Lewis 141
Murdoch, Lachlan 37
Murdoch, Rupert 30, 43, 60–1, 99
Murdock, G. 52–3, 68
Murray, David 125
MUTV 101–4

Nagle, John 109–10
'narrow channel exploitation' 136
Nathan, M. 98
national culture 162
national leagues 135
Nationwide League 32–6, 48, 80, 96, 127
new media 53, 70, 74–5, 88–9, 94–9,

110–11, 114–15, 121, 138–45, 152, 158, 160, 166
Newcastle United FC 16, 81, 110
News Corporation 37, 60–1, 99, 143
News International 42
Nike 76, 85, 90, 102–3
Nottingham Forest FC 36
NTL 32, 34, 47, 100, 108–12, 123, 138, 144, 149

Odam, Douglas 124
O'Farrell, John 27
OFCOM 165
Office of Fair Trading (OFT) 45–6, 101, 132
OFTEL 144
O'Leary, David 81
Olympic Games 156, 165
ONdigital 27–34; *see also* ITV Digital
O'Neill, Martin 159
O'Regan, T. 148
Osborn, O. 10–11, 22–3
Overmaars, Mark 89
Oxford United FC 18, 22

Papathanassopoulos, S. 31, 51–3, 57
Parks, J. 138
'passing off' 77–8
pay-per-view (PPV) 22, 25, 28–9, 37, 55, 57, 59–60, 98, 122, 126, 153
pay-TV 4, 19–22, 25, 27–33, 43–4, 50, 53–9, 62, 67, 69, 96–9, 102–3, 119–24, 128, 135–6, 150–1, 159
Pepsi Cola 88, 102
Perez, Florentino 83
Phillips, Ian 77
Pinz, Matthias 91
piracy 37, 59, 61, 100, 140, 156
Platt, David 82
Prebble, Stuart 30, 33, 37, 40–3
Premier League 13, 21–2, 28–35, 44–50, 64, 72–84, 88–9, 96, 99–104, 112–15, 120–8, 132, 136, 147, 151; *see also* Scottish Premier League
Premier TV 112
Premium TV 109–10
Professional Footballers Association (PFA) 43, 48, 74–5, 83–4
Project Premier 128
promotional activities 88–9
public relations (PR) 23, 39, 83–4, 97
public service broadcasting (PSB) 12–13, 18–20, 52–7, 68–9, 152–3, 158–65

Quokka Sports 145

radio 111–12, 166
Rangers FC 100, 105, 111–12, 117,
    119–26, 129–35, 159
Real Madrid 72–3, 83–9, 115, 161–2
Reed, Matthew 78–9
Reel Enterprises 123, 126
regulation of broadcasting 44–9, 165
replica kit 73, 87
Restrictive Practices Court 46
Revolution 103
Richards, Ed 42
Richardson, Bryan 80
Ridsdale, Peter 81
rights in football, sale of 17–18, 21–5,
    28–9, 32–3, 41, 101–4, 115–16,
    126–8, 132–6, 151, 156, 167; changing
    regulatory context for 44–9; in Europe
    51–68; *see also* image rights
Roberts, S. 98
Robson, Bryan 93
Rogan, David 123
Ronaldo 72–3, 83, 85
Rooney, Wayne 73, 97
Runcorn FC 110
Russell, Richard 165

salaries of footballers 80–2, 96, 162
Samualson, P. 79
Sanchez, Jose Angel 71
Scannell, P. 160, 163
Scottish Football Association 160
Scottish Football League 120
Scottish Media Group 35
Scottish national team 160
Scottish Premier League (SPL) 5, 13,
    120–2, 128, 131–5; *see also* SPL TV
Screen Digest 150
Scudamore, Richard 47, 123
set-top boxes (STBs) 30, 37, 42, 149
short-termism 128, 160
Sloane, Niall 93–4, 151–5
smart cards 37
Smith, A. 140
Smith, Peter 104–5, 113, 116
SMS (short message service) 113–14, 166
Soccernet website 142
'spam' 155
Spanish television 60
SPL TV 118, 123–8, 131, 134–6
sponsorship 18, 81, 87–9, 103, 106, 138,
    155

Sportal 143–5
Sports.com 103, 144
star footballers 72–3, 76, 80–7, 90, 161
Steinberger, Mike 161
Stevenson, Nick 159, 162
strategic alliances 98
Sun, the 42
Sunday Times, the 9
Sunderland FC 16
supporters of football clubs 8, 11, 14–15,
    28–9, 34, 71–2, 116, 124, 138–140,
    160
Supporters Direct 43–4
Swiss Bank Corporation 128

Tait, Sam B. 90
Talk Radio 77
Talksport 77
Taylor, Gordon 84–5
Taylor Report (1990) 9–10
Teamtalk 103
television viewing 147–8
Television Without Frontiers Directive 65
Telewest 32, 47, 138, 144, 149
Telstar 17
text messaging 113; *see also* SMS
Thatcher, Margaret 19, 43, 88
third-generation (3G) mobile phones 66,
    70, 99–100, 113–16
Thompson, Stewart 122
The Times 36
T-Mobile 114
Toft, Torben 45
Tomas, Pedro 60
Tonge, Gary 43
Tottenham Hotspur FC 8, 16, 19, 79, 81
Totti, Franscesco 90
Townley, Stephen 33
trademarks 78–9, 90
Trueman, Fred 77
Tunstall, J. 58

UEFA 13, 31, 36, 62–7, 85, 91, 130–1;
    see also Champions League
UKBetting 144

Vegas, Johnny 35
Venables, Terry 81
Verwaayen, Ben 107
Victor Chandler (company) 146
video games 89, 91
video streaming 108–9, 156
video-on-demand (VOD) 151, 153

'virtual communities' 154
Vodafone 88, 102, 105, 113–14, 138
'vortextuality' 24, 87, 155

Wakeling, Vic 20–1, 46, 118–19, 122
Walmsley, Nigel 33
Walsh, Conal 86
Watkins, Maurice 82
weblogs 142
websites 89–90, 106, 112, 132–3, 141–7, 152, 155–8
West Bromwich Albion FC 36
West Ham FC 81
Westerbeek, H. 140
Whannel, G. 24–5, 87, 155
Williams, J. 13, 78, 80
Williams, Raymond 2–3
Willis, Alison 77

Willoughby, Damian 111
Wireless Application Protocol (WAP) 98, 100
wireless Internet connections (Wi-Fi) 166
Woodgate, Jonathan 81
World Cup 5, 9, 17, 29, 56, 106, 138–9, 152, 155–8, 165
World Intellectual Property Organisation 75, 90–1
Worthington Cup 34–5
Wright, Paul 108–9
writing-off of investments 100

Yahoo 145, 155–7

Zenith Media 36
Zidane, Zinadine 72–3